The Shuster Mission to Iran:

Leaving Something Worthwhile Behind

Joan Gaughan

REAL
Nice Books
Baltimore, Maryland

Copyright © 2021 Joan Gaughan
All rights reserved.

No part of this publication may be reproduced, stored in, or introduced into a retrieval system, or transmitted, in any form or by any means (electronic, mechanical, photocopying, recording, or otherwise), without the proper written permission of the copyright owner, except that a reviewer may quote brief passages in a review.

ISBN 978-1-7355938-76 Hardback
ISBN 978-1-7355938-83 Paperback

Library of Congress Control Number: 2021936823

Published by
Real
Nice Books
11 Dutton Court, Suite 606
Baltimore, Maryland 21228
www.realnicebooks.com

Cover pictures from Depositphotos.com
All photographs are in the public domain, more than thirty years having passed since their original publication or presentation.
Set in Sabon.

Dedication

On May 8, 2018, President Donald Trump stunned the world by unilaterally withdrawing from the Joint Comprehensive Plan of Action, signed with five other nations and Iran in July 2015. The next day, in discussing that tragic withdrawal, a young Iranian-American friend, Ramin, told me, "Americans have also exploited Iran but they have usually managed to do so in a way that left something worthwhile behind."

In gratitude for his continued faith in America's tendency to leave "something worthwhile" behind and for his constant encouragement and invaluable help, I dedicate this work to him.

Acknowledgements

I am especially grateful to Dr. Thomas Ricks for his careful reading of the entire manuscript. The weekly conversations were invigorating, quite often entertaining, and always helpful. I am especially grateful for his insights into the sufferings of the people of Tabriz during the second phase of the Constitutional Revolution.

To Azin R. for providing the maps that are contained in this book. She patiently endured my pickiness and for that I am relieved and grateful.

To Dr. Willen Floor for his somewhat stringent but helpful comments, especially on the Qajar period.

To the staff at the Hatcher Library at the University of Michigan for their unfailing support and help especially in the Map and in the Special Collections rooms. For many years, the members of the Hatcher staff have gone out of their way to answer questions that must, at times, have seemed a bit outlandish.

To Lynn Conway, archivist at Georgetown University for her valuable newspaper clipping, and to Shelly Buring of George Washington University's Gelman Library for sending me the Columbian University yearbooks and course catalog for the period of Shuster's attendance there.

To Lewis Wyman, Reference Librarian at the Library of Congress, I am very grateful for copying and mailing me Shuster's *Diary*.

To my daughter Allison McKenzie, for her English-major comments on several chapters of the manuscript and to her husband, Jeremy, for many spirited conversations on the subject of politics in general, and Iran in particular. The discussions with Allison and Jeremy have been constant reminders that this story is not about an American helping Iranians so much as human beings caring about other human beings.

To Father Tom Helfrich, pastor of St. Rita's Catholic Church in Clark Lake, Michigan, to Ambassador John Limbert and to Jackie Spurlock for their insights, especially on the last chapter of this book, I am truly grateful.

Most of all, I thank the Peace Corps for having given me the chance many years ago to serve as a volunteer in Iran and to the people of Rasht and Lahijan to whom I owe much more than I will ever be able to repay.

Contents

Dedication	iii
Acknowledgements	iv
List of Illustrations	vii
Introduction	viii
I .... A Fateful Treaty	13
II .... The Realm of the Qajars	24
III .... A King Besieged	41
IV .... October 1906. The Constitutional Revolution	62
V .... Anglo-Russian Convention of August 1907	75
VI .... The Second Majles	93
VII ..... Why an American? Why Shuster?	112
VIII .... First Days	131
IX ...... The June 13 Law	148
X .... Creating a Respect for Law	155
XI ...... The Stokes Affair	169
XII ..... Mohammad Ali Invades	181
XIII .... Mohammad Ali Invades: The Military Campaign	200
XIV .... September	210
XV ..... The Shu'a al-Saltaneh Incident	217
XVI .... October. The *Times* Letter	227
XVII .. November. Demands and an Ultimatum	237
XVIII . December	250
XIX ... Making Angels Weep	263
XX ..... Khoda Hafez (Good-bye)	273
XXI ... Conclusion	283
Appendix	292
Glossary	294
Notes	295
Index	325
Bibliography	331

List of Illustrations

Map of Iran	xi
Morgan Shuster	xii
Agha Mohammad Khan	22
Fath Ali Shah	23
Nasr al-Din Shah	58
Amir Kabir	59
Taj al-Saltaneh	60
Jamal al-Din al-Afghani	61
Sir Edward Grey	90
Alexander Izvolsky	91
The Persian Cat	91
Map of the Anglo-Russian Convention	92
Howard Baskerville	109
Mohammad Ali Shah	110
Nasr al-Mulk	111
Edward G. Browne	130
Sir Charles Barclay	146
Stanislaw Poklewski-Koziell	147
Major Claude B. Stokes	180
Ephraim Khan	209
Shu'a al-Saltaneh	226
Frank Cairns	272

Introduction

"I had been ambitious to serve the Persian people."
—W. Morgan Shuster, December 1911

Once, a young boy who had lost one of his legs in a terrible accident and wore a prosthetic device, entered a foot race. As the race proceeded and he fell farther and farther behind, a big, strong Marine also fell behind and ran alongside the boy throughout the race. To no one's surprise, they both lost.

No one remembers who won the race. But they do remember the valor of the boy and they remember the humanity of the Marine.

To those lucky few who win the race, we give praise and trophies, television interviews, and contracts to sell tennis shoes, cars, insurance policies, and perfumes. We quote them as authorities on all sorts of things that they may know little or nothing about. We emulate them and wish that we could be like them.

To the losers, we sometimes give poetry. And often our hearts. Thus, the story of the Shuster mission to Persia (the country now called Iran) is, in a sense, our common story because we have all at one time or another needed a brace and we have all at one time or another failed. But it is also a story of courage and hope and failure and cupidity and avarice and sham and deceit, cowardice and generosity and hatred. Above all, it is about honesty and about personal and national integrity. This is about a man who thought that one's dignity and freedom were worthless if they were not to be shared with others. And it is about other men who struggled to create a modern state under circumstances that crushed many of them.

Scholars have debated whether Shuster's mission was worthwhile or a tragic catastrophe. Perhaps it was a bit of both. In any case, it is not my intention to add anything to the splendid work others have done. Rather it is to try to see the mission as Shuster saw it, in moral terms.

The story of the Shuster mission raises important ethical questions relevant not only for America's relationship with Iran but for our conduct toward any nation: that is, what if doing the right and honorable thing results in the massacre of hundreds, perhaps thousands of people who aren't particularly interested in your right and honorable behavior? Does one have the right to take a moral action that results in the slaughter of innocent people? As the reader will discover, I have not been able to find a satisfactory answer to this question. But the Shuster story is a reminder that it is worth pondering.

A word about names: I have kept the name "Persia" throughout this book because that had been the name of the country until it was changed to "Iran" in 1935. Thus, for the sake of consistency with the citations, it is "Persia" not "Iran" that is most often used.

Other proper names need an explanation. In 1911, last names were not yet in use. Persian men were commonly known by their titles. Neglecting to know or recognize a man's title, therefore, was to ignore his importance, a failing that was neither overlooked nor easily forgiven. Several titles in particular were in wide use among the people with whom Shuster worked: "Doula" or "Dowla" (state), "Mulk" or "Molk" (domain or kingdom), "Saltaneh" (sovereignty), "Nizam" (Guardian) and "Saltan" (sovereign). Thus, the Regent of the country in 1911 was known by his title, Nizam al-Mulk (Guardian of the Kingdom).

The title "Mirza" indicates a prince, and of course "Shah" indicates a king. A "Khan" was a tribal leader. "Atabak" at the time meant a government minister, and so Mirza Ali

Asghar Khan was known as "the Atabak."

The titles "Sepahdar" ("greatest of the marshals") and "Sardar" both indicate high-ranking military commanders equivalent to what we might call generals, with "Sepahdar" falling above the rank of "sardar." Thus Mohammad Vali Khan Nasr al-Saltaneh, the Sepahdar-i Azam (Grand Marshal), was known simply as "the Sepahdar."

Shuster's own name may be a puzzle. Christened William Morgan Shuster, he dropped the use of his first name since he shared it with both his father and grandfather, and normally signed his correspondence "W. Morgan Shuster." Informally, he was simply Morgan Shuster.

Transliterating Persian terms presents a unique challenge. For instance, the name of the Minister of Foreign Affairs with whom Shuster dealt can appear as Vosuq al-Daula, Vousuq ad-Dowla, Vusuqu'd-Daulah and, in Shuster's own case, Wuthuqu'd Dowla. Various attempts for standardizing Persian orthography in English including Ann Lambton's *Persian Grammar* (Cambridge, 1963), the Library of Congress, as well as several others have also been devised. Nonetheless, one searches in vain for uniform spellings of names and terms in works related to Iran, regardless of where or when they have been published. In this work, I've used a slightly modified version of the Lambert-Library of Congress system.

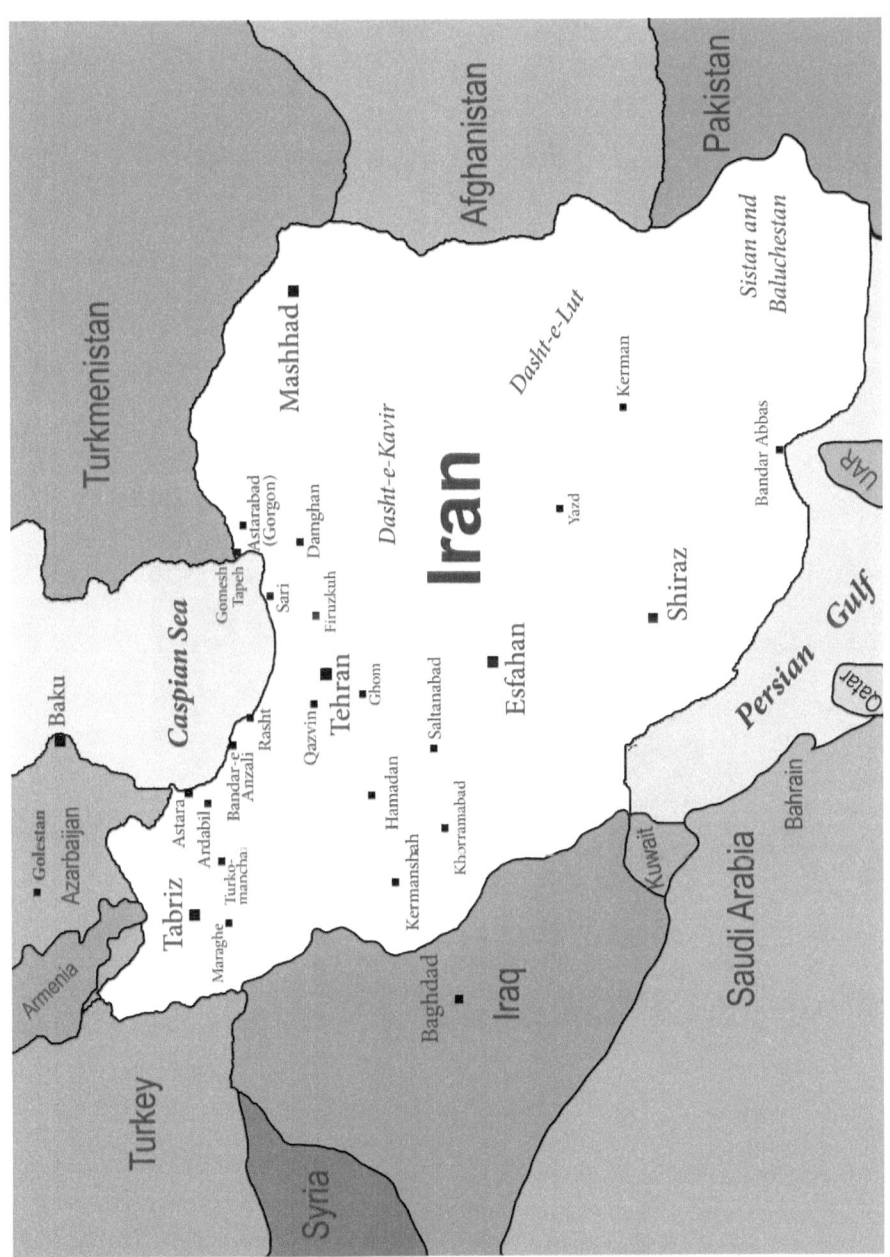

Morgan Shuster

I

A Fateful Treaty

"...the independence and integrity of Persia"

Persia's—and Morgan Shuster's—modern tragedy can be said to begin with the Treaty of Turkomanchai, signed by Fath Ali Shah (r. 1797-1834) on February 21, 1828, ending the second of two wars against Russia. An earlier treaty, also signed by Fath Ali Shah, ending the first war in 1813, had resulted in the loss of Dagestan, much of Azerbaijan, Eastern Georgia, and included such important cities such as Baku, Derbend, Shirvan, and Ganja—territories that had intermittently been part of the Persian Empire since the mid-sixteenth century. In addition, Persian ships had lost full rights to navigate the Caspian Sea and its coasts; henceforth, only Russian ships were to have that right.

From the time of Peter the Great, Russia's expansionist ambitions had come up against not only Persia's historic claims to territories in the Caucasus but to Persia's heartland as well. A loss to Russia in 1723 had forced Persia to relinquish the rich provinces of Gilan, Mazandaran, and Golestan bordering the southern shore of the Caspian Sea. Although they had been recovered about a decade later, Russia had proven to be an existential threat. Thus, the treaty signed in January 1813 at the little village of Golestan, had settled nothing.

In 1823, under some pressure from the Persian clergy, Fath Ali's son and designated heir, Abbas Mirza, had begun preparing for the second expedition with the aim of recovering not only the lost territories but the lost prestige of the previous war. In 1826, with an army larger than Russia's but not as well equipped, and expecting British support which didn't materialize, he marched north. Persia was defeated a second time and the capital of Azerbaijan, Tabriz, was occupied by Russian troops.

Fath Ali Shah's journey to Turkomanchai had begun almost three decades earlier. Born in 1772, he was the nephew of Agha Mohammad Khan, the viciously cruel and wily Turkoman chief who had founded the Qajar dynasty and whose land base had been in Azerbaijan. Following a series of very bloody battles against formidable rivals, Agha Mohammad had become master of the Iranian plateau. Then, in 1795, in order to thwart Russian expansion into former Persian territories, he marched into Georgia which had placed itself under Russian protection twelve years earlier. He had vanquished its capital, Tbilisi, and then marked his victory with the massacre of thousands, and the enslavement of about fifteen thousand women and children. Agha Mohammad had himself crowned the following spring and was assassinated the year after that. Before his death, however, through various bribes, threats, and other inducements, Agha Mohammad had paved the way for Fath Ali to succeed him to be followed by Abbas Mirza.

Upon Agha Mohammad's death, having put down several disturbances in Azerbaijan, Fath Ali punished Agha Khan's assassins, had the old shah's body carried to the holy city of Najaf in present-day Iraq for burial, and then had himself crowned in 1799.

Two years later, the massacre in Tbilisi neither forgotten nor forgiven, Georgia was annexed by Russia followed by Tsar Alexander I's annexation of Persian-controlled khanates bordering Georgia, including Dagestan and parts of Azerbaijan. In May 1804, Fath Ali had demanded Russian withdrawal from those regions. The demand had been rebuffed but it had not been until 1813 that Fath Ali had entered the first Russo-Persian War hoping to recapture those territories. He had expected British support but, shortly before the campaign began, that support had been lost as a result of Britain's alliance with Russia against Napoleon. In what proved to be a dress rehearsal for the second war thirteen years later, Fath Ali had entered the war unaided. And lost.

The Treaty of Turkomanchai drew Persia's northwestern boundary with Russia at the Aras River resulting in the further loss of territory. In addition, Persia was required to pay Russia 20 million rubles in reparations. The sum, equivalent to five million Persian tomans in gold, was nearly twice the size of Persia's annual income and virtually bankrupted the Persian state.[1] Other terms forced Persia to sign economic treaties with Russia as Russia specified and to recognize capitulation rights for Russia that included exempting foreigners, that is to say Russians, from the jurisdiction of Persian courts. Article XI of the treaty gave Russia the right to send consular envoys anywhere in Persia. In return, in accordance with Agha Khan's directive, the Russian tsar approved of Abbas Mirza as the successor to the Persian throne.

To Fath Ali, Russia gave the ungracious choice of either signing the treaty or, in five days, Russian troops would take the city of Tehran which had just become Persia's capital. Fath Ali signed the treaty but a year later, in February 1829, possibly without his knowledge or consent, a mob stormed the Russian embassy in Tehran and slaughtered almost everyone inside including a friend of the poet Alexander Pushkin, a playwright named Alexander Griboyedov who had been instrumental in designing the treaty. To apologize, Fath Ali dispatched not a regular envoy but one of his own sons bearing the large Shah Diamond from his treasury thereby exacerbating the humiliation of the treaty itself.

Fath Ali has received a less than flattering press both in the West and in Persia for a number of things but especially for the ignominy of Turkomanchai. One might argue that the initiator of a war "deserves" to lose and be humiliated. But in Persia's case, the loss of territory that Persia had long held, and the clear prospect that even more might be in jeopardy plus the fact that in the first war Persia had had some expectation of British support should take some of the sting out of whatever infamy Fath Ali has been burdened with since.

Moreover, Turkomanchai gave Persia the benefit of stability on the northern border—something that had long been lacking in that neighborhood. Although he could not possibly have foreseen it, in recognizing the Aras River boundary, Fath Ali was accepting what would prove to be a protective wall. The cycle of raids, wars, general butchery, and mayhem that had characterized life on both sides of the river throughout the eighteenth century was, while not entirely extinguished, substantially lessened. Russia's expansionist ambitions south and eastward would by no means be extinguished but Turkomanchai effectively assured that such ambitions would be halted at the Aras.

In the long run, however, what mattered most about the Treaty of Turkomanchai was not so much its specific terms but its timing. At the signing of that treaty, in addition to Persian and Russian dignitaries, several British officials were present as well. In 1813, when the Treaty of Golestan had ended the first conflict, despite his inglorious retreat from Russia, Napoleon Bonaparte had not yet been finally defeated and was still a threat felt by both Russia and Britain. By 1828, with that threat now extinguished, Britain and Russia would face not France but each other, and not in Europe but in Asia where both powers had imperial interests.

By 1828, the British East India Company had gained fair mastery of India, that "jewel in the crown" that would become the centerpiece of British foreign policy for the next century. Crucial to the defense of that "jewel" was control of the sea and land routes to India and, because of its geographic location, control of those routes involved Persia. The sea routes, including the Persian Gulf and Indian Ocean were guarded by Britain's navy. Thus, it was primarily through Persia's land neighbors lying to the east and north, Turkmenistan and Afghanistan, that British India could be threatened by Russia. Whether or not any Russian government had yet laid covetous eyes on India itself is debatable, but by 1828 Russian ambitions had already made Persia critical to the imperial ambitions of both Britain and Russia—often to Persia's advantage since neither would be able to threaten Persian sovereignty on her own soil without risking war with the other. Thus, in 1828, in the words of a phrase that would become infamous by the time Shuster arrived in Persia ninety years later, Russia and Britain really were genuinely interested in safeguarding the "independence and integrity of Persia." In the diplomatic game that would play out in the Middle East in the nineteenth century, it would be possible for Persia to play one against the other. Shortly after the signing of the Treaty of Turkomanchai, Britain granted Fath Ali a subsidy of £200,000 and Russia withdrew from Tabriz.

Turkomanchai was significant for another reason. It pulled Persia firmly into the orbit of Europe's diplomacy, its economies, and its culture. As unwelcome as the West ultimately proved to be in many areas, its ideas of liberalism, nationalism, secularism, and constitutionalism inevitably challenged the Persians' view of themselves and their relationship both with their own government and with the western world.

To be sure, there had been earlier contacts with both Russia and Britain. In 1598, the English adventurers, Anthony and Robert Sherley, had visited the court of the powerful Safavid monarch, Shah Abbas who later, in 1616, entered a military pact with England in order to wrest the island of Hormuz in the Persian Gulf from Portuguese control.[2] In 1763, Britain had established a residency at Bushehr, a post that gave the British East India Company a commanding commercial and naval position on the Persian Gulf.

Relations with Russia had been less cordial. Nonetheless, embassies from Peter the Great had arrived in Persia in 1708 and again in 1715.

Turkomanchai, however, pointed to a different kind of relationship with the West. Earlier embassies from Europe had been welcomed to an empire far larger, richer, and more powerful than the realms of the Tudors, Valois, and Hapsburgs combined. And the embassies had reciprocated. A fresco in the Vatican shows Pope Paul V receiving a Persian embassy in the early seventeenth century. Persia had not only dazzled Europe but had also been viewed as a potential and powerful ally against the expansionist Ottoman Empire. By 1828, however, torn by a century of internal strife and now twice defeated, Persia was not only smaller and weaker, but its future would not be entirely in its own hands.

An indirect beneficiary of Turkomanchai was that the city of Tehran remained intact. Arguably, the most important act of Agha Mohammad Khan's short reign had been to make Tehran his capital for two reasons. First, a settled capital marked a sharp break from a tribal to an urban regime. Government hereafter was to be located at a specific place rather than at whatever tribal encampment the king and his retinue happened to lodge themselves. What the wars with Russia had shown was that, if Persia were to survive, tribal levies would have to either be supplemented or entirely replaced by a disciplined army with modern weaponry and under a command headquartered at a base close to the center of power. Quite simply, a modern army can happen only if there is a centralized state possessing the bureaucratic machinery to support it. A settled capital provided the possibility for such a modern army to be created.

Secondly, a city rather than an encampment also represented a close tie with the religion of most Persians. Shi'a

Islam is quintessentially urban. And urbane. Thus, Agha Mohammad was offering a hand, albeit a rather bloody one, to a powerful element in Persian society that could either be a support or a thorn, the clergy—the *ulema*.

The choice of that particular site for a capital provides a fascinating insight into Agha Mohammad's thinking. Why Tehran? Why not simply return to Isfahan, the Safavid capital with its splendid mosques, palaces, and gardens and, moreover, with that commodity for which most of Persia, including the area around Tehran, thirsts—a river, a source of water? Or why did not Tabriz, the commercial center and capital of Azerbaijan with its "window" into the Caucasus, become the new capital of Persia? Another possibility might have been the city of Sari, Agha Khan's headquarters in the province of Mazandaran.

The reason may have been that other cities like Isfahan had historical "baggage" or, like Tabriz, were too closely identified with a specific tribal or ethnic group. Isfahan's link with the Safavid dynasty (1501-1736) might have ignited questions of the legitimacy—or lack thereof—of the new dynasty. Tehran was not only "new" but it was also within fairly easy striking distance of Azerbaijan, as well as Isfahan, and close to the rich agricultural provinces bordering the Caspian Sea. Nestled in the foothills of the Alborz mountains and in the shadow of Persia's highest mountain, Damavand, the city was also easier to defend than either Tabriz or Isfahan. In settling on Tehran, Agha Mohammad made it clear that he was a Persian, not simply a Qajar king, thus laying the foundation for the idea of a Persian "nation." In the next century it would be to Tehran that diplomats, merchants, scholars, curious travelers, missionaries, and an occasional scoundrel or two from across the world would come. And it would be in Tehran that they would find embassies, legations, shops, and eventually hospitals, churches, schools, and orphanages where they could exchange goods, news, ideas, and gossip.

Tehran never would have quite the graceful splendor of Isfahan, but from a dusty nondescript village Fath Ali began to turn it into a fairly decent city. It had been a retreat for the Safavid kings, and the remnants of the small Golestan Palace were still there. Fath Ali enlarged this palace and then also engaged in the building of several beautiful mosques possibly to assuage his conscience but also, hopefully, to gain the support, if not the affection, of the ulema. In a further gesture to gain their support, he paid special attention to the holy city of Qom, where he encouraged the rehabilitation of a number of mosques and mausoleums which had been damaged or fallen into disrepair.

Aside from the humiliation of having lost twice to Russia, Fath Ali Shah is usually remembered for little except his long beard, slender waist, the development of elaborate court etiquette and a cache of splendid portrait paintings, primarily of the shah himself, plus his progeny which numbered 130 sons and 150 daughters by about a thousand or so ladies at the court.[3] Some of the ladies were concubines, at least four were legitimate wives, and others were of assorted casual status.

That he is remembered for so little is significant. And perhaps unjust. As had been the case in many Western cultures, marriage or concubinage was a means of consolidating power. Although his numerous progeny suggests no small amount of carnal pleasure, Fath Ali's marriages were often political arrangements—the daughters of tribal chiefs, high-ranking officials, Persian and Georgian slave girls, as well as women captured in war or given as gifts—thereby sparing the country the horror of civil war which had wracked it for most of the preceding century. His numerous male offspring, placed in strategic provincial governorships, gave the Crown at least theoretical dominion over the entire realm. Moreover, despite the losses in the Turkomanchai treaty, Persia lost no further territory and actually made modest economic gains. Most importantly, the country did not lose its independence or disintegrate into autonomous units jealous of the Crown and at odds with each other.

Fath Ali also did his country another, not inconsequential, favor: he lived a long time and, shortly after the death of his designated heir, Abbas Mirza, Fath Ali died of natural causes in his own bed in 1834 without leaving his country bankrupt. For the time being.

Abbas Mirza's son, Mohammad, was approved as Fath Ali's successor, per Turkomanchai, by Russia and Britain over the heads of many rivals. The short reign of Mohammad Shah brought few improvements and what could have been a fatal rupture with the clergy. He fell so deeply under the influence of a Sufi minister, Haji Mirza Aghasi, that the two were often ridiculed as the "two dervishes." His failed attempt in 1837 to re-take the city of Herat in Afghanistan from the British resulted in a humiliating withdrawal and gained him the scorn of those among his subjects who bothered to care.

Happily for Persia, the reign of Mohammad Shah was relatively short and he too, like Fath Ali, managed to lose no further territory and die in bed.

Agha Mohammad Khan (r. 1789-1797)

There is a theory that the pained look on his face as well as the cruelty which intensified the older he became were due to having been castrated as a youth.

Fath Ali Shah (r. 1797-1834)

II

The Realm of the Qajars

"Persia is overrun with tribes."
—Lady Mary Sheil

By the time Mohammad Shah died in 1848, the pattern of Qajar government, constructed roughly on the Safavid model, and one similar to the monarchies of early modern Europe, had emerged. The shah was an absolute monarch who, in his person, combined legislative, executive, and judicial powers. He was the Shahanshah, the Shah of Shahs, the King of Kings, the Shadow of God. To rebel against him was to rebel against the will of God. He had authority surpassed by none and he was responsible to no one. His realm was his possession. To have suggested otherwise would have been an invitation to return to the troubled decades of the period before Agha Khan.

At the heart of the Qajar system lay the fundamental weakness that would be the undoing of the dynasty. No bankruptcy, no threat of invasion, no diplomatic inveigling by foreign powers would so seriously devastate the regime as the fact that it was an autocracy and, like any autocracy, it was a house of glass. The shah was, as Lord George Curzon would phrase it, "the pivot upon which turns the entire machinery of public life,"[4] That was, however, the shah's greatest weakness. When things went well, he could expect full credit and honor, but when things fell apart, he could also expect full blame.

The administrative center was a Court that embraced hordes of royal relatives and a well-populated harem among whom the queen mother and/or favorite wife often played influential roles. There was no hereditary aristocracy that would be recognized in a western court. Nor was there any centralized, organized bureaucracy that could operate independently of the shah. Offices in both the central and provincial governments were bought or gifted by the shah. These appointments usually came from the royal family or from among tribal khans whose loyalty the shah found it prudent to secure.

Provinces were subdivided into districts, cities, and towns each requiring an official whose appointment by the shah was a lever to secure loyalty. Since the sole qualification for an appointment was loyalty, neither service nor competence nor accountability was required or expected. No existing roads or bridges needed to be repaired nor new ones built. No schools, hospitals, or dispensaries needed to be opened or staffed. None of Persia's historic monuments needed to be cared for. No firefighters, police agencies, or sanitation workers needed to be trained, equipped, and salaried. Innovation or experimentation in any area, because there is normally some risk involved, was discouraged while the arts of flattery and sycophancy thrived.

There were no salaries as such. The office holder was expected to derive his income from his constituents, and obviously the higher the office the more was required to maintain his household in the style to which he thought it necessary. What was gifted arbitrarily, of course, could just as arbitrarily be taken away. If the shah were in good spirits or liked the wit or flattery of some court official, or simply acting on a whim, he would grant him a title or an office or perhaps the revenue of a village or several villages as a token of royal esteem. He might also direct that the name of a favored one be put on the civil list for a pension of so many hundreds or thousands of tomans,[5] per year, or for so many *khavars* (about a third of a ton) of wheat, barley, or straw. No province lacked a pension roll, the largest being, of course, Tehran. Most of what budget there was, therefore, went to support the Court and its dependents. In a few cases—very few cases—these pensions, which were normally hereditary, were granted for public services actually rendered.

Aside from the autocracy itself, there were two other barriers to the extension of effective authority emanating from Tehran, and the Court could ill afford to jeopardize the support of either one. These were the Shi'a clergy, the *ulema*, and Persia's tribes. Indeed, that the Qajar rulers in the nineteenth century were often able to maintain the support of both without becoming the tool of either is of no little importance.

Over the ulema, the government had no control since the center of Shi'a religious authority was not in Persia but in the cities of Karbala and Najaf in the Ottoman Empire. Moreover, according to Persia's Twelver Shi'ism,[6] the only legitimate authority came from God and it was only the higher members of the ulema, the *mojtahids*, who could interpret the intentions of the Twelfth or Hidden Imam. Secular authority was inferior and was, therefore, to be simply tolerated.

Traditionally, the clergy had acted as both buffer and mediator between the people and their rulers. Their connections with both the bazaar and the lower classes were strong since members of both classes tended to be deeply religious. The clergy knew the Scriptures; they were literate. To the lower classes, they were therefore, not only a source of religious guidance, but also of social and political instruction as well. To the merchants in the larger cities, the ulema not only served as arbitrators in commercial disputes but lower members of the clergy, the mullahs, themselves were often engaged in trade. As a result of that encompassing influence, the Court often found it wise to offer an office, a gift, a grant of land, a pension, or some other emolument in return for the support of an enterprising cleric who might need to assuage his conscience for tolerating the existence of secular governance.

Beyond the control of the Court, because it was in the

hands of the clergy, was a good portion of the judiciary. It was divided between the Sharia (religious) courts and the secular courts over which the shah theoretically presided. In the Sharia courts, the law and the procedures for its administration were fairly uniform. That was not the case in the secular courts, however, where procedures and decisions were subject to bribery on rather heroic terms, ranging from charges for petty acts barely managing to be criminal to egregious offenses normally meriting capital punishment. Lord Curzon found that, in no other country was bribery "so open, so shameless, or so universal" as it was in Persia.[7]

Aside from the Christian missionary schools, education was also in clerical hands. For the most part, it was traditional, religious, and limited largely to basic reading and writing enough to memorize the Koran which, in Arabic, was often little understood. Western science, philosophy, literature, political and economic theory, technology, and art—the learning, that is, of the *kafir* (infidel)—was thought to be useless at best, toxic at worst. Yet, it is important to note that, throughout the Qajar period, the Persian clergy, like the clergy of the Islamic world in general, was not at all unified in its response to the impact of the West. While many theologians viewed Western ideas and institutions as having absolutely no merit in Islamic society, others, especially during the latter half of the nineteenth century, became convinced that Islam, rightly understood, was compatible with much of what the West could offer.

The divide often centered on whether girls should be educated and, on that question, the girls lost and were educated but rarely. Despite that, by the end of the century, a number of upper-class women had become literate enough to form *anjemans*, or societies that were largely directed at philanthropic and educational work, particularly in the duties of citizenship. What these women discovered, however, was that the duties of citizenship led inexorably to participation in Persia's political life—and participate they would.

The second barrier to the extension of royal power and at the same time, like the ulema, a potential—indeed, indispensable—ally was Persia's tribes. "Persia" wrote Lady Mary Sheil, "is overrun with tribes."[8] Between a quarter and a third of Persia's population belonged to tribes consisting of between two or three to as many as a couple of dozen clans. Lady Mary estimated that, if both the wandering and the stationary clans were taken into calculation, they might have equaled in number all of the other inhabitants of Persia.[9] Often living in arid, mountainous areas, each with its own unique set of social relationships and administrative structures, the tribes were closely bound, largely autonomous, and fiercely proud of their independence. At least as late as the mid-twentieth century, it was possible to meet an inhabitant of Iran who would identify herself or himself as a member of a tribe—a Kurd or Lur or Azeri, for instance, almost as easily as identifying as "Iranian." That independence, that special identity was (and still is) expressed in a variety of ways, including distinctive patterns and colors in crafts such as carpets, jewelry, tiles, and pottery decoration, in dance, music, cuisine, and costume.

In addition to simple banditry, the tribes lived off the wool and meat from the livestock they raised. This was traded in the towns and villages for things they could not provide for themselves such as food stuffs and weapons. In addition to that form of exchange, there was another; towns and villages could be required to pay the tribes for protection against raids, usually in the form of goods, to assure that something would remain at harvest time. Because the tribes were nomadic or semi-nomadic, it was almost impossible to gauge their size or their assets for taxable purposes. Nor was it possible to impose policy on them from Tehran. In 1908, for instance, the drilling of oil by what would become the Anglo-Persian Oil

Company at Masjid-e Suleiman in southwestern Persia had deprived the Bakhtiari tribes of their traditional pastures.[10] As compensation, in return for 5% of the profits over a period of twenty-five years, the tribal *khans* quite independently of the central government, made an agreement to provide what the central government could not, namely, a guarantee of the security of the oil installations.

The tribes provided Persia's best fighting men which made them useful but at the same time dangerous to the Court. Thus, in return for their loyalty, the khans often became provincial governors or other court officials. Nonetheless, as useful as they might be, the tribes were also a divisive presence. Many of them were neither ethnically Persian, nor, in some cases, Shi'a Muslims, nor was Persian necessarily their native tongue. The Turkic-speaking Turkomans in the north and the Baluchis in the southwest as well as the Lur-speaking Bakhtiaris in the west who would play a major role in Shuster's short career in Persia were predominantly Sunni. The Azerbaijani Turks whose homelands bordered the Ottoman and Russian Empires were Shi'a but were as likely to speak Turkish or Russian as Persian and for them, the rest of the population had little affection. The homelands of the Kurds in the west who were also largely Sunni stretched into both Russia and the Ottoman Empire and their affection for those two governments as well as Persia's was, at best, flaccid.

There was a Persian army—of sorts. It was chronically underpaid, ill-equipped, and ill-led largely because armies—as opposed to a tribal levy—required money and the Qajar treasury was chronically short of that. Lady Mary Sheil observed that, while the Persian soldier was good, the officers were the reverse. Rank was often sold or given to men and boys who had no military experience and were never expected to gain any, but who pocketed their salaries and then followed whatever trade in the bazaar in which they were inclined to engage. Because of the prevalence of bribery and favors, Lady Mary noted, a forty- or fifty-year-old man with no military experience whatsoever could suddenly morph into a colonel, a brigadier, a general, or even a commander-in-chief.[11] As Shuster would later point out, with good reason, "nobody paid much attention to the army as a serious factor in affairs."[12] What that meant, however, was that in a time of crisis, the government had nothing to rely on—except the tribes who were far better armed but whose loyalty, as Shuster would painfully discover, depended on whatever personal gain could be extracted from either the government or the spoils of a campaign.

In a country with the abundant natural resources that Persia possesses, the penury of the Qajar army, indeed the increasing poverty of the country itself throughout the Qajar period, seems baffling. The major explanation is that Qajar Persia presented a basic contradiction: in a government that was theoretically an absolutist monarchy, real power was, in fact, diffuse. This was most seriously damaging when it came to raising revenue.

The Qajar method of taxation was one that both an official from the Safavid court and St. Matthew, the publican apostle of Jesus Christ, would have recognized; that is, it was essentially tax farming. There were seventeen or eighteen taxation districts in Persia each containing its own large town, normally the provincial capital. Several hundred local tax collectors, or *pishkars*, were in charge of collecting taxes at a figure set by the central government. The province was then subdivided into smaller districts, each with its own sub-collector, and those districts were, in turn, divided into villages where the taxes were collected by the local headman, the *kadkhoda*.

The pishkar was required to deliver from his district a sum fixed by the central government, but how that sum was arrived at or how it was actually collected allowed for all kinds of creativity. The pishkar would tell the sub-collectors how much he expected from each of them. He would then keep track of what he received from each sub-collector in a little notebook called a *ketabche* which he carried in his own pocket. The office of pishkar and his ketabche were usually handed down from father to son. The notations were kept in a script that even someone who could read Persian well would not have been able to understand.[13] Often prepared generations earlier, the ketabche offered no updated basis for tax collection. Thus, the pishkar would have no idea of the sources from which the sub-collectors were deriving the taxes they delivered to him unless they decided to do a re-evaluation—which the village paid for and which, for reasons that were not necessarily altruistic, did occasionally happen.

Above the pishkars, was a class of seven or eight senior tax overseers called *mostafis,* each responsible for two or more provinces or districts, who actually could read the ketabches. The mostafis were responsible for seeing to it that the tax collectors throughout the country placed to the credit of the central government the sums they were expected to provide. Although Shuster would find a Bureau of Mostafis in the Ministry of Finance, he would also find that the mostafis regarded neither the bureau itself nor the ketabche records as belonging to the government, and they resented any interference from the government. This office was usually hereditary but, like all the officials in tax collection, salaried at a miserably low level. After only a few years' service, however, most of them became wealthy or, as Shuster would delicately put it, "they were deriving a satisfactory reward in some way other than through the pay-roll."[14]

The largest share of taxes came from something called the *maliat* which was levied on land and therefore, affected the majority of Persia's population, the peasants, herdsmen, and craftsmen who lived in small, isolated villages whose kadkhoda mediated their disputes, oversaw the maintenance of common lands, and supervised the rotation of strips of arable land allocated to each cultivator. The office was quasi-hereditary; that is, it normally passed from father to son and thus had the potential to invite tyrannical behavior on the part of its holder. However, since the kadkhoda was someone's uncle, another person's son-in-law, and yet another's nephew or other close relative, the villagers themselves could exercise informal control of his integrity.

The individual cultivator did not technically "own" the land he cultivated; instead, he "held" it as long as he paid rent to the *arbab* or owner of the village through the kadkhoda, who would determine what part of the tax each household in his village would be responsible for bearing. Then, because cash was a rare—and in the majority of rural areas a non-existent commodity—the maliat was paid in kind—wheat, rice, barley, cotton, nuts, rice, tea, tobacco, silk, opium, and occasionally livestock or even labor.

Aside from the obvious challenges to personal integrity, there were several impediments for the government with this system: First, even if the tax collectors were honest, it was almost impossible for the central government to formulate anything like a national budget since it was almost impossible to devise a system for determining exactly what the revenues from a particular village, town, or district might be. Villages that had been prosperous, for instance, may have been hurt by a decline in population due to weather conditions, perhaps, or famine, a succession of tribal raids, the exhaustion of soil or any combination of the above, while others might have become more populous and prosperous. Yet the amount of the tax required from a village normally remained the same regardless.

Second, determining the cash value of commodities was

extremely difficult. Did a kilo of tea have the same value as a kilo of nuts, for instance? It would have been difficult to put equitable cash values on goods in Persia's domestic market but calculating reasonable tax revenues would have required not just honesty but expertise in the functioning of economies far removed from the experience of a Persian mostafi or pishkar.

Third, it was often difficult to determine what a "village" was and what it was not. It was rarely a tidy, compact thing fitting onto a dot on a map—assuming that a pishkar had a map. It could also be a collection of more or less inaccessible hamlets with two or four or maybe half a dozen families. What land they cultivated, where one strip ended and another began, and the value of that land, therefore, would have been difficult for all but the most conscientious collector to assess. Not surprisingly, one observer in 1881 concluded that "The nominal assessment differs so often from the sum really exacted and...anything like exactitude in calculation is impossible." The assessments of an individual village were, as he put it, "valueless."[15] Hence, the real tax that a peasant actually paid was often much higher than the government's assessment.

The lives of these people were dismal. More than a century later, Arthur Millspaugh who would be Morgan Shuster's successor in Persia, said of Persia's people, "Their toil had three simple objects: to exist, to satisfy the demands of the landowners, and to meet the multiplied exactions of an extravagant and rapacious government."[16] James Bassett, an American missionary who worked in Persia in the early 1870s, described conditions of decay, famine, and sickness so severe that some people had been driven to cannibalism. Granted, much of what he saw was the result of an unusually severe famine; nonetheless, the poverty was deep and generations old.[17] And it was not something the central government was eager to ameliorate. The founder of the dynasty, Agha Mohammad Khan, had given Fath Ali advice which none of the

Qajar rulers apparently ever forgot: It is easier to rule your people if you keep them poor, he had suggested. They must be kept occupied with much labor lest they be given time to think. If they are not poor, they become interested in politics and want to change things but if you keep them poor, he advised, you rule them.[18]

Ironically, the "exactions of an extravagant and rapacious government" themselves were haphazard. Everyone was taxed but not everyone actually paid taxes. There were any number of exemptions. Theoretically, the ulema could be taxed and among the higher ranks there was a good bit of wealth. However, as in many Western countries, a significant amount of that revenue came from the ulema's own direct taxation of religious holdings and from *vaghf* donations. Vaghf is an inalienable endowment in money or property given either for charitable purposes such as the support of poor clerical students or for institutions such as schools, hospitals, shrines, or mosques controlled by the ulema and hence, beyond the reach of the tax collector.

As Persia's merchant class grew in the last half of the nineteenth century, merchants, craftsmen, artisans, their guilds, and any and all kinds of tangible goods they produced were taxed. Influential people were taxed but usually found ways to avoid actually sending anything of value to the central government and, if one could secure influence, one could receive an exemption from any tax at all.

To have viewed the system as a kind of pervasive brigandage, as Shuster would, misses the mark. Brigands are normally better organized. It was possible, for instance, for the local pishkar to tell the government that due to "disturbed conditions," it was impossible to collect the required revenues and then not to send anything at all. In a vicious circle, as resources for policing the country dwindled, the pishkar of almost any province could have honestly found quite enough "disturbed conditions" to avoid sending the required revenues to Tehran. And without the revenues, it was impossible to quell the "disturbed conditions" leading to a further decline in revenue collection. Nor, without the revenues, was it feasible to either repair what existing infrastructure there was or to engage in new projects.

Another problem was that transport had to be found—and paid for—in order to get the taxes to a central location. Unless the tax/produce had been collected in the districts near Tehran, it had to pass through many hands which needed to be greased and be transported often under extremely difficult conditions before it reached Tehran. By the end of the nineteenth century, the empire did possess about six or seven main roads connecting the major urban centers. None of them were paved. Outlying roads, where they existed at all, were often little more than dirt paths. Because policing was a haphazard affair, there was little or no security for either the produce or the carriers. Then, either secure storage facilities had to be located and paid for or the "taxes" had to be converted into liquid cash in order to pay the expenses of the government, a procedure that invited no small amount of graft.

****

Whether the Treaty of Turkomanchai was a cause of bringing Persia into the international market or simply coincided with other factors in the development of a fairly vigorous middle class in the nineteenth century is a matter for discussion elsewhere. Certainly, the stabilization of the northern frontier with Russia benefitted Persia since it allowed merchants from both sides to carry on a trade the value of which doubled, tripled, and then quadrupled in value.[19] From cities in the north like Tabriz, Ardabil, Rasht, Sari, and Mashhad, wool, cotton, silk, almonds, and pistachios, and eventually tea and rice could be sent by rail to Russia and thence to markets in Europe.[20] At the same time, the presence of the British navy in the Persian Gulf allowed the safe transport of carpets, tobacco, herbs, textiles, and wheat, to be shipped from Shiraz, Kerman, Yazd, and Bushehr to markets in British India, the Levant, and thence to Europe.

Ironically, while the international market brought wealth into Persia, and the natural resources and labor potential were there to develop even more wealth, there were not many wealthy Persians. While a small number of entrepreneurs benefitted, and as the increase in the export of agricultural goods especially increased, the value of those goods either remained stationery or decreased. Robert McDaniel notes, for example, that the amount of wheat exported from Bushehr between 1869 and 1894 increased as much as eight times in volume but the value remained almost the same.[21]

Part of the explanation for that is that entrance into the global market also subjected Persia to the fluctuations within that market. Persia had been on the silver standard but in the mid-1860s, much of the industrialized world went on gold, thus dropping the value of silver which drained the country of its bullion. Then in the late 1860s, the Caspian province of Gilan which had produced some of the world's finest silk was devastated by a silkworm disease from which it never fully recovered. In 1871, a global depression caused a huge drop in the price of all agricultural commodities but especially Persia's wheat. The depression in that market was unfortunately accompanied by drought, and then famine so severe that an estimated one-tenth of the population died.[22] The suffering led to riots. And repression. And more discontent. And more repression.

Persia's international trade was of little interest or value to the vast majority of the population, however, who remained dependent on the cultivation of land. Imported goods tended to provide unfair competition for Persia's own produce. In the 1890s, for instance, American cotton was introduced. Its seeds produced a more abundant crop and one of better quality than the Persian variety. This should have been a boon to the grower of the cotton. Instead, although the price of this cotton increased with demand, in order to meet that demand, a cultivator's landlord would need to acquire more land, and that went with a commensurate increase in the tax burden on that land. Squeezed between the landlord and the tax collector, the peasant's benefit from international trade was negative.

The years from 1869 to 1872 were disastrous. Rainfall was light and, in some areas, there was none at all. For the peasant, this meant starvation; for the towns, discontent, and for the economy in general, the outflow of silver in order to buy on the world market what could not be produced at home was devastating. [23]

During the last quarter of the nineteenth century, entry into international markets saw the emergence of a new class of merchants, tradesmen, artisans, mechanics and laborers, government officials, and members of the clergy whose status rested on money rather than land. Self-conscious and often literate if not well-educated, these people managed their own affairs with little interference from the government. Young Persian merchants in Istanbul, Calcutta, and Mumbai, Cairo, Tbilisi, Paris, Vienna, and London not only developed a taste, albeit an often unsophisticated one, for the goods and often the manners of that wider world, but they also became increasingly critical of the closed, insular world of stern clerics and ignorant rural folks into which they had been born. And from the West came a technology that would have far more impact on Persia than railroads or steamships, or mechanized looms, technology that carried not goods but ideas—the newspaper.

The Shuster Mission to Iran

****

Robert McDaniel opens the second chapter of his study of the Constitutional Revolution and Shuster's role in it with the statement, "In the eighteenth century there was no Persia, there were only Persians."[24] That his statement accurately describes Persia's bloody, fractious history following the decay of the Safavid empire in the early part of that century is clear, but contemporaries and some modern scholars have wondered if such a thing as Persian "nationalism" existed even by the twentieth century when Shuster arrived in Persia. As Homa Katouzian argues, except for a small, educated elite, most Persians identified their village or tribe or possibly their town or province as their *vatan*, that is, their homeland.[25]

In one sense, the question of whether a Persia actually existed assumes that what the West understands by "nation" is the only construct worthy of being taken seriously; that if it was not a "nation," then that land called "Persia" naturally invited other actual "nations" to step in and "correct" its perceived defects. Criticism that Persia was not a nation is also ahistorical since it ignores the fact that "nationalism" is almost as recent an idea in the West as it is in the Middle East.[26] Until the middle of the nineteenth century, there was, for instance, no Germany or Italy, only Germans and Italians. Indeed, the psychological historian A. Maurice Low wondered what, or if, there was even such a thing as an American race or nationality in his two-volume *American People: A Study in National Psychology*, published just as Shuster entered Persia, in 1909-1911.[27]

Yet what Michael Axworthy calls an "empire of the mind" definitely did exist. Or, as Katouzian also asserts, "There certainly was a sense of Iranian community and culture, largely centered on the Persian language and literature, and a sense of what most of that community held in common, including religious beliefs and passions."[28]

Persian intellectuals who thought about a "nation" often identified it with Shi'a Islam, made Persia's state religion by order of the Safavid Shah Abbas in the sixteenth century. The Shi'a branch of Islam itself derives from the claim of Ali, the Prophet Mohammad's cousin, son-in-law, and first male convert to Islam, to be the rightful heir of the Prophet—a claim denied by adherents of the majority Sunni Islam community.[29] The martyrdom of Ali in 661 A.D. at the hands of the supporters of Mu'awiya who would found the Ummayid dynasty, and then of Ali's, son, Hussein, and his tiny band of about seventy-two followers at Karbala in the year 680 by an Ummayid army numbering about 4000 has given to Shi'ite Muslims a sense of belonging to a righteous, persecuted minority against an illegitimate, unrighteous majority. Moreover, transcending religion, there were few Persians, literate or not, Muslim or not, who did not, and still do not, share that sense of having been somehow dispossessed, betrayed, deprived of a rightful heritage, and humiliated by history.

Almost paradoxically, however, the very fact of being on the "losing" side of history has also given Persians the habit of adapting to and transforming misfortune to their advantage. The Arab conquests of the seventh century, for instance, had given Islam to Persians but it was Persia's arts, mathematics, science, poetry, manners, mysticism, its expertise in diplomacy and government that had transformed and enriched the Islamic civilizations of the subsequent centuries. As it gave, Persia also received. The Arabic of their conquerors gave Persians a new script in which to write their language but for at least a millennium, their own language itself then became the language of learning and culture throughout the Islamic world.

Despite the disapproval of the more conservative ulema,

there were other Persian intellectuals who looked back to the pre-Islamic past and the glories of the Achaemenid, Sassanian, and Safavid dynasties to trace an Iranian or Persian "nation." Whatever the source of "nation" might be, there was among most thinkers a sense that there was a common culture, something that most of the people who lived in Persia held in common. Although Persian might not have been the native tongue of everyone, the heroes and heroines of the great Persian epic, the *Shahnameh (Book of Shahs)* written by the eleventh century poet, Ferdowsi (940-1020 C.E), were part of a shared heritage as were other poets such as Khayyam, Hafez, Sa'adi, Nezami, and Rumi. At least well into the twentieth century, illiterate women could be heard disciplining their children and wrangling with bazaar merchants in couplets from Hafez or in a local or tribal dialect sprinkled with aphorisms from Omar Khayyam. Indeed, one observer noted that "...the influence of Hafez is greater in the long run than that of all the mullahs."[30] The shared calendar was Islamic, with the years dating from the Hejira, but with months calculated and named on one developed by Khayyam. And the most joyous date on that calendar, Nowruz (New Year), a feast dating back to Persia's Zoroastrian past, was celebrated by everyone.

Upon whatever basis a Persian nation might be conceived, however, the divisive elements within Persia were so formidable that the development of loyalty to something as abstract as a Persian state that transcended local identities was going to bedevil not only the Qajars but their successor dynasty, the Pahlavis, as well. Nonetheless, if there had not been a sense of "nationalism" by the end of the nineteenth century, the reign of Nasr al-Din would foster its creation.

III

A King Besieged

"...a selfish despot...most averse to the introduction of liberal ideas amongst a people whose natural quickness, intelligence, and aptitude to learn cause him nothing but anxiety."

—Taj al-Saltana

At Mohammad Mirza's death in 1848, his seventeen-year-old son, Nasr al-Din, ascended the throne. His reign would span almost the entire second half of the nineteenth century—a moment in history when the technologies of the Industrial Revolution linked to the service of European imperialism would permanently transform the countries of the Middle East, including Persia.

By the time Nasr al-Din reached the throne, a pattern of deep and ever-expanding indebtedness had already taken root. Lady Mary Sheil, the wife of Sir Justin Sheil who had been appointed British envoy to the shah's court about a year after Nasr al-Din's coronation, observed, "The entire nation seems to be in debt, commencing with the Shah, who is in debt to the Emperor of Russia, and ending with the humblest muleteer."[31] The annual net revenue, including the value of revenue paid in kind, was 2,677,000 tomans, but of that amount 2,656,601 was consumed in expenditures which could be listed. What was not listed in that figure were the expenses connected with the maintenance of the Court which, she noted, were "considerable" and the little that was left over was spent in "various uncertain expenses" such as diamond-hilted swords, decorations, and "extraordinary" military expenses caused by insurrections.[32] Salaries for various functionaries were absurdly high. The salary for a provincial governor, for instance, could be on the same scale as that of the Governor-General of India.[33] That would not have included the allocations for his retinue which could number in the hundreds of followers.

Nonetheless, three ministers would attempt to place Qajar government on a sound economic footing. The first of these was Mirza Taqi Khan Farahani.

According to Qajar custom, Nasr al-Din, as the crown prince, had been serving as governor of Azerbaijan. When his father's death was announced, it was to his tutor, the forty-year-old Mirza Taqi Khan Farahani, that the young king turned for assistance in reaching Tehran and securing his throne. On the evening of his coronation, Nasr al-Din named Mirza Taqi Khan his chancellor and awarded him the title by which he is still known, Amir Kabir.

Born in 1809, the son of the chief chef to Qa'im Maqm, the chief minister of Abbas Mirza, Amir Kabir had quickly risen to prominence at the court and, beginning at the age of twenty-two, he had undertaken several important diplomatic missions. As a result, he had become convinced that Persia could not advance unless it adapted along Western lines, and so he had established Persian embassies at London and St. Petersburg. As an envoy to the Ottoman Empire, he had become familiar with the positive effects of that government's liberalizing and westernizing reform program known as the Tanzimat.[34] Unlike in the Ottoman government, however, Amir Kabir found a treasury in Persia that was entirely bankrupt. Recognizing that fiscal stability was the *sine qua non* for political independence, he attempted to balance the state budget by doing two things that Shuster would also attempt sixty years later and that, although they made perfect sense, would be all but impossible to accomplish: curbing expenditures while increasing sources of revenue.

The largest single expenditure was the Court. Nasr al-

Din possessed eighty wives and concubines each of whom had about ten or twenty maidservants and other assorted domestics. Thus, at any one time, the population in the royal harem reached between five and six hundred.[35] In addition, each lady had a residence, a stipend, her own staff of servants, and all the necessities a royal household required. Amir Kabir's first belt-tightening measure was to cut the allowances of the Court, including those of the very influential and ultimately very dangerous Queen Mother. The salaries of government officials were also cut and many of the stipends paid to pensioners and courtiers who had given the government little if any service were also either drastically reduced or entirely eliminated.

In his efforts to augment the flow of revenues into the treasury, Amir Kabir recovered the Caspian fisheries from Russia in whose hands they had been since 1828, and placed them into the hands of Persians. He earned the support of Tehran's merchants by laying the foundation for the great bazaar in that city. The bazaar in any city is a tightly knit unit with its own sense of independence but the one in Tehran would play—and has continued to play—a crucial role in Persian politics.

Amir Kabir sent assessors and collectors to every province of the country to collect overdue taxes from provincial governors and tribal chieftains. And he made the collection of Customs duties which had been farmed out to individuals, the direct responsibility of the government. Unfortunately, as Shuster would also later learn, enforcing honesty and discipline in tax and Customs collection earned not gratitude or even minimal cooperation but rather, the hostility of scores of officials who had long viewed graft as their solemn, hereditary right.

More importantly, and destined to outlive him, Amir Kabir established the Dar al-Fanun, a state-funded polytechnic institute, similar to one established in the Ottoman Empire. Designed to train military officers and civil servants, its curriculum quickly came to mirror that of a European university. Among the subjects taught were medicine, natural history, mathematics, surgery, and science. Most of the instructors were Europeans who knew no Persian, so interpreters had to be used. In this, too, Amir Kabir earned the ire of the conservative clergy, the ulema, who viewed education as their prerogative, and western education as useless, if not downright heretical.

Amir Kabir's reforms were sound and wise, and thus won the hostility of other influential groups as well. No one at Court approved of him. He was also disliked by both the British and the Russians who saw that his reforms would lead ultimately to the kind of financial independence which would have impinged upon their own "interests" in Persia. The hostility of the Queen Mother, however, was mortal. After three short years, in 1851, he was dismissed, exiled to Kashan, and shortly thereafter, taken to the "Fin Bath" in that city where his veins were cut and he was bled to death.

Shortly before his dismissal, there had been an even uglier blood-letting that had everything to do with Persia's religious identity. Sayyid Ali Mohammad had been born in 1819 into a merchant family in Shiraz. In 1844, when he was about twenty-five years old, he declared himself to be the *"bab"* or gate who would announce the coming of the Mahdi, the savior who would bring about the spiritual and moral regeneration of mankind. He taught three unities: of God, of mankind, and of religion. The third of these, unity of religion—the idea that all religions were valid—was anathema to orthodox Islam as it might have been as well to either orthodox Judaism or Christianity. Moreover, the *bab's* insistence on the equality of the sexes, the harmony of science and religion, the elimination of extremes of wealth and poverty, and universal compulsory education also won him the enmity of the ulema. His teaching did, however, appeal to the educated middle classes who found the conservative orthodoxy of the ulema stifling. It also represented something of an urban revolt against the insular and aloof ruling order in both mosque and state, and was thereby a threat to both.

The bab announced his separation from Islam in 1848 and was executed in Tabriz two years later. Then, in 1852, while hunting, Nasr al-Din was slightly wounded by a bullet fired apparently by three of the bab's followers. In the harsh backlash ordered by Amir Kabir, not only were those three executed but also a number of other Baha'is, including a charismatic woman named Qorrat al-Ain.[36] As things like this often do, the courageous demeanor of these people under torture which can only be described as barbaric won sympathy for the religion and its adherents and disdain for the perpetrator of their suffering. Baha'is went underground and then into exile under the leadership of a successor, Baha'ullah (1819-1892) who claimed in 1863 to be not merely the bab but the "one whom God shall manifest."

The execution of the bab and the continuing persecution of his followers, coinciding with the fall of Amir Kabir coming only about four years into Nasr al-Din's reign, marks such a sharp break that Peter Avery calls the twin events "fatal errors."[37] Reform in both the political and religious spheres was effectively ended. Compounding the damage, in 1856, apparently not wanting to appear inept, Nasr al-Din engaged in a second costly attempt to take Herat. He succeeded in holding the city, briefly, then was turned back by a British force and forced to renounced all further claims to Herat or any other part of Afghanistan in the Treaty of Paris in March 1857.

As his indebtedness to Britain continued and worsened, the twin "fatal errors" coincided with Persia's deeper absorption into the Western economies. Nasr al-Din needed money, but loans came with interest. Concessions, however, did not.

Amir Kabir had been careful not to grant concessions, but without his or any other restraining hand, the shah and his courtiers found that they could use the British-Russian rivalry to further their own interests. Ruling now without the check of a strong prime minister, Nasr al-Din was willing to grant foreign companies and individuals exclusive and valuable concessions over Persian imports and exports as well as natural resources in exchange for lump cash payments or loans on which there were varying rates of interest. Instead of investing it to develop the country's resources, the shah spent the money maintaining his lavish court, trips abroad, and pensions to a burgeoning number of Court favorites, provincial governors, revenue collectors, and an array of officials with brilliant titles who did little but whose loyalty the shah could not afford to forfeit.

Jockeying for influence at the Persian Court became a precarious balancing act for the Russian and British governments who, by the middle of the nineteenth century, had become the principal protagonists in something called the "Eastern Question." One might think of two animals, the Russian bear and the British lion, jealous of each other, wary of each other, each coveting a sick animal, one tearing off a limb here while the other tore off a limb there. If the shah granted a monopoly of one commodity to a British individual or company, for instance, that would have to be balanced by a Russian entity profiting somewhere else. In 1841, the British gained a commercial treaty with a Most Favored Nation clause which meant that any concessions granted to them would apply to other nations as well. In 1874, Russians received the right to build a railroad from the northern frontier to Tabriz; in 1876, Russia regained the monopoly of the fisheries on the southern coast of the Caspian that it had lost under Amir Kabir; and in 1881, Russia acquired a highway concession in Azerbaijan. To balance the Russians, a British company gained a telegraph concession in 1864; Russian companies then received highway and mining concessions in 1893, 1898, and 1899.[38]

Ultimately, the two Powers came to regard meddling in Persian affairs as a quite legitimate extension of their diplomacy justified by the weakness of the Persian government, the rampant corruption and venality among officials, and the rising discontent of the Persian public.[39] That weakness and corruption were also sufficient justification for another set of capitulations which gave *all* foreign subjects rights of immunity from prosecution by Persian courts.

In 1871, twenty years after the dismissal of Amir Kabir, Nasr al-Din appointed a second powerful man, Mirza Hossein Khan, as his prime minister. Like Amir Kabir, Mirza Hossein Khan had served as a diplomat in Istanbul where he also had seen the positive effects of the Ottoman Empire's Tanzimat, and he encouraged the shah to embark on a similar course.

One of the reforms that he inaugurated and that Shuster later would encounter was the organization of a Cabinet to be named by a prime minister approved by the shah. The Cabinet was to meet regularly, on a weekly basis, at a fixed place. Originally there were three ministries: a prime minister (not surprisingly, the first prime minister was Mirza Hossein himself), a Minister of Finance, and a Minister of Foreign Affairs. Later, six more were added: Internal Affairs, Finance, Justice, Public Works, Commerce and Industry, a Ministry of Sciences (Education), and a Ministry of Court.

This body could have become a lever to not only balance the autocracy but to bring about needed reforms. The country badly needed infrastructure which a strong Ministry of Public Works, for instance, might have been able to bring about. A Ministry of Finance might have been able to bring some regularity and integrity to the assessment and collection of taxes.

Two things, however, prevented the separate ministries

or the Cabinet as a whole from carrying out these reforms or from playing a meaningful role in governing Persia. One was Nasr al-Din himself. He had inherited and he would jealously maintain a system that tolerated the grant of not a sliver of responsibility to any person or agency beyond his own absolute control. Second, and related to that, by the time a Cabinet was inaugurated, the system of patronage and nepotism was so deeply ingrained in civic life that meaningful change was almost impossible to effect—a system, incidentally, that would arguably be the biggest obstacle confronting Shuster.

The result was a system highly susceptible to self-aggrandizing sycophancy and outright graft. One of the more ingenious examples was in the ministry that would later give Shuster major headaches, the Ministry of War. In the early 1890s, Na'ib al-Saltaneh, Nasr al-Din's son, became Minister of War. He would receive pay for the army in silver from the Treasury but then dispense it in copper leaving a tidy 15% profit in his own hands. Plus, he would keep all the salaries in his own hands as long as possible in order to earn interest on the short-term loans he made from them.[40]

The Ministry of Justice presented a different kind of problem. Since justice was essentially the domain of the clergy, the Ministry of Justice could neither establish courts nor execute civil law without their involvement, and some clerics did manage to find ways of assuaging their consciences while finding lucrative positions within that Ministry. Nonetheless, non-clerics also found their way into that Ministry and by the time Shuster arrived, a number of men employed in positions within that Ministry tended to be Qajar princes rather than clergy, thereby widening the gulf between the Crown and the ulema.

Perhaps the most intriguing innovation in the new Cabinet because it was a recognition of the potential power of the press was an office overseeing publications. By the middle of the century, there were three or four official newspapers whose news sources were largely government functionaries. The "news" was therefore rather bland and made more insipid by the presence of a secret police which stifled any public criticism of the government. Nonetheless, in the last third of the century, independent newspapers, critical of the government, and published by the Persian diaspora in London, Cairo, Calcutta, Paris, Istanbul, and Mumbai began appearing in Persia. Two of these were especially influential: *Qanun* (*Law*), published in London, was so caustic in its criticism of the government that it became a criminal offense to own an issue. *Habla al-Matin,* founded in Calcutta in 1893, railed at the corruption not only in the government but in Persian society in general.

Unlike Amir Kabir, Mirza Hossein Khan was careful not to require any belt-tightening of the Court. Instead, he focused on an ambitious program of internal development that involved agreeing to an extraordinary concession from Baron Julius de Reuter, a German-born British Jew and the founder of the news agency that still bears his name. The concession included construction of a railway from the Caspian Sea to the south, mining rights, and many industrial improvements. In return, the shah would receive an advance of £40,000. The scheme failed, partly because of Persian criticism but more because of objections from Russia, and by Reuter's failure to consult the British government. Under pressure from the two Powers, the shah cancelled the concession but held on to the £40,000. As compensation, Reuter was allowed to set up an Imperial Bank of Persia with exclusive rights to print currency along with provisions for a loan to the shah. In addition, the Russians were permitted, in 1891, to found a bank, the Banque d'Escompte, which became largely a political instrument extending loans to the shah as well as to government officials, clergy, and others favored by the shah.[41]

In the severe famine of 1870-71, about a tenth of the population died. Even if the government had had the will to provide relief for the suffering, it lacked the resources to do so. But the famine did give the shah an excuse to force Mirza Hossein Khan out of office in 1873. He had served one year less than Amir Kabir. The lesson of the two ministers was not hard to miss, a lesson that would bedevil Shuster: reform was a good idea that many in the Persian government could applaud as long as their own purses and/or prestige were not affected. What was also clear was that Nasr al-Din was unwilling to tolerate an autonomous ministerial office separate from the control of the Crown.

In 1879, the shah visited Russia and was so impressed with Tsar Alexander II's Cossacks that he decided to found his own imperial bodyguard, the Cossack Brigade, officered by Russians but financed by Persia. By the time Shuster arrived, it would number between 1200 and 1500 men and would be the only regularly paid, disciplined and thus, effective fighting force Persia had. Not only would the Brigade prove to be useful in supporting the throne against protesters, but, naturally amenable to Russian use, the Cossack Brigade also allowed for the possibility of Russian military intervention in the likelihood of any internal disorders, real or fabricated.

Throughout the 1880s, the shah continued to negotiate concessions to foreigners. In 1883, at the apex of the British-Russian rivalry, Nasr al-Din appointed the third of the reforming ministers, Mirza Ali Ashgar Khan, also known as Amin al-Saltan (confidante of the sultan) who would soon be given the title of the Atabak, by which he would thenceforth be known. Wily, Machiavellian, shrewd, and, despite (or because of) a European education and opposed to any kind of liberal reform, he was able to develop friendly relations with various factions at Court, and, as Abbas Amanat phrases it, turned the office of premier into a "lucrative racket with shares for the shah, himself, and other willing partners."⁴² Motivated by sheer pragmatism as far as Persia was concerned and by his own substantial self-interest, the Atabak was not at all hostile to the sale of concessions from which he earned handsome profits, some of which enabled him, before his assassination in 1907, to construct the lovely palace and compound into which Shuster and his family would move in May 1911.

By the end of the century, as court favorites and local brigands looted cities and villages, neither life nor property remained safe. A British soldier, Edward Stack, traveling to Europe through Persia in 1882 noted:

> ...the traces of decay and ruin which one meets within so many villages, the empty bazaars falling to pieces in Isfahan, the neglected garden-palaces of Shiraz, the crumbling walls of even commercial Yazd and Kerman, the long lines of choked qanats on the great plains, the old bridges left unrepaired, and the total absence of public works of any kind—and the whole forms a picture sufficiently discouraging.⁴³

Rightly or wrongly, Nasr al-Din's subjects linked their misery directly to the shah's dependence on foreigners. One traveler noted that:

> ...the jealousy with which the Persian people are prone to regard these railways, tramways, monopolies, concessions, and companies...is both natural and reasonable. These things, so far as they are sources of wealth at all, are so, not to the Persian people, but to the Shah and his

ministers on the one hand, and to the European promoters of the schemes on the other.[44]

Russian influence in the latter years of the nineteenth century increased such that it tended to outweigh that of the British. A subsidized shipping line between the Black Sea and the Persian Gulf was inaugurated ostensibly to increase trade but also conveniently cemented a Russian presence in the Gulf allowing Russia to become a player in the rivalry between the Ottomans and the British for control of Kuwait and Bahrain. A treaty negotiated in 1889 and renewed ten years later bound Persia to grant no concession for the building of railways to any other power without Russian consent. Huge sums of money were spent constructing roads leading from northern Persia to the Russian border over which motor car traffic was in operation by 1905, thus assisting Russian commerce in the region where it already had a virtual monopoly.[45]

The most egregious outrage, however, came not from Russia but from Britain when, in 1890, the shah granted a 50-year monopoly on the production, handling, sale, and export of all tobacco raised in Persia to the British Major Gerald Talbot. The annual profit was expected to be £500,000. Of that amount, the shah would receive £25,000 and the prime minister £15,000. The purpose of the Concession had less to do with tobacco which obviously could have been obtained from the United States than extending British commercial interests in Persia as a counterbalance to those of Russia.

So openly crass was the bargain that the clergy's declaration of a boycott of tobacco in 1891 was whole-heartedly obeyed. Tobacco shops were closed down and, at least in public, the use of the popular *ghalian* (water pipe) came to a halt. Throughout 1891 and into 1892, rioting erupted throughout Persia as western-educated intellectuals, students, secularists, bazaar merchants, and landowners joined with the powerful ulema in the boycott.

Large numbers of women of differing social classes who would later play a significant part in the events of December 1905, 1909, and 1911 also joined the protests. Even in the women's quarters at court, Anis ad-Dowla, Nasr al-Din's favorite wife, led a number of other royal wives in joining the protests against the Tobacco Concession.[46]

The opposition to the Concession was particularly vigorous in Tabriz. There, placards of the Tobacco Corporation were torn down and the Tabrizis, in a protest to the shah, announced their intention of defending their rights against foreigners by force, if necessary. A Tabrizi woman, Zinat Pasha, described as "passionate, brave, and enlightened," led a protest that closed down the bazaar.[47]

The indignity of having to buy from the British a commodity that the Persians had themselves cultivated was in itself demeaning. Nonetheless, although most Persians used tobacco in one form or other, such a fuss over a commodity that, after all, is hardly a necessity, seems to make no sense. Peter Avery, however, puts the Concession into the wider context in which an individual Persian would have experienced it, that is, not simply as the imposition of an additional expense from which he would derive no benefit but also as an invasion of privacy, a penetration into his entire way of life. Noting the great charm, the love of talking, the exquisite courtesy, and hospitality of the Persian people, Avery writes:

> The lack of privacy necessitated by social conventions of unfailing hospitality…make the preservation of privacy, the guarding of the secrets of the heart and mind, an art in whose acquisition special rules and gestures have to be learned…

> and the effort to retain Iran's separate identity under the threat and actuality of invasion and devastation at alien hands has not been easy.... Therefore, penetration of Iran's way of life by foreigners was... the cause of serious concern in the minds of many of the people....[48]

The shah was finally forced to void the Tobacco Concession but was also compelled to pay half a million pounds indemnity at an interest of 6% (£30,000/year)—borrowed from a British bank—to compensate Talbot.[49] Ironically, the monopoly itself was continued when an Ottoman company took over the export of tobacco with the shah receiving fit compensation.

So widespread had been the opposition that most scholars have dated Persia's national awakening to this moment. The Tobacco Riots gave the disparate elements of Persian society a common sense of being wronged, of being humiliated. More importantly, as one observer put it, "The Persian people...had shown that there was a limit to what they would endure, that they were not the spiritless creatures which they were supposed to be, and that henceforth they would have to be reckoned with."[50]

The Tobacco Riots had another significant impact. Regardless of the role it had played in the race for concessions, as a liberal, democratic state, Britain had hitherto been viewed more favorably than autocratic, conservative Russia. The Tobacco Concession changed that, and Britain now began to be tarred with the same animus as Russia.

Often regarded as a dress rehearsal for the 1906 Revolution, there were several important dimensions to the protests. Throughout the reign, a new intelligentsia of reformers had emerged—all hostile to the monarch and to Western influences, albeit for different but often overlapping reasons. Similarly, the opposition of the clergy to the Tobacco Concession shredded the bond between it and the Court, a bond which, admittedly, had often been tenuous at best. But was that hostility to the monarch the same thing as hostility to the institution of monarchy itself? And did hostility toward Britain and Russia translate into the abrogation of all things Western, such as secularism, constitutionalism, rationalism and scientific inquiry, a free and independent press, the education of girls?

There was another interesting facet to the protests. At one point, Nasr al-Din invited the Russian government to intervene to put down the disturbances in Tabriz. While offering to help in the abolition of the Concession, that government wisely refrained.

Outside academia, it would be hard now to find an Iranian who has anything good to say about the Qajars in general or Nasr al-Din, in particular. Most would agree with a British traveler in 1887 who described the shah as:

> ...a selfish despot, devoid of public spirit, careful only of his own personal comfort and advantage, and most averse to the introduction of liberal ideas amongst a people whose natural quickness, intelligence, and aptitude to learn cause him nothing but anxiety.[51]

A more damning indictment, because it came from one of his own daughters, and, indeed, one who loved him very much, was this from Taj al-Saltana:

> How much better it would have been if... my imperial father had devoted himself...

to the betterment of his nation and of education and the arts....Had he not been so uxorious and so corrupted with carnal pleasures, and instead spent every hour of his life in governance and advancement of agriculture, how much better off we would be today.[52]

That indictment does not, however, convey quite the entire story.

For half a century, Nasr al-Din had preserved stability in his realm. That was no mean accomplishment. He had had to face the diplomatic and commercial rivalries of two formidable powers—one, Russia, menacing him from the north and the other, Britain, entrenched in India and ready to repulse pressure from any outside power on Persia's frontier with Afghanistan or through the Persian Gulf. Nasr al-Din had faced tribal khans, a fractious and fractured religious establishment, selfish and jealous princes, a rising middle class and an increasingly vocal and restive intelligentsia—none of whom were any longer eager to heed the authority of their sovereign. With few military and financial resources, Nasr al-Din had become increasingly autocratic as the reign progressed, and the Tobacco Riots seem to have made him even more hostile to any suggestion of liberal reform.

There had been many voices crying out in the shah's wilderness stressing Persia's historic and unique character. One of these was the cleric, Jamal al-Din al-Afghani. Born in Persia in 1838, he visited the holy sites of Najaf and Karbala in his youth and then traveled widely to Istanbul, Cairo, and then India—places where, as in Persia, Islam was facing the challenges of Westernization and secularism. Eventually, he reached Vienna and then Paris by which time he had developed a strong antipathy to Western, especially British influences.

However, he had also become convinced that the only way to counter the West was to use reason and science to reform Islam. Islam, he insisted, should and could be revised in the light of Reason to adapt to different conditions. Moreover, he was convinced that the scientific and technological achievements of the West could be at least equaled or surpassed by a science based on Islam.

By the time he returned home, he had developed an international reputation as a fierce opponent of Western imperialism but also as a powerful voice for reform within Islam. When he tried to play the role of counselor to the shah, however, he was rebuffed as a heretic, as a result of which he became a fierce opponent of the monarch.

In 1896, after nearly half a century on the throne, Nasr al-Din was assassinated by Mirza Agha Khan al-Kermani, a disciple of al-Afghani.

Nasr al-Din Shah
(r. 1848-1896)

Amir Kabir
Minister to Nasr al-Din Shah

Taj al-Saltaneh
Daughter of Nasr al-Din Shah

Jamal al-Din al-Afghani

IV

October 1906.
The Constitutional Revolution

"The National Consultative Assembly represents the whole of the people of Persia...."

—Article 2, Fundamental Laws of December 30, 1906

The decade after Nasr al-Din's death is often viewed as an unhappy interregnum punctuated by protests, which led to repression, which led to more protests, which led ultimately to the formation of Persia's—and the Middle East's—first democratically elected Majles (parliament) and its first constitutional government. There is substantial evidence to support that view.

Nasr al-Din's successor, Mozaffar al-Din, was frail both mentally and physically, and even less inclined than his father to give up a life of luxury. Like him, he also sought loans from European bankers at exorbitant interest rates to finance his life style. His sister, Taj al-Saltaneh, would describe him as timid and simple, weak-willed, fearful, irresolute, and extremely gullible.[53] By playing the Russians and the British against one another, Nasr al-Din had kept the state finances in some order, but at that game, Mozaffar al-Din as shah was neither capable nor willing. His frail health provided an excuse for three expeditions to Europe for medical treatments which not only failed but also drew further expenditures from a treasury whose health was even more fragile than his own.

In 1898, three Belgians were hired to raise money on the Customs, and in 1899 they took charge of the import-export trade at two Customs posts, one in Azerbaijan and the other at Kermanshah near the border with the Ottoman Empire. In short order, they would extend their control over the bulk of Persia's fiscal affairs.

Grants of concessions, including the one to William d'Arcy in 1901 for the extraction of oil,[54] multiplied and Mozaffar al-Din Shah continued to negotiate loans from the British at exorbitant interest rates when he could and, when his credit with the British ran dry, from the Russians. The result, again in the words of Taj al-Saltaneh, was that "All the nation's affairs were governed by a bunch of vile, dissolute riffraff.... Fraud, thievery, and swindling were the order of the day."[55]

There is, however, a little more to the story than that. Nasr al-Din's chief minister from 1887 until the latter's death, Mirza Ali Asghar Khan, the Atabak, had helped Mozaffar al-Din secure the throne and then was dismissed after serving a few months only to be reinstated in that position less than two years later. Notoriously unscrupulous, he had nonetheless put in motion—or allowed—a number of reforms that realistically could not have been stopped. Although navigable roads were few and far between, there were telegraph connections linking at least the major population centers. Education was expanded which, along with Koranic studies, included increasingly modern curricula. Instruction for girls and, in some areas, even co-education was attempted.[56] Censorship was lifted, encouraging a relatively free and vigorous press which not only saw the influx of western works but also facilitated criticism of the government.

Another significant technology was the cinema. On his first visit to Europe, in July 1900, the shah was introduced to the "cinematographe" in Paris and was so entranced with it that he ordered his court photographer Ebrahim Khan Akkas Bashi to introduce cinema to his own Court.[57] The new technology rapidly spread beyond the Court and other cinemas opened in short order. In addition to opening Persia to Western tastes and values, they also served as cultural unifiers in that native cinematographers quickly learned to record and spread images of Persia to Persians themselves.

Cultural and educational *anjemans* also began to flourish. One might think of them as something between a guild and a political party. While many of them represented occupations, ethnic, or religious groups, social, economic, and cultural interests were also aired. Thus, it was virtually impossible to avoid political discussion. Several anjemans were, in fact, elected city councils. Most of them were liberal, even radical, but there were also clerical and court-oriented anjemans slanted toward varying degrees of dissatisfaction with the regime. While dissatisfaction with the regime was common, there was no universal agreement among or often even within the anjemans on how to deal with it.

Augmenting the intensity of political activism was the fact that the number of Persians educated abroad along with graduates of the Dar al-Fanun and missionary schools became increasingly numerous and increasingly vocal in their criticisms of the existing order. So too, did the ulema who particularly disliked the Atabak for roughly the same reason they had disliked Amir Kabir—the new schools had weakened their hold on education, and the liberal press had encouraged a sense of national identity that was associated with the pre-Islamic past. Thus, the Atabak's dismissal at the dawn of the new reign signaled the tension between two powerful forces: that of reform along secular, liberal, and western lines which, to a large degree could be reconciled with Persia's pre-Islamic past, and a conservatism arising from Persia's identity as a Shi'ite bulwark against not only a Sunni but against a secular world order that threatened its very soul. Had Persia been left to work out its destiny without outside interference and had it been blessed with a prudent ruler, those two forces might have been brought into balance. Persia was not to be so blessed.

Immediately on his accession as shah, Mozaffar al-Din approached Britain for a loan of a million pounds. Persia's credit rating was so low, however, that the British refused. So the shah turned to Russia who offered a loan of twenty million Russian rubles at 5% interest payable within seventy-five years and guaranteed by Customs receipts which, because they were in Belgian hands, linked animosity toward the one nation with hatred of the other. The shah accepted the terms and set off on his first tour, visiting Paris, Istanbul, and St. Petersburg but not London where, to show their pique at his having approached Russia, the British snubbed him. By the time he returned home, he had consumed eleven million of the twenty million.[58] Of this sum, four million rubles (£500,000) was used to pay off the loan from the Imperial Bank which had been used in 1891 to indemnify the Imperial Tobacco Company.[59] What remained did not leave his court.

In 1901, a locust plague followed by famine devastated southern Persia. The government's response was to impose a heavy tax on several necessities including meat.

In 1902, again strapped for cash, Mozaffar al-Din approached the tsar for a second loan and was granted ten million more rubles. But this time there were strings attached. In return for the loan, the shah mortgaged the Customs taxes from the northern frontiers, that is, those bordering Russia. Since he couldn't find reliable henchmen in Persia, the shah was pressed into relying on the Belgian tax collectors. Thus, on Christmas Day, 1903, one of them, Joseph Naus, became Director-General of Customs and effectively the Minister of Finance. Eventually, the industrious Mr. Naus would add to these two titles that of Minister of Posts and Telegraphs, High Treasurer, Head of the Passport Department, and Member of the Supreme Council of State. Six more Belgian officials were appointed to various posts in the Persian Excise. Allied with the Russians, the Belgians lost little time earning the hatred of almost every Persian who had anything to do with them. To add extremely bad manners to a most sublime arrogance, in 1905, Naus appeared in a photograph dressed as a mullah.[60]

Naus was efficient. Under his management, there was a 35% increase in Customs revenues. However, the British and Russians required those revenues as collateral for loans to the shah. Foreshadowing one of the reforms Shuster would later insist upon, rigorous accounts began to be kept. In another area, Naus would succeed where Shuster would fail—tax farming was almost eliminated but that earned him the hostility of the great land owners who had profited from it. Naus also earned the enmity of the powerful bazaar merchants who, because of the increase in Customs duties, were paying more for their goods than foreign traders were.

The discontent following the Tobacco Riots had never dissipated. Now it threatened to boil over. In 1903, Persia saw riots throughout the country targeted primarily against foreigners, particularly the British and Russians whose rapacity, arrogance, and dishonesty had long been tolerated by the Qajar monarchs and their ministers. In response, the Atabak's second tenure was terminated. The official reason given was that he had failed to secure yet a third loan from foreign financiers.[61] He was replaced by what was described as an arrogant, ignorant, old-fashioned Persian nobleman, named Aynu ad-Dowla.[62]

Growing anger over the shah's travel and other extravagances, plus new Belgian tariffs and the arrogance of the administrators intensified. As with the Tobacco protests earlier, these too cut across class, geographic, gender, and tribal lines—and were met by harsh repression. Even that most powerful and influential class, the clergy, was not exempt from retaliation; several important *mojtahed*s, senior clerics, were bastinadoed in Kerman and Qazvin.[63] But the unrest was now reaching the highest circles. Popular discontent drove one of the shah's uncles, Shu'a al-Saltaneh, the governor of the province of Fars, out of office. He was reappointed in 1904.[64] This man would play a major role in Shuster's downfall in 1911.[65]

To worsen matters, as a result of the strikes and unrest in Russia that would culminate in that country's own October Revolution in 1905, imports of wheat and sugar had become scarce, thereby sending prices in Persia skyrocketing. That led to more serious protests. And more repression. In December 1905, amid protests, the governor of Tehran, Alau ad-Dowla ordered that the feet of two Tehran sugar merchants be bastinadoed for not lowering their sugar prices. That was the last straw.

A few weeks later, on January 6, 1906, as the shah's carriage was taking him to the house of a grandee, masses of women surrounded it, forcing it to stop. Proclaiming their loyalty to Islam, they cried, "...O, King of Islam, if Russia and England come to your support, upon the masters' [ulema's] command, millions of Iranians will declare *jihad*." But, while acknowledging the shah as king, one of them handed him a note which read, "Fear the time when we shall finally take away the crown off your head and the royal cane off your hand."[66]

The fact that the demonstration and the threat had come from women and that they had linked their threat to the powerful ulema should have been more than a little alarming. As Shuster would discover, there was a saying in Tehran that when women took part in a *sholugh* (disturbance), the situation was indeed serious.[67] In another sense, however, it should not have been surprising. Although denied access to formal education, women of the upper classes had frequently acquired not only basic literacy in Persian but access to western publications as well and several dozen anjemans for women had evolved. In their discussions, the women could easily draw the connection between the constraints on their own freedom and their country's.

The role that women played in the Revolution was under-appreciated at the time, but Shuster would give them their full due. The women of Persia, he would find, "...had become almost at a bound the most progressive, not to say radical, in the world." And he would go so far as to claim that without the "powerful moral force of those so-called chattels of the oriental lords of creation, the...revolutionary movement... would have early paled into a mere disorganized protest...."[68]

Six months after that threat, demonstrations again flared in Tehran during the month of Moharram (June/July) that, like the Tobacco protests earlier, fused economic and religious elements. The bazaar was closed and this time roughly two thousand merchants, religious students, and ulema, led by two liberal mojtaheds Sayyid Abdullah Behbehani and Sayyid Mohammad Tabataba'i, took sanctuary at the Hazrat-e Abdulazim mosque in Rey just outside Tehran. From there, they demanded the dismissal of the prime minister, Aynu ad-Dowla.

Others took sanctuary (*bast*) in the British legation at Golhak north of Tehran.[69] From sanctuary, in addition to the dismissal of Aynu ad-Dowla, they also demanded the removal of Alau ad-Dowla who had ordered bastinadoing, the dismissal of Naus, and now they also demanded the establishment of a House of Justice. The shah promised to dismiss Naus but then immediately reneged on that promise and ignored the other demands as well.

And the violence accelerated.

With business in Tehran at a virtual standstill, the shah finally dismissed Alau ad-Dowla. But what had begun as a simple demand for a redress of grievances—for justice—by the middle of summer had evolved into a demand for an entirely new system of government. And in early August, the

October 1906. The Constitutional Revolution

shah reluctantly ordered the convening of a constituent assembly. Interestingly, there was little talk of overthrowing the monarchy completely. Rather, the discussions turned to simply limiting the shah's power with a constitution.

Elected on a partial suffrage defined by wealth,[70] the one hundred fifty-six delegates who met on October 7, 1906, were a fair, albeit not entirely perfect representation of Persia's diverse population. That included primarily landowners, merchants and bazaar guild members with average or above average assets, and members of the clergy. Ideologically, there was a fairly even balance between liberals, moderates, and conservatives, who generally supported a monarchy but wanted to place limitations on it.

The task these men set for themselves was almost ridiculously Herculean. From its start, this Constitutional Revolution had been in opposition to two things: the corrupt Qajar monarchy and malignant foreign influences. What the Revolution was *for* was less clear. A significant number of the makers of the Revolution had been exposed to Western political ideas and institutions, but how would these fit in a predominantly Islamic country that had never been exposed to secularism, republicanism, and capitalism except in the guise of those who sought to exploit it?

Moreover, would/could a government untethered from a monarchy and economically almost entirely reliant on outside powers, actually be constructed? If so, out of what? There was no money in the treasury and hence, no way to put down any kind of disorder, no way to pay for the defense of the country, and no way to provide for the most minimal public services. To make matters worse, there was already talk of an agreement between Britain and Russia in which it was rumored that Persia would figure prominently and, it was understood, not advantageously.

Then there was the matter of law. Law is essentially an

abstraction, a set of ideas. There is about law a certain predictability. If one does or does not do this or that, then there is this or that consequence, invariably. But the notion of a uniform, secular, comprehensive law based neither on custom nor religion, a law that covered everyone, regardless of tribe, village, social class, or religion was foreign. Capricious and subject to bribery, law in Persia was anything but predictable. In a village, law was whatever the kadkhoda, acting with his fellow villagers, decided it was. In the tribes, law was custom enforced by the khan. In a merchant guild, it was whatever the wealthiest merchants, the ones with "connections" determined that it was. And in the larger realm, it was whatever the shah or his minions decided it was.

Could this group of men in Tehran create a set of ideas, of laws, that would have any meaning at all to people who were long accustomed to managing their own affairs according to customs whose antiquity far outdated any new regulations? And how would any laws created in Tehran be enforced anywhere else in the country where means of transport and communication were still, at best, primitive? The law would be written in Persian but many people in the country did not speak, let alone, read Persian.[71] Moreover, a law that covered everyone needed courts and enforcement mechanisms that did not then exist. Even if they had existed, provincial governors and other officials appointed by the shah or someone close to him were hardly going to support them with any enthusiasm.

More troublesome was that the notion of abstract, secular law was essentially a Western import. And by 1906, not only the ulema, but many Persians had come to regard anything Western as pernicious. Could secular law be somehow reconciled not only with the Shariah but with a society that was coming to view much of what the West had to offer as suspect?[72]

And at the heart of everything was the larger question:

October 1906. The Constitutional Revolution

What exactly was "Persia"? The National Assembly represented "the whole of the people of Persia"[73] and a Supplementary added a year later declared that "The deputies...represent the whole nation, and not only the particular classes, provinces, departments, or districts which have elected them."[74] That same Supplementary proclaimed that the "people of Persia are to enjoy equal rights before the law."[75] Roughly two-thirds of Persia's population was tribal. How did those tribal identities mesh with "the people of Persia"? What was to be the role of women if, indeed, they were to have any political role at all?[76]

A central facet of Persia's identity was its religion but if "Persia" were to be identified with Shi'a Islam, what then would be the place of Baha'is who had been grievously persecuted at their founding under Amir Kabir? And what about other religious minorities—Jews, Christians, Zoroastrians, whose presence in Persia pre-dated Islam, in some cases by millennia? What about the many Sunni Muslims who had little use for the Shi'a majority? Article 1 of the October 7 Supplementary declared Shi'a Islam to be the official religion. And further, "At no time must any legal enactment...be at variance with the sacred principles of Islam...."[77] Clerical courts were given a significant role and a committee of five senior ulema would scrutinize legislation passed by the Majles to verify its conformity to the Shariah. Nonetheless, in a triumph of pluralism, the rights of religious minorities were not only protected but members of several groups were granted seats in the Majles.[78]

Notwithstanding obstacles that might have baffled a Solon or a Hammurabi, by the end of 1906, through peaceful, dignified protest, and almost entirely without bloodshed, the Persians, with a democratically elected Majles, had drafted the first, and for several decades, the only constitution in the Middle East, a construct that would last until the 1979 Revolution. Based upon Western, secular models, it explicitly stated that the shah's sovereignty derived, not by divine right, but from the consent of the people.

Not surprisingly, given the history of economic rapacity Persia had endured for nearly a century from foreigners, the Fundamental Laws added in December 1906 also declared that "no concession for the formation of any public company of any sort shall, under any plea soever, be granted by the state" without the approval of the National Council."[79]

There is about this Majles an almost breathtaking optimism and hope, a sense of a beleaguered people coming together to throw off a corrupt, debased regime in order to create something new, something that Persia in all its long history had never dared dream before, a dream that despite its ethnic and religious diversity, despite its poverty and enslavement to outsiders, an independent, liberal state could be created. There had been no Reign of Terror, no bloody recriminations, no public executions, no "enemies of the Revolution" lists, no frenzied crowds yelling "Death to _____." No anguished screams echoed from dark torture chambers. No laws decreed the manner in which one dressed in public. No nation's flag had been burned. No embassy had been looted. The foreign officials in their legations slept peacefully in their beds as did the hundreds of members of the royal court. For a brief sunlit hour, the heirs of Cyrus and Darius, of Shahpur the Great and Shah Abbas, of Khayyam and Ferdowsi, of Sa'adi and Hafez breathed the air of men who are free, their dignity intact.

But despite a shared culture, despite the poetry, the arts, the history that bound these people together, the grubby tools of statecraft were simply not there. The rules of parliamentary procedure and etiquette were known only to the very few who had travelled outside of Persia. And perhaps because of, or as the result of that absence, the idea of compromise for the greater good was underdeveloped when it was there at all. Thus, a dispute over where to allocate monies, for instance, could cripple or even topple a government. What kind of people should serve in the ministries? There was a valid argument for appointing Qajar notables who had experience but there was an equally valid argument for younger men who might not be tainted by contact with the corrupt old guard. Curtailing the power of the monarchy had ushered in a sense of freedom but it also granted greater autonomy to tribal khans and provincial governors who were understandably jealous of their prerogatives. Finally, although there were men who could be identified as democrats, moderates or conservatives, there were no political parties that could set an agenda or discipline debates.

Shuster would recognize the difficulties constitutionalism in Persia was facing at this moment when he wrote:

> I believe that there has never been...an instance where a people changed suddenly from an absolute monarchy to a constitutional or representative form of government and at once succeeded in displaying a high standard of political wisdom and knowledge of legislative procedure....
>
> It would be strange indeed if an absolutely new and untried government in a land filled with the decay of ages should, from the outset, be able to conduct its business as well as governments with generations and even centuries of experience behind them.[80]

Tragically, at what essentially was the birth of Persia as a modern nation, it was not given the chance that the United States, for instance, or Britain, had been given—to work out its problems on its own terms. Before the Constitutional

Revolution had even celebrated its first anniversary, Persia's evolution into a functioning modern state was given a series of crippling blows, many facilitated by its own shah. On New Year's Day, 1907, Mozaffar al-Din accepted the Constitution and then died on January 4. His son and successor, Prince Mohammad Ali Mirza, would take exquisite pains to unravel the limits the Constitution had placed on his authority and would come close to destroying the Majles itself.

As shah, Mohammad Ali would have support from Russia, whose own revolution, only a few months earlier, had resulted in the tsar being forced to grant a Duma (parliament) in April 1906. The Russian government was not going to tolerate a popularly elected body that had written a constitution stating that power derived from the people on its southern border. On September 13, 1906, a St. Petersburg newspaper scowled that obtaining reforms in Persia and "even a Constitution ... would be another heavy blow to Russian prestige in Asia."[81] It was understood that such a blow would not be tolerated.

Liberal England was not thrilled either. An independent, democratically elected government in a Muslim country bordering India where a vigorous nationalist movement involving Muslims as well as Hindus had begun to evolve was as unsettling to Britain as it was to Russia.

And Britain and Russia were already fashioning the noose that would strangle Persia.

V

Anglo-Russian Convention of August 1907

*Ne'er may that evil-omened day befall
When Iran shall become the stranger's thrall!
Ne'er may I see that virgin fair and pure
Fall victim to some Russian gallant's lure!
And ne'er may Fate this angel-bride award
As serving maiden to some English lord!*

—Mirza Aqha Khan al-Kermani shortly before his execution for the assassination of Nasr al-Din Shah.[82]

One of the great heroes of the British Empire, Charles "Chinese" Gordon, once wondered, "Here is a stretch of conscience.... What right has a man of one nation in another nation's territory? What right has he to subdue that nation?"[83] Gordon had written those words from Sudan where he was working to bring European-style order and law to people who weren't particularly interested in either one, and his sympathies often lay with them rather than with the policy makers in either London or Khartoum.

Despite the misgivings about the morality or even the practicality of empire that Gordon and others might have had, and despite the rivalries among themselves which intensified in the last decades of the nineteenth century, there was one thing upon which the Great Powers did agree, and that was that the business of the rest of the world could best be managed by themselves. Notwithstanding parliaments and elections and constitutions and liberalisms (an exception was Russia) the governance of the Great Powers was in the hands of an aristocracy—a class which, at its best—and worst—often viewed human affairs from a sense of noblesse oblige that assured them that it was they who could do the managing. These were men who had been educated in the same kinds of schools with curricula heavy on the classics, history (European), languages (European), mathematics, and the physical sciences. Sociology, psychology, economics, statistics, and even anthropology were taught, but on the very basis of their utility were regarded as inferior disciplines unbecoming a gentleman.

Admittedly, since Waterloo in 1815, these men had not done a bad job of managing affairs. They had kept Europe at peace, largely by outsourcing their squabbles to Africa or the Far and Middle East. If things fell apart in other parts of the world—or even if things didn't fall apart—it would necessarily be Europeans of the upper classes who would pick up the pieces. Moving within the same fairly narrow social orbits, these men would know how to run things, if not as outright colonies, then under the rubric of something like "protectorates" or "spheres of influence" or "spheres of interest" or, after World War I, as "mandates." In what was cynically called the Great Game, the question was not whether the pieces did or did not want to be picked up, but rather, who would pick up what pieces? Who would manage whose affairs?

Colonized people might occasionally prove useful in the lower echelons of governance but on the whole, it was understood that although "Orientals" could be somewhat lovable, compliant, and generally decent on occasion, by and large, notions of truth, law, justice, and rationality were such alien concepts that it was fairly useless to try to impose them on "natives" who were, by nature, emotional, decadent, prone to violence, and deceitful.

In the last decade or so of the nineteenth century, the delicate jockeying for influence among the Powers that had characterized diplomacy for over half a century was threatened by the ambitions of a relative newcomer to the Great Game, Germany. The increasing bellicosity of Queen Victoria's grandson, Kaiser Wilhelm II, had put Europe on the edge of the proverbial tinder box. Eager to acquire his own "place in the sun," Wilhelm had embarked on an arms race that enabled him to bargain for influence in Africa and, in 1903, he had begun to probe the Middle East as well by embarking on the construction of the Berlin to Baghdad Railway. A proposed additional spur from Baghdad to Basra would have put Germany on the Persian Gulf, thus threatening Great Britain's sea route to India. And in 1905, while visiting Morocco, which the French regarded as theirs, the Kaiser had promised the sultan his support in the event that he chose to rebel against France. There was a conference at Algeciras to resolve the issue, but the continuing arms buildup in Germany, and the Kaiser's obvious eagerness to disrupt existing colonial arrangements kept the nerves of everyone, but especially Britain, on edge.

An expansionist Russia on Persia's northern frontier and an aggressive Germany threatening Persia's southern border made the prospect of a Russo-German alliance a nightmare of its own for Britain. And the very real possibility of a wider European coalition that might include France as well was an even greater nightmare. Great Britain's navy did indeed command the world's seas but its army, strung out over an increasingly restive empire, would have been hard put to defend Whitehall.

Then, at the turn of the century, both Britain and Russia suffered humiliation at the hands of non-Europeans—Britain in South Africa and Russia at the hands of Japan. Although Britain technically won the Boer War, it had suffered military disasters at the hands of what were essentially farmers. And Russia had been defeated by people presumed to be racially inferior—non-white Asians.

The Russo-Japanese War (1904-5)[84] had devastated and demoralized both Russia's navy and army, and the country badly needed to rebuild an industrial core that had never matched that of its European neighbors even before that war. Unfortunately, revolution following immediately on the heels of that defeat threatened to topple the Romanov dynasty, and inaugurated a period of profound instability. Battered, humiliated, and now fractured, Russia was determined to at least maintain, if not extend, its influence in Asia.

Thus, for both Russia and Britain, such questions as whether or not empire was a good thing or a bad thing or whether it was worth the blood and treasure of maintaining or expanding it, or whether—or how—one should get rid of the colonies in the odd event that that should become wise or expedient were academic matters to be discussed over cigars and brandy in one's club—questions that policy makers could not afford to ponder. And in considering those questions, especially as they related to India, Persia by virtue of her geography and potential wealth took center stage.

The thinking of Russia and Britain about Persia had not fundamentally changed since the signing of the Treaty of Turkomanchai in 1828. Neither Power had ever thought outright occupation of Persia either possible or prudent. Since trade with Persia was of some profit to them both, the country was to kept moderately prosperous and that involved assuring at least some measure of inner stability. Neither government would benefit if Persia fell apart. But neither government would benefit either if one or the other achieved dominance in Tehran where the art of identifying and then flattering cooperative courtiers close to the shah had become a crucial element in one's diplomatic kit.

By the end of the nineteenth century, Britain had become fairly resigned to Russian influence predominating in the north of Persia and at the Court in Tehran. With eyes always on India, Britain had to safeguard its position in the Persian Gulf while maintaining the integrity of India's northern and western frontiers. That entailed establishing a secure cordon that rested on two fronts: (1) the Persian Gulf and the Mediterranean Sea lanes that led into it and into the Indian Ocean, and (2) India's northern frontier in Tibet and Afghanistan. With borders on both fronts, whether it wanted to or not, whether there would be any economic, diplomatic, political, spiritual, cultural or any other kind of benefit or not, Persia was the key link in weaving and maintaining that cordon.

The idea of an Anglo-Russian understanding on the Central Asia question, and Persia in particular, had been in the air since at least 1903. Newly allied to each other and to France, and concerned about Germany's ambitions, Britain and Russia buried their differences, largely over the Indian frontier, and began negotiations to settle their differences over Tibet and Afghanistan as well as Persia in June 1906. Not a single representative of the three Asian nations was included in the negotiations.

For their part, the British perhaps could have found no friendlier Russian minister with whom to negotiate than Alexander Izvolsky, who had been appointed Foreign Minister in late 1905. He had attended university at Edinburgh, spoke fluent English, was mildly liberal, and therefore expected to be friendly toward the British. However, as might be expected, he was also intensely patriotic, and the disorders in Russia in the wake of the 1905 Revolution made him look more toward autocratic Germany than to liberal England as a model for Russia's own future. He was vain, sensitive to criticism, and had had no prior experience with Persia.

As far as Persia is concerned, the choice of Sir Arthur Nicolson as Britain's chief negotiator was an even less happy one. In the three years he had been in Persia between 1885 and 1888, first as secretary of the British Legation at Tehran, then as chargé d'affaires, Nicolson had developed no affection whatsoever for the country. In itself, that would not necessarily have been a misfortune but what was more vexing, according to his son, Harold, was that his father was "neither imaginative nor intellectual: ... he was essentially English [and believed] that it was the duty of every Englishman to render his own country more powerful, richer, and larger than any other country."[85]

Arthur Nicolson had become convinced that the advance of Russia toward the Indian frontier was "some slow tidal movement...."[86] which, at least as far as British interests in Persia were concerned, could be dismissed. "This part of the world is lost to us," he wrote, "and we should devote the modicum of attention which we seem disposed to give to Persia to the south alone." The idea was to avoid conflict with Russia in the north and instead, concentrate on consolidating Britain's position in the south.[87]

Nicolson's willingness to come to an agreement with Russia on Persia was strongly supported by the British Foreign Secretary, Sir Edward Grey, who had come to that office in 1905 with a Liberal government and who felt that "If we regard Russia as incurably smitten with bad faith, it would... be useless to make any agreements with her and we should have to resign ourselves to a continuance of the former unsatisfactory relations."[88]

The negotiations, lasting only about two months, resulted in a Convention that split Persia into three "spheres of influence."[89] The northern portion that went to Russia included not only Tehran but most of Persia's major cities—Astara, Ardabil, Bandar Anzeli, Rasht, and Sari all of which were on or near the Caspian coast, as well as Tabriz in the northwest, the holy city of Mashhad in the northeast, and the old Safavid capital, Isfahan, in the center. That area was Persia's most fertile and was crossed by most of Persia's major roads.

A neutral zone, roughly in Persia's center, angled sharply north to just south of Kermanshah then down along the Shaat al-Arab River, the border with what then was still the Ottoman Empire, and along the Persian Gulf coast as far east as nearly to Bandar Abbas. Important cities such as Shiraz, Dezful, and Bushehr were in that zone.

The third and smallest zone went to the British. It was largely desert with Kerman being the only city of any significance. The port of Bandar Abbas was also included but its future importance as an oil entrepôt was not yet realized. However, Bandar Abbas did give Britain what she valued most, that is, access to the Persian Gulf which had become virtually a British lake, as well as, in the east, a border with Afghanistan, both of which were critical to her hold on India.

The Convention was signed at St. Petersburg on August 31, 1907. Tehran did not learn of it until almost a week later when it was published on September 4.

What made this Convention a travesty and ultimately a far heavier blow for Persia than the 1828 Treaty of Turkomanchai had been was that at its heart was a fundamental dishonesty. While the two Powers agreed to respect the "independence and integrity" of Persia so that Persia, "aided and assisted by these two powerful neighboring States, can employ all her powers in internal reforms," not a single Persian representative had been involved in the discussions leading up to the Convention. Nor, unlike the 1828 Treaty, were there any Persians involved in the division of their own country. And, in fact, the pledge to respect the "independence and integrity" of Persia was dismissed almost before the ink was dry by none other than Sir Edward Grey, who admitted that the "integrity and independence of Persia" did not in fact exist.[90] Articulating a rationale that had by now become a common theme in imperial discourse, he noted that Persia's internal troubles were such that they compelled or at least

81

invited interference in order to protect the lives and property of foreigners.[91] Further justifying the Convention was that "The inefficiency of Persian Governments, the state of their finances, the internal disorders, not only laid Persia open to foreign interference, but positively invited and attracted it."[92]

While Russia had acquired what Grey called a "perpetual advantage" in the struggle between the two Powers, he acknowledged that Britain had also now acquired a new burden. The Convention would protect Persia from being completely eviscerated by one or the other Power. The Convention would not change Russian behavior, but now her conduct, according to Grey, would "concern us in a way that it had not done before."[93] It was, the British Foreign Office claimed, a "self-denying ordinance by which Persia could only benefit." To that claim Arthur Nicolson dryly commented, "The Persians, who for generations had maintained themselves by playing on the rivalry between Russia and Great Britain, were not in the least solaced by this explanation."[94]

In Britain, the Convention was generally hailed with feeble enthusiasm. Those who praised it argued with Grey that it was about the only realistic defense against an expansionist Russia, and nothing better could have been expected.

Opposition to the Convention was based on both strategic and moral grounds. The strategic argument against the Convention came not only from the opposition Labour Party but was also advanced by, among others, none other than Lord George Curzon, one of Britain's most dedicated imperialists and one who had traveled extensively in Persia from September 1889 to January 1890. Curzon had earlier warned the British not to be deceived about Russian ambitions in Persia. Russia already had, he said, "made up her own mind as to the share which she will require in the division of the spoils." And he had added, "Not content with a spoil that would rob Persia at one sweep of the entire northern half of her dominions, she turns a longing eye southward, and yearns for an outlet upon the Persia Gulf and the Indian Ocean."[95] As for aiding Persia in making internal reforms, he scoffed that Russia was "interested, not in the reform of Persia, but in her decay. In the background of her ambitions is the vision of a country and a people falling from inherent debility into her grasp." And he saw in the partition of Persia the possibility that the northern zone, including Tehran, would become essentially a Russian proconsulate.[96]

The moral argument against the Convention was articulated from business interests, labor unions, from the Government of India, and branches of the Fabian Society as well as a number of other leading socialists. Whatever strategic benefits might be gained from the Convention, or regardless of the seeming inevitability of having to deal with a Russian presence in Persia, an alliance with a despot who had just abolished Russia's first Duma seemed a betrayal of the liberal benefits upon which the British defended the legitimacy of their own empire.

The morality of the pact, or rather the lack thereof, also worried Curzon. Aside from the ambitions of Russia, he had earlier harshly criticized Britain's entire attitude toward Persia. About a decade and a half before the signing of the Convention, in what looks almost like a prediction of Britain's complicity in the future betrayal of Persia as well as a criticism of her past policy, he had complained that Persia

> ...has been treated with penurious meanness....We have made treaties with Persia....When the occasion arose for redeeming them, we have shirked responsibility and have subsequently bought our release from the self-inflicted tie....We have at once pampered and neglected the Persian people.[97]

The strongest opposition, however, came from the London Persia Committee which included in its membership the Persian scholar, Edward G. Browne, as well as H. F. B. Lynch, its chairman who, although he belonged to the same party as Grey and had business interests in Persia, had hoped for a more progressive policy from Grey's government. The Convention, Lynch feared, would not only fail to improve British relations with Persia, but what was worse, in his eyes, was its moral callousness.

> While the feasting is in progress and the toasts are being exchanged, this small nation—which has contributed so much to the artistic and intellectual wealth of the world, and whose prospects looked at least promising before this Convention was signed—is lying between life and death, parceled out, almost dismembered, helpless and friendless at our feet.[98]

In Russia, the chief and apparently only argument against the Convention was strategic. A former prime minister, Count Witte, argued that "...the northern part of Persia was naturally destined...to become a part of the Russian Empire." Since Russia already had that part in fact, the Agreement had served only Britain's purposes.[99] Therefore, Witte lamented, "Persia has slipped out of our hands." What little moral argument there was came from Russian socialists such as Georgii Plekhanov and V.I. Lenin then in exile in Switzerland, and from the novelist Maxim Gorky.

And what of Persia itself?

Persia's predicament was caught in an article in a Persian language newspaper in Calcutta, then the capital of British India:

> The beauty of the thing is that Russia grants permission to England to open the doors of her commercial influence in the North, while England kindly vouchsafes the same permission to Russia in the South! But what business has Russia in Persia either to grant or withhold such permission? From North to South, Persia is ours: we are neither minors needing a guardian, nor a lunatic needing a keeper... the Persians have reached years of discretion and need no tutor. If they did, they would not have a Parliament.... At any rate we fail to perceive on what ground these two Powers give permission to one another to enter someone else's territory, or why they should 'spend money out of the guest's purse.'[100]

Meanwhile, a cartoon in the London *Punch*, October 2, 1907, entitled "The Harmless Necessary Cat" perfectly illustrated Persia's plight. It shows a Persian cat with an alert but startled glance flanked by the British lion and the Russian bear. The lion is telling the bear, "Look here! *You* can play with his head, and *I* can play with his tail, and we can *both* stroke the small of his back." And the Persian cat: "I don't remember having been consulted about this."

Even in the British diplomatic mission in Tehran, there was discomfort. Sir Cecil Spring-Rice, recently appointed British Minister to Tehran in 1906, had quickly developed sympathy for the Persians and opposed the Convention on both moral and practical grounds. Agreeing with Curzon that Russia wanted not merely to annex any part of Persia but rather aimed at getting the whole, he remarked that Persia was the route by which Russia intended to reach the sea, and "one end of a road is not much use without the other."[101] Feeling that Britain had sold Persia to Russia as part of a general scheme of buying and selling which, he said, "we call peace negotiations," he further mused, "Politics here [in Tehran] are highly amusing."

> The Russians are engaged in spoiling their own Duma at home and teaching the Shah how to spoil his Mejlis [sic] here. The dear Liberals at home are trying to get social recognition from the Russian Emperor, and to obtain this are encouraging him in his policy of extinguishing the liberties of Persia. Someday I shall have the great amusement of showing the whole game up. I shall be dead then; but won't my ghost have a good time![102]

Nevertheless, on September 5, 1907, the day after word of the signing of the Convention reached Tehran, Spring-Rice delivered a letter, written in Persian, to the Persian Minister of Foreign Affairs, declaring that Sir Edward Grey and M. Izvolsky were "in perfect accord on two fundamental points."

> First, neither of the two Powers will interfere in the affairs of Persia unless injury is inflicted on the persons or property of their subjects.
> Secondly, the negotiations connected with the Agreement between the two Powers must not violate the integrity and independence of Persia.

> ...Neither of the two Powers demands anything of Persia, and so Persia can devote all her energies to the settlement of her internal affairs....The Agreement... only binds Russia and England not to embark on any undertaking injurious to one another, and delivers Persia for the future from those demands which in the past have proved so hurtful to the advancement of her interests....
>
> They have no sort of intention of attacking Persia's independence...they do not seek a pretext for intervention....The two Powers...hope that in the future Persia may be forever delivered from the fear of foreign intervention, and will enjoy complete freedom to manage her own affairs in her own way....[103]

Less than five years later, on December 14, 1911, with the imminent collapse of Persia's Constitutional Government, Sir George Barclay, then Britain's Minister to Tehran, would deny any knowledge of the existence of that letter. Morgan Shuster, however, would know of it and assume that it meant what it said.

The Tobacco Concession had tarnished Persia's view of Britain as a liberal, enlightened, progressive alternative to authoritarian Russia. Despite the fact that it had been the British Legation in which the revolutionaries had found refuge only a year earlier, the Convention now solidified the view that Britain was capable of making an alliance with the Devil himself. At no time did the Persian Majles accept the Convention. Therefore, at no time did a democratically elected Persian government ever recognize the validity of the terms of that agreement.

In terms of the strategic goals for both Powers, the question might be asked, why did neither of them consider making Persia an ally? For tsarist Russia, that possibility would not perhaps ever have been given serious consideration. First, her age-old push for a warm water port had always involved domination, not cooperation. Second, with her own internal affairs in turmoil, the Russian government was *not* going to tolerate a popularly elected body that had written a constitution stating that power derived from the people, not the shah/tsar. So, the Russian interest in Persia was as much about checking constitutionalism on its southern border as it was about checking British interests in the area.

For Britain, the question is more intriguing. Ironically, at one point, in the 1870s, Lord Salisbury, then Britain's Foreign Secretary, had actually considered a plan whereby Herat which had, at one time, been part of the Persian Empire, would be turned over to Nasr al-Din along with a subsidy to help with internal reforms. Rather than a pawn in the Great Game, Salisbury had hoped that, with reforms, Persia might have become an essential ally in Britain's defense of India. Salisbury had also wondered if the capital should not be transferred from Tehran back to Isfahan. Unfortunately, Nasr al-Din had broken off the talks possibly because of Russian intervention.[104]

Ironically, the real threat to the British Empire in India came not from Russia at all, but from India itself where a lively nationalist movement that included Muslims had begun to take hold. Recognizing that "one of the strongest things" in Britain's rule in India was the "loyalty and contentment" of that population, Lord Curzon urged England to show the Muslims of the world that it was prepared to make every sacrifice on their behalf. And with none of them, he added "ought [we] to have more sympathy than with Persia."[105] That

Muslim element might have been somewhat placated by elevating Persia to the status of a partner in the Convention, or at least allowing Persian participation in it. That might have been a long stretch since hostility to British rule was already deeply rooted among Indian Muslims. Nonetheless, the dismissal of a Muslim nation as even worthy of participation in the conversation did nothing to quench that hostility. Besides, it was an article of faith almost akin to belief in the Ten Commandments that only another Great Power like Britain itself could dislodge the Russian threat from India.

Moreover, given Persia's size, although Russian forces could and did brutalize it terribly, it is doubtful that Russian control throughout Persia could ever have been effective for any significant period of time. Not only had the fragility of the tsar's armed forces been proven against Japan, but the turmoil within Russia itself following the 1905 Revolution was also well-known. Yet, in his dealings with Persia in the ensuing years, Sir Edward Grey would fatally underestimate Russia's weaknesses. Despite clear evidence to the contrary, he assumed that threats to the British Empire in India could only come from another Great Power.

In a sense, Persia may have been beyond Grey's ability, or willingness, to manage. Persia, he would later lament, would try his patience more than any other subject. Sadly, had he chosen to walk away from the Convention at any time and for any reason, given the opposition to it at home, it seems rather unlikely that he would have suffered a great deal of political harm. But his world was Europe and even there, his vision was marred. Had he fully understood Russia's weakness, Persia might have tried his patience less.

Sir Edward Grey
British Foreign Minister

Alexander Izvolsky
Russian Foreign Minister

English lion and Russian bear playing with the Persian cat

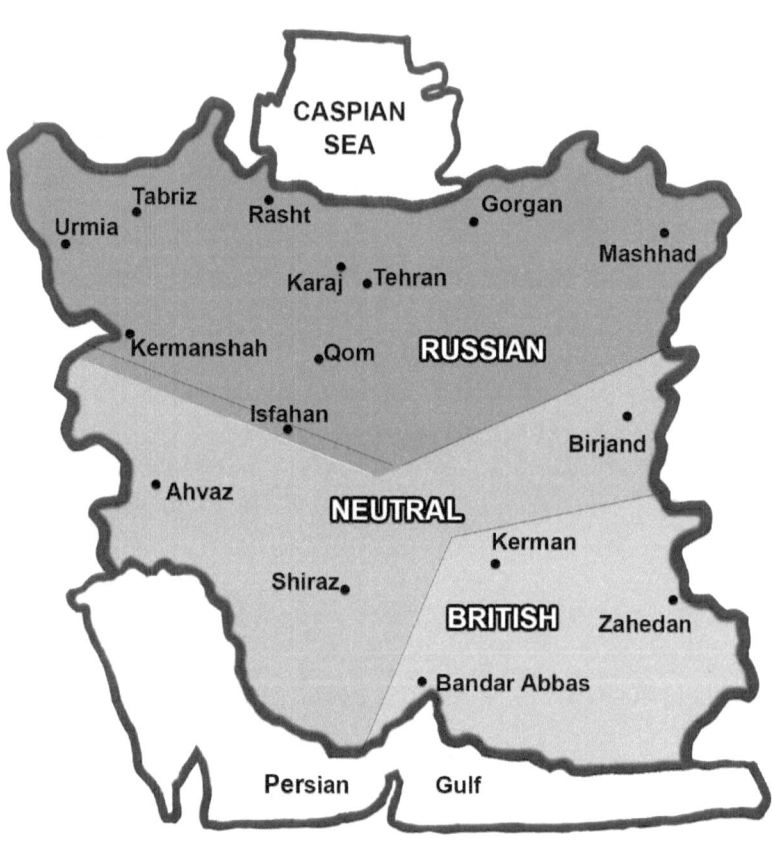

Russian, British, and Neutral zones

VI

The Second Majles

"...the most perverted, cowardly, and vice-sodden monster that had disgraced the throne of Persia in many generations."

—W. Morgan Shuster

Mohammad Ali Mirza Shah was crowned on January 19, 1907. Although he swore fidelity to the Constitution granted by his father a few weeks earlier, his hostility to it became known immediately; the deputies of the Majles pointedly were not invited to the coronation ceremony.

Shuster would label this man "the most perverted, cowardly, and vice-sodden monster that had disgraced the throne of Persia in many generations." His disgust with the man was shared even by those who would find him useful for their own ends. Although his Russian tutor had been what Shuster called a "notorious scoundrel,"[106] it was a Russian who thought his mind was "not well-developed" and characterized him as "dull, greedy, and [prone to take] the most shameful bribes." Such were this monarch's lack of scruples that, as that same Russian also reported, he at one point had "quietly sold battalions from one commander to another for two or three thousand tomans." And, for good measure, the Russian added that, according to his own brothers, the shah had been infected with syphilis.[107]

The struggle between Mohannad Ali Shah and his people began immediately. Under the Constitution, the regulation of all financial matters was subject to the approval of the Majles and, not surprisingly, given Persia's experience with concessions, it specifically provided that no loan or concession, internal or external, nor any state loan was to be contracted without its consent.[108] About the time of Mohammad Ali's coronation, negotiations had begun for a fresh loan of £400,000 to be raised equally from Russia and Britain. The Constitution also provided that, although the Cabinet ministers were appointed by the shah, they were responsible to the Majles. However, the ministers responsible for negotiating that loan—thus further deepening Persia's indebtedness—found it "unnecessary" to appear before the Majles for questioning about it. Fortunately, the Majles refused to sanction yet another step in the further selling of Persia's independence. The prime minister, prudently understanding that his life might not be entirely safe if he did not support the Majles' decision, refused to push the matter forward. And while he did not appear before the Majles, he—again, prudently—caused the other ministers to be present during the deliberations.[109]

With the aim of freeing Persia from reliance on foreign assistance, the Majles voted to prevent any fresh loans from either Russia or England and embarked on plans to establish a Persian national bank to be capitalized from internal sources. On February 10, under compulsion from the Majles, Mohammad Ali dismissed the hated Joseph Naus who returned to Belgium to enjoy the spoils he had accumulated at Persian expense. By itself, the disposal of Naus, says Shuster, "vastly increased the prestige of the Majles with the people."[110] For that very reason alone, however, if the shah had not been determined to undermine the Majles before, he now was more determined than ever to destroy it.

Unfortunately, the dismissal of Naus turned out to be no solution to the problems he had represented. The Customs still remained in Belgian, not Persian, hands. The twenty-five or thirty other Belgians who had worked with Naus remained, and Naus' replacement was an equally acquisitive person, Joseph Mornard, who, like Naus, had the active support of the Russians. There was a critical difference, however. The extra titles and offices that Naus had accumulated were denied Mornard. He had wanted the post of Treasurer General but the Majles withheld that. To Mornard's vast chagrin, two years later that post would go to Morgan Shuster.

To counter the Majles, and despite hostile telegrams from northern anjemans, the shah invited Aminu's Sultan (Atabak) to return to Persia to serve as his prime minister. Atabak, it will be remembered, had been forced into exile in 1903 for his role in securing two Russian loans in 1899-1900 and again in 1902. When the shah's interest in welcoming Atabak back to Persia became known to Russian officials, he was conveyed in a gunboat across the Caspian Sea to the port of Anzeli with the highest official honors. At Rasht, the capital of Gilan, however, he was received with far less warmth. There, he was compelled to swear fealty to the Constitution before the people of the city would permit him to travel on to Tehran.[111]

On reaching Tehran on April 26, Atabak found not only the chronically empty treasury but a country verging on chaos. Anti-monarchical uprisings had occurred in Tabriz, Isfahan, and Hamadan and, to make matters worse, a Turkish force had crossed the northwestern frontier and threatened the city of Urmiyeh. By summer, political anjemans had begun to recruit and arm a nationalist militia. In the midst of this, Atabak began negotiating a loan with the Russians which he must have known could not be secured without the approval of the Majles. The loan became a moot issue, however, when Atabak was assassinated on August 31, 1907.[112] That same day, eight months after he had been crowned, Mohammad Ali Mirza thought it wise to accept the Anglo-Russian Convention which the Majles had adamantly rejected and would continue to reject.

However, on November 4, under public pressure, the shah came to the Majles and swore on the Koran to abide by the Constitution. About a month later, however, on December

15, he sent for the members of the Cabinet and forcibly detained them, including Abul Qasem Khan Nasr al-Mulk who was imprisoned in a cell, his neck enchained.[113] This man had been associated with reform in Persia under Mozaffar al-Din. He had been Minister of Finance and also president of the Council of Ministers in the first Majles. He was an Oxford graduate and had been a classmate and close personal friend of both Sir Edward Grey and Lord Curzon. Now threatened with execution, he was rescued through the intervention of the British legation and then immediately left for Europe. Like Grey—and unlike Curzon—Nasr al-Mulk would come to feel that Persia could actually benefit from the newly-signed Anglo-Russian Convention and he thought that Persia could survive only by working with the Powers. He would, therefore, become an advocate for cooperation with Russia and Britain while trying to introduce a real two-party system into the Majles.

Meanwhile, the shah's *luti* (ruffians) began agitating in the streets against the Majles, which continued to meet in a building called the Baharistan, its approaches guarded by armed volunteers who had come to protect their representatives. With neither the *lutis* nor the Cossack Brigade bold enough to attack those volunteers, the shah had little choice but to dismiss a number of his court favorites who had been particular targets of the demonstrators, punish the *lutis,* and place the Cossack Brigade and other royal troops under the Ministry of War. He also—again—pledged under solemn oath on the Koran to abide by the Constitution.[114]

Five days later, on December 20, 1907, the shah proposed a new Cabinet whose members, not surprisingly, were as little interested in constitutional government as he was. The Majles continued its efforts to be conciliatory but at the end of February 1908, a bomb landed on top of the shah's automobile as he was being driven through the streets of Tehran, slightly injuring his chauffeur. The shah was unharmed but shaken, and he blamed the Constitutionalists for the attempt, thereby putting a new strain on an already fractured relationship. Six months later, on June 1, 1908, again compelled by the government, the shah reluctantly dismissed several more of his courtiers who then took refuge in the Russian legation.

By now, the British and the Russian legations had decided that they had no choice but to intervene—but on behalf of the shah, not the democratically elected Majles. Thus, the following day, the Russian minister, N.G. de Hartwig, with the British chargé d'affaires, Charles Marling, called on the Persian Minister of Foreign Affairs to warn him that further obstruction of the shah's plans would lead to Russian intervention.[115] That this was in direct violation of the Anglo-Russian promise to respect the "independence and integrity" of Persia less than a year after the Convention had been signed apparently disturbed nobody in either London or St. Petersburg.

On June 3, 1908, the nervous Mohammad Ali Shah, escorted by Colonel Vladimir Liakhoff, commander of the Cossack Brigade, left the city and took up residence outside the city walls at the Bagh-i Shah (the King's garden). From there, for the next two weeks, he ordered the arrest of a number of deputies while collecting troops, arms, and munitions. He also had the telegraph offices seized, thereby cutting off communications between the Majles and the provinces. He declared martial law in Tehran and placed Liakhoff in supreme command as military governor of Tehran. He then sent an ultimatum to the Majles threatening bombardment of a major mosque if a number of people who had gathered there to protest him did not disperse. In response, crowds took to the streets the next day demanding his deposition.

Then, just before sunrise, on June 23, 1908, over a thousand Cossacks and other troops surrounded the Majles in the Baharistan and occupied the adjoining streets. Deputies were allowed to enter the building but not to come out. About an hour later, Liakhoff and six other officers arrived, and placed the troops along with six cannon in such a way as to command the area. Liakhoff then rode off and the troops opened fire on the Majles building. Although about a hundred armed volunteers managed to put up a resistance for about seven or eight hours, the odds clearly were not in their favor. With the collapse of the building, many well-known Constitutionalists were either killed or arrested. Others escaped overseas, many of them to Turkey where Shuster would meet with them two years later.

For several days, Liakhoff and his troops engaged in systematic bombardment and looting of the homes of persons disliked by the shah. Majles records were destroyed while Liakhoff, as the virtual dictator of Tehran, insisted that, although he wore a Russian uniform, he was, as indicated by his departure before the firing had actually begun, simply carrying out the orders of the shah. Hence, he could claim that he, that is, Russia, was in no way violating the terms of the Convention.

Thus, the autocracy was restored. But not everywhere and not without considerable resistance. And it was resistance that, as in the Tobacco Concession disturbances of the previous generation, crossed not only tribal and class but also gender lines. That September, the *Manchester Guardian* reported that a committee of Persian women from Istanbul had sent a telegram to the "Sovereign Ladies of Europe," a group that included the British Queen, Alexandra, begging for their intervention in order to bring about an end to the massacres in Persia. Grey's response to the telegram was that it was his desire "consistently with the independence of Persia to promote the restoration of order in Persia." To his credit, he at least did acknowledge that "massacres" were happening.[116]

The destruction of the Majles provoked riots and vicious

retaliations in many of Persia's major cities including Rasht, Kerman, and Isfahan. The bloodiest protests however, were in Tabriz, the home of some of the most liberal members of the Majles. By October 12, the Constitutionalists were in control of the city. The day before that, however, 400 Persian Cossacks with four guns had already left Tehran for Tabriz to overthrow them on the grounds that the Constitutionalists presented a "serious and imminent danger" to Europeans.[117] The Russian Consul-General at Tabriz, Ivan Fedorovich Pokhitanov, who had vehemently opposed the 1907 Anglo-Russian Convention on the grounds that it restrained Russian intervention in Persian affairs, had been openly supplying the Royalists with arms and ammunition. This gentleman would prove to have a lively imagination. There was ample evidence that the "serious danger" to European lives and property did not, in fact, exist but two years later in 1911, Pokhitanov would pull an equally imaginary tale out of the stratosphere to justify Russian intervention again.[118]

By early January 1909, the Cossack force in Tabriz had been augmented by bands of brigands under the command of a notorious bandit named Rahim Khan, plus a Royalist force commanded by Aynu ad-Dowla, a grandson of Fath Ali Shah, who had made himself unpopular as a Minister of Interior and then briefly as a prime minister under Mozaffar al-Din. For ten months, the Constitutionalist government in Tabriz would battle not only the Royalists embedded in the city itself but would also wage a heroic struggle against famine caused by a blockade of the roads leading into the city by Rahim Khan and the Cossacks. By March, the people of Tabriz were dying of starvation with many more subsisting literally on grass.[119] With no access to fuel, severe cold added to the misery.

As Tabrizis watched their children and elderly relatives wither, any hope of relief seemed futile. There were provisions in the surrounding villages but they were in the hands of Royalist forces, outlaws, or Russians. In defiance of an order to post white flags as a sign of surrender to royal forces, local leaders such as the charismatic Sattar Khan and his colleague Baqer Khan and their followers went about the city pulling the flags down. Desperate sorties to open the blockaded roads were frequent, bloody, and supported by women as well. Following one of the bloodier battles to break the siege, twenty female bodies, clad in men's garments, were found among the dead.[120]

One of those whose sympathy lay with the defenders of the city was W.A. Moore, an Irish-born employee of the London *Times* who would remain a close observer and reporter on Persian affairs throughout the course of the Constitutional Revolution.

Another was a 24-year-old American named Howard Baskerville. The son and grandson of Presbyterian ministers, Baskerville had been born in North Platte, Nebraska, and graduated from Princeton University in 1907. While at Princeton, Baskerville had applied to be a missionary to Persia and had received a recommendation from his history professor, the future American president Woodrow Wilson.[121] That fall, he had come to Tabriz to teach English, history, and geography to a mixed class of boys and girls at the American Memorial School. From among his students, he organized and trained a force of about a hundred volunteers called "Save." On April 19, 1909, while trying to break the siege, in the battle of "Sham Ghazan," he was killed by a sniper.[122] His grave can be seen in Tabriz where he is often hailed as Persia's American Lafayette.

His heroism was not appreciated by Washington, however, where a policy of non-intervention and the avoidance of any political entanglements whatsoever had resulted in a blank refusal to grant asylum or shelter to refugees, regardless of their plight. The policy, albeit harsh in its individual application, made sense at that point. Even if the United States had been inclined to enter Europe's quarrels, which it was not, it was singularly unprepared to do so. Neither its army nor its navy were of sufficient strength to engage in combat against either a British or possibly even a Russian force anywhere, least of all on the other side of the globe. Ironically, the State Department had relied on Russia to rescue the American Consul-General William F. Doty and the Presbyterian missionaries when it seemed they would either be slaughtered or starved by Rahim Khan and the Royalists.[123]

Eleven days after Baskerville's death, four squadrons of Cossacks, three battalions of infantry, two batteries of artillery and a company of sappers entered the city. To the starving population, the Russian government gave assurances that the troops would remain only as long as might be necessary to guarantee the security of the lives and property of foreigners and would refrain from taking any part in the political conflict.[124]

The agony of Azerbaijan and especially Tabriz would continue for many years, but what the citizens of Tabriz probably did not know was that the nationalist cause for which they were suffering was on the verge of success. On January 5, 1909, a troop of 100 Bakhtiaris under their chiefs, Samsam al-Saltaneh and Zargham al-Saltaneh, had dispersed what there was of a Royalist force at Isfahan and the city had come under their control. At Rasht, the Constitutionalist movement was aided by Mohammad Vali Khan Nasr al-Saltaneh, the Sepahdar-i Azam, or simply "the Sepahdar," whose loyalties would ultimately prove to be rather fluid. He had served as governor of Astarabad under Nasr al-Din Shah and a few months before that had commanded the Royalist forces attacking Tabriz.

During March, the Rashti Constitutionalists had been able to occupy the road leading from the Caspian to Qazvin, about ninety miles north of Tehran. The two forces entered Tehran on July 13 and the next day the Cossack Brigade under Liakhoff wrote to the Sepahdar proposing terms for the city's surrender. On July 16, the shah fled with a large number of his retainers and took refuge at the Russian legation at Zargundeh, outside the city. That evening, he was forced to abdicate in favor of his twelve-year-old son Ahmad, who became shah under the regency of Azud al-Mulk.[125]

After prolonged negotiations, a Protocol was drawn up and signed on September 7, 1909. The Protocol specified that Mohammad Ali Shah after his abdication would return to the state any Crown treasure he had appropriated/stolen. The Persian government would assume the shah's debts (1,413,434 tomans to the Russian bank alone) and would take over the shah's estates but would pay him and his family 100,000 tomans a year starting from the day he left Persia. In return, the Russian government promised "to take all effective measures in order to prevent any such agitation on his part." Further, if Mohammad Ali were to leave Russia and if he conducted political agitation against Persia from a country other than Russia, the Persian Government would have the right to stop the payment of his pension.[126]

Constitutional government was thus restored. Unlike the first Majles, this second one was far more democratic since elections were on the basis of population rather than simple property. On November 15, the second Majles was convened and provincial assemblies were restored. By the time Shuster arrived in Persia ten months later, the Majles had eighty deputies. To this body was submitted for approval a Cabinet of seven members nominated under the direction of the Regent but with the proviso that the Majles could depose any Cabinet at any time by a vote of lack of confidence.

Unlike the first Majles, two political parties were formed. The democrat party, liberal and secular, favored centralization as the only way to reign in tribal and clerical forces in order to foster economic development. It encouraged land reform and a uniform income tax as well as toleration of religious minorities and equal treatment of women but not to the extent of granting them full suffrage. The moderate party, led by Ayatollah Behbahani, included members of the ulema as well as notables from the old ruling class and represented a more traditional order. Unfortunately, not only would it be difficult for the two parties to cooperate with each other on matters affecting the country as a whole, but even within each party, factions and individual egos as well as local interests constantly hindered cooperation when it most mattered. The democrats tended to represent Turkish Azerbaijanis whose ancestral connection with the Qajar dynasty and the recent heroic stand of Tabriz against the shah and his allies on behalf of the Constitution gave them an air of perceived and often real arrogance which many other deputies found difficult to swallow.

A year after Mohammad Ali's abdication, Azud al-Mulk died and was replaced as Regent by Nasr al-Mulk, Sir Edward Grey's friend who had fled to Europe following his escape from execution in December 1907. In July 1909, shortly after the restoration of the Constitution, he had returned to Tehran.[127] There had been another short trip to Europe but on February 11, he again returned, and the premier (since July 1910) Mostafi al-Mamalik, handed him his resignation and Nasr al-Mulk took the oath of office as Regent on March 7.

Meanwhile, the unity of the new Majles itself quickly began to fray. Throughout 1907 and the first half of 1908, the Majles had been able to pass several measures for the reform of taxation, finance, education, and the judiciary. But the last two, especially the reform of the judiciary, disturbed the ulema, who were particularly vexed by the prospect of secular law and courts acting beyond the purview of the

Shariah. However, as noted before, the ulema themselves weren't united. Several mojtaheds, senior clerics, including Behbahani and Taqizadeh, thinking along the lines of Jamal al-Din al-Afghani, were willing to accept western ideas and political structures which, they argued, were fully compatible with Islam. Others, however, including Persia's most prominent cleric, Sheikh Fazullah Nuri, supported the shah largely on the grounds that the Constitutionalists were importing the customs and practices of the "abode of unbelief," that is, Europe. Upon the abdication of the shah, several of these men, including Sheikh Fazullah Nuri, were executed. Behbahani would also die, and Taqizadeh would be forced into exile.

But the precarious unity of the Majles was by no means Persia's only problem. At the heart of most of her difficulties lay finances. Even without the new burdens of the ex-shah's debts and the annual 100,000 tomans due to keep him out of the country, the government could barely meet day-to-day expenses. And without the money to pay its bills, it was simply impossible to maintain order since it could not afford a paid, equipped, and trained military or police force. Such forces Persia did not have but Russia did, and Russian troops remained on Persian soil in Tabriz, Qazvin, and Rasht on the grounds of "preserving order."

Almost immediately, the new government approached the Imperial Bank of Persia for a loan of £100,000. It might be remembered that this bank had been established in 1872 as part of the Reuters Concession and was therefore seen by the Russians as an agent of British interests in Persia. The British were willing to approve the loan but reluctant to antagonize the Russians, who were simply not going to allow a financially independent Persia to happen. The existence of a viable constitutional regime in Tehran *ipso facto* threatened not only Russian influence in Persia; it also threatened conservatives in Russia who had had to submit to the creation of a Duma.

Thus, as a condition for approving the loan, the Russians attached demands that were unacceptable to the Persians, and Sir Edward Grey, unwilling to antagonize the Russians, felt that he had little choice but to acquiesce in order to save the Anglo-Russian alliance. The Persians let the negotiations for that loan die.[128]

Over the next year, as the Persians tried several more times to get loans from the two Powers and from private sources, that pattern would be maintained. The Russians would protest and the British would back down, albeit more or less reluctantly.

A major private source was a London firm, the Seligman Brothers. Seligman had originally been an American firm but, although they still worked together, the London branch had become independent of its American parent before the 1906 Revolution. In October 1910, the Persian government applied to the Seligman Brothers for a loan of £1,200,000 which would have been enough to pay off its debt. Although the firm was perfectly willing to negotiate such a loan and although it had no connection with the British Foreign Office, Grey felt, again, that he had no choice but to support Russian opposition to it.[129]

Meanwhile, as Persian anger at the Russian presence mounted, Grey's efforts to get some measure of financial help for Persia and to get the Russians to agree to withdraw their troops were going nowhere. "As to [Russian] troops," Grey told Hugh O'Beirne, the British chargé d'affaires at St. Petersburg, their indefinite stay "...would be inconsistent with the maintenance of any native government at all in Persia, especially when combined with refusal or prevention of all financial help to [the] Persian government."[130] Yet, as Firuz Kazemzadeh puts it, "London did not want to hear evil, see evil, or speak evil."[131] And while he was ready to admit Russia's bad faith, Grey was determined to prevent the breakup of the 1907 alliance at any cost.

The presence of Russian troops became a matter for debate in the Majles when it convened in early 1910. Why didn't the Russians just go home, wondered several deputies? But Russia had been given a convenient reason not to "just go home" in the person of the brigand, Rahim Khan who, after terrorizing Tabriz, was captured by the Russians in August 1909, but released about three weeks later. A month after his release, he attacked Ardabil, about a hundred miles east of Tabriz, thus giving the Russians an excuse to send fresh troops into Persia.[132] In December, he had been surrounded by an army led by a Turkish-Armenian, Ephraim Khan, but had been assisted by the Russians to escape across the Russian frontier. In early 1911, he was allowed to "escape" once again and in the single month of February, at a village near Astara, sixty people, including women and children, were massacred. The Russians could therefore argue that "disorders" in northern Persia required the presence of their troops there. Indefinitely.

Rahim Khan was useful in another way, too. Russia was willing to provide him with sanctuary, placing him beyond the reach of government troops while granting him quarters where he could store the loot he had taken in Persia. But since he also had looted property in Russia, the Persian Government would periodically receive demands for payment for the damage he had caused there. Both Sir George Barclay, the British Minister in Tehran who had replaced Cecil Spring-Rice, and Stanislav Poklewski-Koziell, who had arrived as Russian minister to Tehran in September 1909, protested that practice, but to no avail.[133] The Russian government decided that Rahim Khan was not a common bandit but instead an "insurgent."[134] Sir Edward Grey again demurred. And Persia suffered.

That summer, revolts in Fars and Kermanshah, clashes with Russians, and an unsteady government seemed to justify

The Second Majles

the continued Russian presence. And complicating things was the talk in Tehran of the possibility of a loan to the Persians from Germany, underlined by the presence of a representative of the Deutsche Bank, and the apparent willingness of two Cabinet ministers to talk to him.[135] That German presence in Tehran was far more disquieting for Sir Edward Grey than Persian discomfiture over the presence of Russian troops in Azerbaijan.

A few months before Shuster arrived on October 19, 1910, Hussein Quli Khan, the Foreign Minister and a leading Constitutionalist, informed the British and Russian legations that the Persian government had discovered treasonable correspondence between the ex-shah, Mohammad Ali, and some of the Turkoman chiefs on the Persian frontier east of the Caspian Sea. And he proposed, in accordance with the terms of the Protocol, to stop the payment of the next installment of the ex-shah's pension until further investigation could be made. The two legations not only refused to pay attention to that demand but insulted him by sending two servants from the Russian legation, in uniform, to follow him through the streets and stand outside the door of his private residence until the payment was forthcoming.[136]

As if that outrage were not enough, a month later, the Russian Minister demanded an apology from Hussein Quli Khan for an alleged insult to a Russian consular agent at Kashan whom Shuster describes as "an evil Persian" to whose appointment the Persian government had strongly objected. The Russians clearly wanted Hussein Quli Khan gone. He resigned a month later but without granting an apology.[137]

In Isfahan, an ex-official of police wounded the Constitutional governor, killed his cousin, and then took refuge in the Russian Consulate there. Five days later the Persian Minister of Finance and a leading moderate, Sani ad-Dowla, who had been trying to negotiate a loan for Persia, was shot and killed in the streets of Tehran by two Georgians, Russian subjects, who also wounded four Persian police before they were captured.[138] The Russian consular authorities refused to allow these men to be tried by the Persian court and, in defiance of the 1909 Protocol, they were instead handed over to the Russian legation in Tehran beyond the reach of Persian justice.[139]

There was no protest from Sir Edward Grey.

Howard Baskerville
American missionary and teacher, killed attempting
to help defend Tabriz from Russian-led Royalists

Mohammad Ali Shah
(r. 1907-1909)

Nasr al-Mulk
Regent of the young Ahmad Shah

VII

Why an American? Why Shuster?

> *"...a man of considerable force of character and unquestioned integrity...He is said to have also taken up the cudgels for the natives ..."*
>
> —British Ambassador James Bryce

If Persia had been a human patient, by the spring of 1911 one might have been justified in calling in the coroner. Bankrupt and effectively barred from borrowing funds, with no army or police force of its own to control the crippling disorders within its borders, and with its northern provinces virtually, if not legally, occupied by a foreign power, Persia's prospects for survival as an independent, integral state were beyond dismal.

What was needed was to place Persia on a firm enough financial footing so that it could manage without foreign financial help. That meant creating the machinery to control its own revenues and expenditures, but the experience of Persian financial reformers from Amir Kabir to the Atabak, had proven unhappy to say the least. That the Majles had no realistic choice but to consider inviting a foreign financial expert to create that machinery should not, as Arthur Millspaugh who would later come to Persia in the same capacity as Shuster, argued, "be construed to indicate any inherent incurable incapacity for self-government or even for technical administration." Millspaugh saw it "...rather in the spirit that... an American municipality...appoints a city manager, budget director, or police chief from another part of the country."[140]

Inviting a foreigner was one thing. Deciding on the

nationality of that foreigner, or foreigners, was quite another. More Belgians were absolutely out of the question. The Belgian Customs officers from top to bottom had become hated not only for their arrogance but precisely because they had been imposed. Indeed, the association of Belgians with both Russia and the monarchy had been a key trigger for the 1906 Revolution.

Equally if not more out of the question were British or Russian advisors. Even if they had shown some interest in Persia's financial viability, finance had never been a strong point for the Russians, but a British advisor in Tehran, that is, in the Russian sphere, was also out of the question. Advisers from any other European country might have been acceptable to the Persians but, as Sir Edward Grey worried, they would have been suspected, certainly by Russia and probably by Britain, of using whatever influence they had to favor the interests of their own countries.[141]

Nonetheless, on August 10, 1910, when the Persian Cabinet presented a proposal to the Majles to reform the administration of the ministries that most needed it, Europeans were suggested. The Ministry of Finance was to get seven Frenchmen, Interior was to have four Italians and two Swedes, and Justice was to get one Frenchman and one Egyptian. The proposal was referred to a Majles committee who made only one change, that Swiss rather than French advisors be sought. The government, however, insisted on French advisors. The committee held out briefly for Swiss advisors but then the idea of Americans was raised and received wide support from the Majles deputies to whom Charles W. Russell, the American Minister in Tehran, had suggested that only in America could really honest people be found.[142] That support might have been due to the nationality of Russell himself.

Americans were not unknown in Persia. In 1835, five American Presbyterian missionaries had become established in Urmiyeh in the province of Azerbaijan. By the end of the nineteenth century, they had also opened mission stations in Tehran, Tabriz, Hamadan, Kermanshah, Qazvin, Rasht, and Mashhad. They genuinely meant to leave Persia with "something worthwhile," and for them, that ultimately would have been conversion to Christianity. The number of converts they managed to get, however, never amounted to more than a mere handful, and those were primarily from among Nestorian Christians. Although achieving little in the realm of conversions, the missionaries had made a significant impact in two areas: education and medicine. Besides introducing modern medical practices to Persia, several dispensaries and hospitals had been built, and Persia's first modern medical school had been opened in Urmiyeh. A cholera epidemic in 1892 had led to the establishment of a hospital in Tehran in 1893 and that hospital had then become the center of relief during another cholera outbreak a year later.

The educational system established by the missionaries, while Christian in orientation, provided schooling from primary to college level in secular subjects such as mathematics, science, and often business methods in a nation that, except for the Dar al-Fanum, had literally no secular education. Several of the graduates of the missionary schools had played major roles in the Constitutional Revolution and had become prominent figures in the Majles. Others were among the country's leading lawyers, doctors, engineers, and literary figures. The missionary schools had also afforded the first opportunity for the education of women in Persia by creating a school system that included Sage College for women in Tehran.[143]

While Howard Baskerville's sacrifice on behalf of Persia was unusual, it was not unusual for American missionaries to spend their entire lives in Persia often with few, if any, returns to their homeland. And although there had been a measure of suspicion on both sides of the religious divide, open hostility was rare. Where there was distrust on the part of the Persians, it was primarily on religious grounds only. It was not the religion but the nationality of American missionaries that made them tolerated and often welcome. The work of the missionaries of other nationalities was overshadowed by the imperial and economic interests of their governments. The work of the American missionaries was *sui generis*. Persians would have been unable to separate the work of British missionaries, for instance, from the fact that the British, along with the Russians especially, were despoiling their country. The Americans, at that time, were not. While the Americans, like the other Europeans, were *kafir*, infidel, they seemed uninterested in exploiting the weaknesses of the Qajar dynasty.

America was wealthy and while it lately had demonstrated in the Spanish-American War and in its earlier conquest of the continent at the expense of dozens of Native American nations that it was not immune from imperial ambitions, it had not yet exhibited any political designs or interests in the Middle East. The few American investors that were in Persia could be safely dealt with and, with both financial and missionary interests at stake, the republican United States might be expected to act as a champion of Persian independence.[144] So, when the Majles deputies discussed the proposal to invite foreign financial advisors again in early September 1910, at the suggestion of a mullah, Agha Sheikh al-Raïs, it was Americans that they voted to hire.[145]

Historically, however, the American government's enthusiasm about involvement in Persia beyond being of some assistance to the Presbyterian missions had been limited. It was not until 1883 that the United States and Persia had exchanged diplomatic representatives, and Mr. J.G.W. Benjamin, who was himself the son of missionaries in the Ottoman Empire, became the first American minister to Tehran. Protecting the missions, however, was the primary and really the only American interest in Persia. Emphatically so. In 1888, the Persian government had made an impassioned plea to the United States to help stave off the Russians and the British. A message from Nasr al-Din to President Grover Cleveland had read in part:

> The Government of Persia, which is an old established and independent Kingdom of the world, have a Special message to Her Young and prosperous and powerful sister…we have two great neighbours which…are entirely repulsing us from our progress…and we cannot carry their proposes, because if the Government accepts what they say, it seems She wants to hand her country to them….

The shah then had made two requests, neither of which was for financial or military aid. What he wanted was assistance in "your diplomacy and justice, and when any of those powers want to prevent our advancement do you assist us in preventing them." A second request was for American science and industry, for "your companies and merchand [sic] and manufactures" in order to establish the "modern civilization and development of the country and progressing the people."

Instead of a reply, in his fourth annual message to Congress, President Cleveland briefly mentioned the establishment of a new legation which he hoped would lead to improved commercial relations. He did not bother to tell the shah that involvement in Persia's political struggles was contrary to America's foreign policy of strict non-intervention.[146]

In 1910, any involvement in Persian affairs on behalf of its "diplomacy and justice" was something that neither President William Howard Taft nor his Secretary of State, Philander

Why an American? Why Shuster?

Knox, would relish. However, both men were enthusiastic advocates of something called "dollar diplomacy," that is, the idea that by supporting stable, well-run governments, Americans would be encouraged to invest capital abroad, thus enriching investors at home. The last thing the State Department wanted was another Howard Baskerville or anyone else for that matter, who, while he might be a hero to Persians, by siding with revolutionaries against Russia, had jeopardized the safety of not only missionaries but any American who wanted to do business in Persia. Independence movements were all well and good; Americans instinctively cheered such things on behalf of freedom, self-government, and democracy. But not at the expense of endangering its misionaries. And not if the investment in freedom brought no financial return. However, sending an American financial advisor to Persia to stabilize its fiscal structure fit nicely with "dollar diplomacy."

On Christmas Day, the Persian Foreign Minister, Hussein Quli Khan, who had just been so gravely humiliated by the Russians in October, wired the following instructions to the Persian chargé d'affaires in Washington D.C., Mirza Ali Quli Khan. His letter to the American State Department of December 25, 1910, reads in part:

> Request immediately Secretary of State put you in communication with Imperial American financial people and arrange preliminary employment for three years subject to ratification by parliament of disinterested American expert as Treasurer-general to reorganize and conduct collection and disbursement revenue assisted by one expert accountant and one inspector to superintend actual collection in provinces secondly one director to

organize and conduct direct taxation assisted by one expert inspector similar to above...avoid other methods of proceeding who may offer advice and services...[147]

Meanwhile, the patience of the American minister in Tehran, Charles Russell, with non-intervention had worn thin. The Persians, he kept reminding his superiors, were enthusiastic for Americans, and the reluctance of the State Department to recommend anyone was wearing on him. Thus, that same day, Russell wired, "Shall I assure Minister for Foreign Affairs you will cooperate with Persian chargé d'affaires in selecting assistants if requested or leave impression we do not care to be consulted as to what is the character of American citizens employed by order of Parliament?"[148]

Instead of rejecting the two requests, President Taft promptly dispatched a letter on December 28 to Philander Knox that not only embraced the idea of sending an American advisor to Tehran but specifically named W. Morgan Shuster, who was then a partner in a Washington, D.C. legal firm.[149] The letter read, in part, "I do not know a man in the country or the world who is more competent to [organize their entire Customs and revenue services] than this same Morgan Shuster. I wish you would talk with me about it."[150]

The mystery is who suggested Shuster to Taft? More than likely, the project originated with Russell who had connections in Washington legal circles and whose daughter suggested as much to Robert McDaniel in 1967. While Russell's reports don't entirely clarify the matter, as McDaniel points out, Taft had noted in his December 28 letter to Knox that he had been "looking into this matter for several months past."[151] Russell also must have been aware that Taft knew Shuster personally. He had worked with him in the Philippines and, as the letter suggests, had developed a high regard for him.

WHY AN AMERICAN? WHY SHUSTER?

As a result of negotiations with the American State Department, Shuster was contacted and accepted a three-year contract to serve as Treasurer-General of the Persian Empire to "organize and conduct the collection and disbursements of the revenues of Persia."[152] At the same time, the State Department "took pains" to point out that Shuster would have no official connection with the U.S. government which "assumed no responsibility for his actions."[153] His name along with that of four assistants was forwarded to the Majles which, on February 2, 1911, confirmed the contracts of the Americans for a period of three years.

Sir Edward Grey would later claim that it was he who suggested an American advisor[154] but European diplomacy does not seem to have been informed of the negotiations between Persia and the United States until nearly a month after they had begun, that is, until January 26, 1911, when the British ambassador in Washington cabled that information to London. London then informed St. Petersburg where the Foreign Minister, Sergei Dimitrovich Sazanov, objected to the appointment of an American, arguing that the appointment of an American would establish a precedent for the penetration of Persia's administration by America's citizens and thus limit the influence of the Great Powers. Yet, when Washington rejected Sazanov's request to refuse the Persian proposal, Sazanov gave way and the proposal went forward.[155]

The fact that neither Grey nor Sazanov objected more strenuously to an American raises the question of why they did not? What did they expect of an American?

They would not have anticipated an American to be a significant player in matters related to Persia. The United States was not considered a Great Power and its policy of strict non-intervention suggested that it would present no threat to the increasingly precarious balance of European diplomacy. Moreover, unlike members of the European diplomatic community, an American would not be a member of that class accustomed to managing affairs. And, as a simple financial advisor, neither would the American be a professional diplomat, and would not, therefore, be familiar with the diplomatic protocols and machinery, the delicate nuances, and subtleties to which the representatives of the Powers were accustomed. And perhaps the expectation was then that whoever was sent from the United States could be safely "managed."

Who was Morgan Shuster?

A native of Washington D.C., Shuster was born in February 1877 into a leading District family. His grandfather had been a prominent businessman and his father was a well-known member of the District Bar. Following his graduation from high school in 1895 where he had earned high honors and served as president of his senior class, he had attended Columbian University[156] on a scholarship which he had won in a competitive examination. There, he played the position of lineman on the University's football team.[157] After his third year, he enrolled in the Columbian Law School, but then he left the University in order to work in the law firm of Carlisle and Johnson. That employment was short-lived, however, because in the fall of 1898, in the aftermath of the Spanish-American War, Shuster took service in the War Department initially as a stenographer. In a short time, however, it became clear to a correspondent for the Associated Press, that "when something of special importance had to be done, it seemed natural to entrust it to him" and he became the Deputy Collector of Customs in Havana, Cuba.[158] There, he also organized and then became the head of a bureau of statistics and "did good service in unearthing and suppressing attempts to defraud the government."[159] The Cuban tour was shortly followed by service in the Philippine Islands where, as a member of the Second Philippine Commission (the so-called Taft Commission), he served first as Customs Collector and then as Secretary of Public Education.[160] Praising the fact that Shuster filled one of the most important positions in the administration of the Philippines with "dignity and honor," the Associated Press correspondent proudly called him "a splendid example of the possibilities of American youth."[161] He was not yet twenty-five years old.

James Bryce, the British ambassador in Washington, however, was less lavish in his praise of Shuster. His tendency to enforce regulations, thought Bryce, "occasionally became vexatious, and certainly rendered him unpopular." But that was not all. Bryce further commented:

> He is described as a man of considerable force of character and unquestioned integrity. He seems to be also rather unbending in temper and rigid in methods.... He is said to have also taken up the cudgels for the natives with a vigour which caused some little embarrassment to the administration, and which would appear to have led to his return home.[162]

Those three qualities, his integrity, his "force of character," and the vigor with which he had "taken up the cudgels for the natives," should have been a warning to the Powers that the American who was coming to Persia would not be at all easy to manage.

Shuster also possessed a keen intellect and a quick wit that could find its way into withering sarcasm. He would find the Persian army, for instance, to be "a mythical corps worthy to take rank with the gnomes who disturbed the slumbers of Rip Van Winkle."[163]

Some of his harshest sarcasm, however, would be reserved for the British Foreign Office and especially for Sir Edward Grey. After admitting that Grey was a man of good birth, manners, and a splendid education, the Foreign Secretary would receive this scornful judgment: "...[his] most tangible accomplishment during a lengthy public career is an authoritative treatise on dry fly-fishing." He would, thought Shuster, have made an excellent minister for Switzerland or Belgium or perhaps for Ruritania.[164]

Often, however, he was more amused than critical when he was faced with the banality and pomposity of the officials, both Persian and European, whom he would encounter. At a party he attended shortly after his arrival, he wondered at the various types of top-hats worn by the "gallant" secretaries of one of the legations. He noticed that "...most of them [were] of rare vintage (the hats), and many...were prevented from engulfing their entire countenances only by their ears..." He later learned that the supply of "these social weapons" was limited in Tehran and had to be transported over the Alborz mountains, so the junior diplomats treated them like "official" heirlooms. "From which I take it that megalocephalia was prevalent among their predecessors in office."[165]

Shuster had never dreamed of going to Persia but, as he put it, "the eloquence" of Mirza Ali Khan, together with the opportunity to "help a people who had certainly given evidence of an abiding faith in our institutions and business methods" removed his doubts.[166] As an American, he took a Constitution and a rule of law for granted and, like most Americans, thought that what was good for Americans was good for the rest of humanity as well.

His experience in the Philippines may also have influenced his approach to Persia. In 1901, civil government had been established in the Islands under Taft who, first as Civil Governor then as Governor General, would serve with a bicam-

WHY AN AMERICAN? WHY SHUSTER?

eral legislature. Despite an ongoing, very bloody insurgency, Shuster had been able to cultivate the cooperation of Filipinos in inaugurating institutions of self-government among people who, like the Persians, had never had such a thing. He had had a role in founding the first university in the Philippines and creating a secular educational system. That had been no small achievement. In the Philippines, as in Persia, education had been in the hands of the clergy; in the case of the Philippines, that had been the powerful Jesuit order. He had helped organize a Chamber of Commerce and he had seen the development of a judicial system including a legal code as well as a civil service, and the establishment of autonomous provincial and municipal boards whose members were empowered to collect taxes, manage local properties, and carry out infrastructure projects. Thus, Shuster had no reason to think that institutions such as those being brought to life in the Philippines could not also be established anywhere else—in Persia, for instance.

Also, like many Americans, and as his experience in the Philippines had seemed to demonstrate, he was fairly certain that there was no problem that could not, with intelligence and skill, be solved. In Persia, however, that approach was not always useful. Generations of dealing with often ruthless oppressors, their own as well as from abroad, had given Persians consummate skill in bargaining, negotiating, and engaging in a system of excessive flattery called *"ta'arof"* that may have had nothing at all to do with solving the problem at hand.

Energetic, idealistic, honest, Shuster, in many ways, resembled the earlier missionaries who had preceded him as well as many other Americans, including the Peace Corps volunteers of the 1960s and 1970s who would go to Iran with no other motive than to give that country and her people "something worthwhile."

So, what should Shuster have known before he arrived in

123

Persia?

First and foremost, it would have been extremely helpful to have known Persian. Grammatically, the language is fairly easy to learn, but mastering the cultural nuances embedded in the spoken language takes years. He would later acknowledge that his lack of knowledge of the "habits and modes of thought" of the people was a great handicap.[167] He did manage to pick up at least a few vocabulary items and phrases while in Persia, but most of his communication was either directly in French in which he was quite fluent, or in English or translated into one of those languages from a Persian speaker.[168]

More significantly, it was not only in language that Shuster's education had left him intellectually under-prepared for Persia. As at any university in either the United States or Europe, the liberal arts curriculum at Columbian University was Eurocentric. Courses in history did not extend beyond Europe and the United States. Thus, at the time of his appointment, Shuster's knowledge of Persia's history beyond Alexander the Great's burning of Persepolis was probably minimal. And that mattered. The most illiterate Persian would have been aware that the monuments in his land speak of glories and triumphs belonging to a past far beyond the Achaemenid period but a past that is also littered with defeats and humiliations. As the history of Amir Kabir had illustrated, prosperity and power both for the country and for the individual were fragile. Neither last for long. The lesson was simple: one takes what one can at the moment, for in the glance of a minister's eye, in the whisper of a powerful woman in the royal harem, in the sneer of a favored courtier, one's fortune and perhaps one's life could be forfeited.

Before he left the United States, Shuster had tried to acquaint himself with the land in which he would be working by reading Edward Granville Browne's "magnificent work" *Persian Revolution, 1905-1909*.[169] That book was critical, possibly even more so than his experience in Cuba and the Philippines, in shaping his approach to the situation he would confront. In fact, it is not too much of a stretch to maintain that Shuster's approach to his role in Persia cannot be understood apart from Browne.

Browne had traveled to Persia in 1887 when he was twenty-six years old. He spent a year traveling about the country with only one servant, going from Tabriz to Tehran, then to Isfahan, the once-beautiful capital of the Safavid monarchs and then down to Shiraz, and finally to Yazd and Kerman, ready to engage in any kind of conversation, whether it was about theology, poetry, politics, architecture, Baha'ism, history, food, anything at all with anyone he met, peasants, tribesmen, craftsmen, clerics, merchants. In short, Browne fell in love with Persia and with the Persian people—defensively so.

> ...for while all who know them have admitted their wit, their quickness of mind, their pleasant manners, their agreeable address, their amusing conversation, their hospitality and dignity, they have been charged with falsehood, treachery, cowardice, cruelty, subserviency, lack of principles, instability of purpose, and corrupt morals.[170]

Upon his return home, Browne had published *A Year Among the Persians* and had become Persian lecturer at Cambridge University, where he would remain until his death in 1926. Although he never returned to Persia, he followed events there very carefully and became a leading member of the London Persia Committee. In 1910, reflecting on the Persian revolution, Browne forsook the "pleasant paths of Persian literature to enter into the arid deserts of international politics." But, he said, the call was "imperious" and the summons urgent: "[T]o neglect nothing of that little which lay in my power in order to arouse in the hearts of my countrymen some sympathy for a people who have, in my opinion, hitherto received less than they deserve."[171] He had published *The Persian Revolution.*

Browne's narrative began with the revolutionary movement in the latter days of the reign of Nasr al-Din Shah, specifically with the activities of Jamal al-Din al-Afghani and the tumult of the Tobacco Concession. What Shuster knew of Persia's history before that period or how much weight he would have given to the impress of that history on the Persian mind is hard to gauge. Often, when a Persian official would show lukewarm enthusiasm for reforms he suggested, reforms which would manifestly strengthen the Constitutional regime, Shuster would be baffled and frustrated, apparently not appreciating the depth of distrust that the official might have had in the stability and permanence of that or any regime. To his chagrin, he would learn that, despite the lofty ideals of the Constitutional Revolution, the principal object of holding office was usually not to perform a public service but to enrich oneself and one's friends. In the very next breath, however, he would also remark that "a correct reading of her history" was essential to understanding the character and motives of the men who were shaping Persia.[172]

Temperamentally, Browne and Shuster also resembled each other. Neither was particularly interested in what is called realpolitik, that is, diplomacy conducted on pragmatic rather than ethical principles. Sir E. Denison Ross, in his "Memoir" to Browne's *Year Amongst the Persians*, described Browne as

> ...perfectly fearless...and his views, if idealistic...were always based on love

of justice...for him there was no such thing as compromise and [he] who was so apt to tolerate all shortcomings in his fellow-men, was in politics intransigent and unforgiving—and usually on the losing side."[173]

That description could have been applied to Shuster as well.

From Browne, Shuster would have learned that he would not be the first non-Persian to attempt financial reform in Persia. Beginning in early 1908, M. Bizot, an "eminent French finance-doctor"[174] had been contracted to untangle the finances. Not surprisingly, the Court had been uninterested. It was not until early September that Bizot had even managed to obtain an audience with Mohammad Ali where he intended to expose the "scandalous way" in which revenues were being squandered. He had been met with a cold reception "almost to discourtesy."[175] Earlier, the Cabinet had been no more cooperative. Not only had Bizot found it impossible to obtain needed information but, earlier, in late April, when the Minister of Finance presented a budget to the Majles, Bizot found that his own proposals to control expenditures were completely ignored. Contrary to his advice, the Minister's budget included raising tariffs on a number of items including tea and sugar while showing no signs of cutting expenses. Moreover, the Majles was assured that the Powers were willing to agree to the changes. They were not since there was no sign that the changes would benefit the country.[176] Two years later, under attack from all sectors of the government, Bizot was forced to resign having left behind a thirty-page report expressing his opinion as to *what somebody should do* to reorganize the fiscal system.

Shuster's later contempt for Bizot was perhaps unduly

harsh. He was under the impression that Bizot had done little during his tenure but "drink tea, play bridge, and ride out for his health." He also scorned Bizot for having been "thoroughly entranced by [the] good fellowship and the numerous social festivities given at the different legations."[177] As he would find later, his own efforts at financial reform would be confounded by the same forces Bizot had faced.

The key factor shaping Shuster's approach to Persia was Browne's condemnation of the Anglo-Russian Convention. But not without some reservation. In Browne's *Persian Revolution*, Shuster had read the September 5, 1907, communique of Sir Cecil Spring-Rice to the Persian Office and had become hopeful, if not convinced, that the purposes of Britain and Russia in Persia really were those expressed in the language of the Convention "and not ulterior and undisclosed ones."[178] To his chagrin, he would learn otherwise, and the lesson would be harsh.

What Shuster could not have been aware of was the diplomatic correspondence that had passed between London and St. Petersburg in the months preceding his appointment. In September of 1910, Grey had instructed Sir George Barclay that unilateral Russian action in Persia must be prevented "at all costs." However, he added,

> It is absolutely essential...that the solidarity of action of the two Powers in Persia should be maintained, and care should be taken not to allow any divergence of views with your Russian colleague.... If joint action of the two Powers should lead to resignation of Cabinet it would be unfortunate, but consideration should not be allowed to impair the harmony now existing between the two legations.[179]

Why an American? Why Shuster?

What Shuster also could not have been aware of was that by that same autumn, Russian opposition to any kind of loan to Persia, its insistence on maintaining troops in the north, and British acquiescence in both actions, had hardened. Throughout the summer of 1910, the Persian government had pleaded with Russia for the removal of her troops and the answer had remained the same: Russia needed "real proofs of the willingness of the Shah's government [this was written a full year after Mohammad Ali's removal from the throne] to establish firm, sincere relations with Russia, which would be possible only if it met our wishes." And the Russians began to talk of "the necessity of entering the path of reprisals."[180]

St. Petersburg's recognition that the government in Tehran belonged to the deposed shah and not to the Majles, and the insistence that that government "meet our wishes" might have been a warning to Shuster had he known of it. And if he had known, the question then is, would he have taken up the task anyhow?

He probably would have because from an early date, possibly even before he left the United States, he seems to have viewed his task not simply as a financial one but as a moral summons. "I finally decided to do what I could to help a people who had certainly given evidence of an abiding faith in our institutions and business methods," he wrote. Notwithstanding his initial ignorance of Persian and his perhaps limited reading of Persia's past, Shuster had borrowed from Browne his "...high opinion of, and desire to secure justice for the nascent constitutional movement in Persia, [and it was that which] strengthened my own determination to proceed."[181] If a particular minister's faith in the Constitutional movement might have wavered, Shuster's would not.

On Saturday, April 8, 1911, Shuster, his family, and four assistants who had served with him in the Philippines sailed from New York. A little less than a month later, they would arrive in Persia believing that there would be no objection "to the fair and honest accomplishment"[182] of giving to Persia "something worthwhile."

Edward G. Browne, British writer and Persia scholar

VIII

First Days

"The Majles was insistent from the very first that I should do nothing which would either directly or otherwise recognize the existence of...spheres of influence within Persia. This I gave them my promise at the outset not to do."

– Morgan Shuster

About 9 o'clock on the morning of May 7, 1911, almost exactly one month after sailing from New York, three American men accompanied by their wives and children disembarked from a little Russian side-wheeler, the *Bariatinski*, at the Caspian Sea port of Anzeli having sailed the afternoon before from the Russian port of Baku. Morgan Shuster, accompanied by his wife and two daughters, was one of the men.[183] The other two were Charles McCaskey, who would hold the office of Inspector of Provincial Revenues, and Bruce Dickey, who would become the Inspector of Taxation. Later, on May 25, they would be joined by the fourth member of the team, Ralph Hills of Washington D.C., who had been compelled to remain behind in Istanbul because of the serious illness of his daughter. However, just after their arrival in Tehran, another one of his children got sick and the Hills family had to return home on June 2. Frank S. Cairns, who had been Collector of Customs in the Philippines would become Shuster's principal assistant as Director of Taxation. He arrived on June 19. All of these men were in their early to mid-thirties, except for Cairns who was forty-two years old.

They were met by a gentleman named Hormuz Khan who had been sent by the Ministry of Finance to act as courier and guide. This worthy presented his card on which he described himself as an "American student" and who actually did speak English fairly well.[184]

After Customs formalities which took about two hours, the little party traveled by a crowded launch, then a small boat and finally by carriage inland to the city of Rasht, the capital of the province of Gilan. The journey of about twenty-five miles took three and a half hours.

At Rasht, they were met by the acting governor of the province who entertained them "very hospitably"[185] for two days while arrangements were made for the next leg of the journey to their destination, Tehran, 220 miles to the south.

Fortunately, an American missionary, a Dr. Douglas, had warned them to sew their bags in native felt; otherwise, after three days of alternate dust and rain, their baggage would have been useless. Traveling in four unwieldy, dilapidated, springless post-chaises drawn by four tiny, scrawny ponies which were changed at stations every ten or twelve miles, they traveled on winding dirt roads up into the cold of the Alborz mountains where the last of the winter snows were melting.

Interestingly, except to note that the road from Rasht to the first overnight stop at the station of Manjil was "good but hilly," Shuster says nothing of the landscape which, despite the rain, in May is quite pretty. Bordered by colorful wild flowers, sage and lavender, clover, daisies, and blossoming shrubbery, the road would have wound past gurgling little streams and lush green fields of tea and rice. At the stations where they changed ponies, they would have seen the thatched roofs that should have reminded Shuster, as they reminded Turin Boone who joined his team several months later, of the dwellings he had seen in the Philippines.[186] They also must have encountered the hospitality for which Persians were, and still are, famous. Surrounded by curious onlookers, they would have been refreshed with tea, sweets, nuts, fruits, and cigarettes. Yet, of this, Shuster also says nothing except to mention "interesting adventures" which he does not describe.[187]

The journey was hard and the days long. They covered between fifty and seventy miles in the space of ten to twelve hours a day. The second night was spent in Qazvin, another provincial capital and, for about forty years at the end of the sixteenth century, the capital of the Safavid dynasty until it was replaced by Isfahan. Their lodging in Qazvin most probably would have been in the massive caravanserai of Sa'ad al-Saltaneh, but of this building he also says nothing, possibly out of sheer exhaustion.[188]

Intent on seeing to it that the American visitors received a favorable impression of his country, Hormuz Khan relieved much of the monotony of the journey with his conversation and songs, pointing out the beauties strewn about the landscape. Although he was a good Muslim, he did not mind an occasional cup of cognac and was not shy about reminding someone in the party that a sufficient time had elapsed since the last one.[189]

Sunburned, dirty, and tired, they descended to the heat of the plain, reaching the outskirts of Tehran on the afternoon of May 12. There, Hormuz Khan reminded them that his personal services had been of such worth that he should immediately be assigned the post of Assistant Treasurer-General or Chief Tax Collector. Since neither title was within Shuster's power to grant even had he been disposed to do so, Hormuz Khan left disappointed and never returned to Shuster's story.

The incident, however, prefigured something that Shuster would deal with frequently. The remuneration expected for the performance of a task could often be far greater than the effort required to perform that task.

Four miles outside the Qazvin gate of Tehran,[190] the party was met by the American minister Charles Russell with his family and a number of American missionaries as well as several Persians. From there, they were escorted to Atabak

Park. This would be Shuster's home for the next seven and a half months. There is no indication that, following that difficult trip, he was eager to embark on another one anywhere at any time during his stay in Persia.

This residence and park had belonged to the Atabak, whose acquisition of those qualities normally associated with civic virtue had been less impressive than the magnificent palace he had acquired while serving as prime minister under Mohammad Ali Shah. Since his assassination in August 1907, the Atabak compound had come into the hands of a wealthy Parsee merchant named Arbad Jamshid. From E.G. Browne's *Persian Revolution*, Shuster would have known the Atabak's history, but if he had a twinge of foreboding about his lodgings, he does not reveal it.

Arriving at the park in the early evening, the Shuster party was met by a crowd of "strikingly uniformed servants and guards" and conducted through a driveway under trees sparkling with lanterns which made Tehran itself "almost a fairy land."[191] Surrounded by high mud-baked walls, the eight-acre park, studded with several artificial lakes and water courses, was crowned by a two-story, white stone residence that contained about thirty rooms, a number of which were quite spacious, and filled with "strange" furniture and "a most remarkable collection of curious bric-a-brac," including fine and rare Persian rugs. After dinner, they spent several hours listening to the nightingales singing in the trees surrounding the palace. To add to that sense of grace, Shuster would soon find that a large number of Persians permanently attached to their household spoke either English or French and were "always ready...to help in any way merely in the hope of being found useful by those to whom they looked to aid their country and their people."[192] That night, in that place, Morgan Shuster could drink in the Persia of poetry and nightingales, of roses and fragrant perfumes, of romance and ancient kings and stately cypress trees and mystery, the Persia of Khayyam's *Rubia'yat* and Sa'adi's *Golestan*.

The Persia of nightingales and poetry, however, was not the Persia he would face the next morning.

Before they were able to unpack their trunks, in a procession that would continue for two months, callers began pouring into the compound, each one "an important personage" seeking an interview in which to explain his views on the situation and offer steps to reorganize the government. Rather than being annoyed by the great amount of time that was consumed by these interviews, Shuster found them a great "fund of valuable information."[193]

In those first days, too, he met three men who would remain his constant friends throughout his stay in Persia. All three were as deeply committed to the Constitutional government as Shuster himself and, thus, from all three, he would receive firm support. On May 16, he met the first of these, the man who would become his best and truest friend in Persia. Arbab Kaikhosro was a Parsi, a merchant and property owner, who had been educated abroad but returned to Persia, thrown his lot in with the Constitutionalist movement and had been elected to the second Majles from Tehran to represent the Parsi community. Like the other officials Shuster would meet, Kaikhosro promised to give Shuster and his team every assistance he could and "to defend the American finance officials against intrigues and attacks from every source."[194] Shuster would discover, however, that Kaikhosro actually meant what he said.

A few days later, he met Colonel Beddoes, late of the Royal Dublin Fusiliers who represented the Seligman Brothers in Tehran. Shuster would meet with him quite often to discuss the possibility of a loan from the Seligman firm which had, the previous October, shown a willingness to offer financial aid to Persia. That willingness, Shuster would discover, remained.

The third friend was the London *Times* Correspondent, W.A. Moore, who, it will be remembered, had led the sortie with Howard Baskerville in Tabriz against the ex-shah in 1909 in which Baskerville had been killed. Moore's sympathies lay firmly with the Constitutionalists and therefore, with Shuster.

Before he had left the United States, Shuster had come to a decision that would have the most beneficial and, at the same time, a most detrimental effect on his work in Persia. On his arrival, eschewing normal diplomatic protocol, Shuster avoided making courtesy calls on any of the foreign legations in Tehran, including the British and the Russian. There were two reasons for that: first, by agreement with the United States State Department, he would not be going to Persia as the representative of the American government. To have made the usual courtesy calls could have been perceived as tantamount to asserting a diplomatic role that, in fact, the American government did not intend for him to play and that he had no intention of playing. However, it also automatically deprived him of the support of his own government which, given its policy of strict non-intervention, may not have amounted to much in any case.

Secondly, a key condition of Shuster's employment had come from the Majles itself and it was unequivocal.

> The Majles was insistent from the very first that I should do nothing which would either directly or otherwise recognize the existence of so-called spheres of influence within Persia...For me to have done so would have been to break faith with the Government which employed me and to betray a trust which had been placed in me.[195]

Throughout his tenure in Persia, Shuster's fidelity to the

Majles and his fidelity to that trust, even when his own life was in danger, never wavered.

Apart from the obligations imposed upon him from both his own government and from the Majles, Shuster promptly became unimpressed with the diplomatic corps in Tehran. At that time, it was composed of the British, German, American, French, Italian, Turkish, Russian, Austro-Hungarian, and Dutch ministries, all of whom except for the Russian, British and Turkish ambassadors according to Shuster "had no greater task than to keep a number of their citizens and subjects on the salary and pension rolls of the bankrupt Persian government."[196] Most of the corps, he found, had splendid titles. One Italian official "dimly" connected with the Persian War Office bore the "self-created" rank of full general, while another aged and incapacitated gentleman of that same country but on Persia's payroll did "nothing more active than passing his time in an arm chair."[197]

> Imagine, if you will, a fast decaying government amid whose tottering ruins a heterogeneous collection of Belgian Customs officers, Italian gendarmes, German artillery sergeants, French savants, doctors, professors and councilors of state, Austrian military instructors, English bank clerks, Turkish and Armenian couriers, and last, but not least, a goodly sprinkling of Russian Cossack officers, tutors and drill instructors all go through their daily task of giving the Imperial Persian Government a strong shove toward bankruptcy, with a sly side push in the direction of their own particular political or personal interests.[198]

About a week after his arrival, he was asked when he would find time to call at the legations. His initial response was to prevaricate. He answered that he had not yet gotten settled in and was busy preparing a basic financial law for submission to the Cabinet and Majles; thus, it would be at least a month before he could make any calls.[199] This was a misstep that could have been avoided by simply making it clear that both the instructions he had received in Washington and his commitment to the Majles sharply discouraged such calls.

Much would be made of this refusal and in retrospect, Shuster conceded that perhaps he should have called upon the foreign diplomats "certainly as soon as the pressing matter of establishing and defining by legislation our official status and positions had been arranged."[200] He also felt, however, that, largely because of the publicity the snub received in the days following his arrival, to have yielded would have cost him the confidence of the "already suspicious and oft-deceived Persian people." However, he had to admit that "we have been charged with the high-crime of lack of tact."[201]

On the face of it, the fussiness about diplomatic protocol seems almost laughable. Nonetheless, in that insular diplomatic world, there was no such thing as a small discourtesy. The snub Shuster gave was not only never forgotten; it was never forgiven and when his mission encountered difficulty later, there would be no sympathy.

Ironically, despite Shuster's disdain for British and Russian machinations in Persia, and given that his greatest difficulties would come from St. Petersburg and London, with the ministers of those two Powers, Sir Charles Barclay, the British minister, and Stanislaw Poklewski-Koziell, the minister for Russia, he would develop cordial, if not, warm personal relationships. He found both men to be "most pleasant and polished gentlemen" but as he also noted, "one must at times separate a gentleman and a diplomat from his official acts performed under orders from his…government."[202] And as he made that separation rather often, so did these two diplomats.

He met these two men in early June at a garden fete at Sepahdar-i Azam's lovely and spacious park. Arriving at the entrance to the tent, Shuster and Charles McCaskey and their wives were ushered into the middle of "a gloomy and forbidding circle of European ladies and gentlemen who, posed in attitudes of studied indifference, stared stonily at the intruders." And although the tent was closed on three sides and the air was stifling, Shuster detected "a distinct atmosphere of frost."[203]

After about ten minutes, the ice did begin to thaw somewhat and the guests mingled. McCaskey, who had earlier become acquainted with Barclay, informed Shuster that the British minister wanted to meet him. The two did meet a few minutes later and had a friendly chat during which Barclay noticed "a very distinguished gentleman whose uneasy expression suggested…a diplomat of high rank" standing about eight feet from them. The "uneasy gentleman" was Poklewski-Koziell who, just at that moment passed them, swinging his cane. Barclay touched him on the arm and by that gesture, the American and the Russian met "without further disturbing the diplomatic balance of the world."[204]

Such was the personal regard that Poklewski-Koziell would develop for Shuster that, later, in early August when the fall of Persia's government seemed imminent, he would make him a most extraordinary offer. Shuster had gone to a dinner given by Colonel H.R. Beddoes, who had arranged the dinner in order to discuss a loan from the Seligman firm to the Persian government.

At the dinner were Barclay and Poklewski-Koziell as well as W. A. Moore. The dinner proceeded on what were at least cordial, if not, friendly terms. When it was over, they played several rubbers of bridge where Shuster's success at the game impressed Poklewski-Koziell with what he assumed was the ability of all American financiers. Afterward, on the balcony, Poklewski-Koziell asked Shuster bluntly whether he might be willing to remain as Treasurer-General or vazir when (not *if*) the ex-shah, Mohammad Ali, was restored to power. Poklewski-Koziell assured Shuster that he would retain the full powers he then possessed as well as securing the "full support" of the Russian government and be "suitably compensated." All Shuster would have to do is remain passive until the change took place. "The proposal was delicately worded," Shuster wrote. And he was certain that

> ...the Russian Minister regarded it as a highly proper suggestion, and that no insult was intended. Stripped of all diplomatic trimmings and phraseology, however, it was plainly proposed that I should cease to aid or advise the existing Persian Government, allowing it to hurry into bankruptcy and ruin....

He told Poklewski-Koziell as politely as he could that, whatever the outcome, he would not think of remaining under Mohammad Ali.[205] As cordial as the personal relationship between Shuster and Poklewski-Koziell was, and would remain, his refusal here to accept the offer did nothing to endear Shuster to the Russian government in St. Petersburg.

There is another way of looking at this dinner, though. Despite the criticism Shuster received for failing to make the usual diplomatic calls when he arrived in May, this dinner and especially Poklewski-Koziell's remarkable offer four months later indicate that neither he nor Barclay held that against him. Moreover, despite the difficulties Shuster would face from their two governments, and despite the problems he would present for them almost to the day he left Persia, it would remain very possible for Shuster to work with these two ministers.

Getting Started

The Americans had barely arrived in Tehran when they were greeted with the inauspicious warning that they would never be able to accomplish anything in Persia. Other foreign advisors who had attempted to bring about reforms had either been forced to leave or had "made their peace" with the clique of Persian officials, usually men whose wealth, power, and influence had been gained under the Qajar regime, and who had concluded that it was far safer and easier to become the tools, agents, and protégés of the Russians than to throw their lot in with their own people. It became a joke of the diplomatic corps in Tehran that the Americans wouldn't last three months, and the idea that any serious attempt would be made to straighten out Persian financial affairs met with laughter.[206]

For about a week, however, things went well. The day after their arrival, on May 13, Shuster, Bruce Dickey and Charles McCaskey accompanied by Charles Russell met with the Persian Minister of Finance, Mumtaz ad-Dowla, "a very intelligent man" and a former president of the Majles. The offers of assistance and assurance of cooperation that he met with from Mumtaz ad-Dowla as well as from a number of other Persian officials that he met early on, as well as the fact that they were all fluent in either English or French pleasantly surprised Shuster. That afternoon, driving through the streets of Tehran, he became aware that the Americans were "objects of very unusual curiosity" and, in apparent ignorance of the work of the missionaries, Shuster could not imagine what the name "American" conveyed or what any American had done previously that should have excited the interest of the Persians to the extent that they had.[207]

Three days later, May 16, was a busy day. Again accompanied by Russell, and by previous arrangement with Mumtaz ad-Dowla and the Minister of Foreign Affairs, Mutashamu as-Saltaneh, they called upon the latter at his office and indulged in the "necessary" official ceremony of taking tea. That afternoon, they were taken to the official reception palace of the Regent, Nasr al-Mulk, whom Shuster then would find to be "a most kindly and intelligent looking man." The ten to fifteen-minute conversation was free and cordial, and the Regent invited Shuster to call upon him any time, without ceremony.[208]

The next day, with Russell, Shuster called on the prime minister, Sepahdar-i Azam, who also held the portfolio for the Ministry of War. He was a tall, thin, wizened man about sixty years old, with small black eyes and a "very nervous manner" and one of the few Shuster met who spoke neither French nor English. Shuster was aware of the prominent role he had played in the capture of Tehran by the Nationalist forces and the deposition of the shah in July 1909. However, he was also aware that before that, he had been regarded as a supporter of the shah and, perhaps with that in mind, found him to be "rather more an arch intriguer than the leader of a victorious army."[209] It was at his garden party that Shuster would meet Sir George Barclay and Poklewski-Koziell a few days later.

Also present at this interview were Mumtaz ad-Dowla and the Vice Minister of War, Amir Azam, "a fat and oily giant" who spoke French well and acted as interpreter.[210] Shuster would later find that Amir Azam had been regarded as a supporter of the shah and "whose general reputation would warrant a long sentence in any workhouse."[211]

First Days

On May 21, Shuster gave an interview to the leading newspaper editors outlining the work the Americans hoped to accomplish. One of the newspapers, *Estekal (Independence)*, was the organ of the moderates, while *Irani-Noh (New Iran)*, had become the organ of the democrats. That interview may figure as his most significant and lasting accomplishment in Persia. From that time, the American mission had the undivided support of the Persian press, not only in Tehran but throughout the country. Shuster noted, however, that one evidence of Persian inexperience in political affairs was their sensitivity to any form of newspaper criticism and, despite the Constitution's guarantee of freedom of the press, it was a "frequent occurrence" for the Minister of the Interior, in a habit carried over from the Qajar regime, to suppress one or more papers in Tehran for casting even some very general aspersion on the government's actions or motives.[212]

These early days were spent exchanging more visits, smoking countless cigarettes, and drinking copious amounts of tea with members of the Cabinet. However, Shuster was also meeting deputies in the Majles. En route to Persia, the party had spent five days in Istanbul where Shuster had met with a number of Persians, many of whom such as Sayyid Taqizadeh had been members of the first Majles and who had warned him of the difficulties and dangers he would face, including the possibility of foreign intrigues against his work and even personal injury. But they had also convinced him that the Majles was more unified than, in fact, it was. That had reinforced his understanding from E. G. Browne who had believed that the Majles represented "the best aspirations of the Persians more than any other body that had ever existed" in Persia.[213] In Istanbul, he had been told, "Gain the confidence and good will of the deputies of the Majles and half of your work will already be done." But that injunction had been coupled with a warning, "Fail to obtain its cooperation, and you may as well give up your efforts to accomplish any real results."[214]

It was Browne's distinction between *mellat* (the people or nation) and *dolat* (the government), that Shuster would shortly begin to see in the chasm between the Majles and the Cabinet. Browne's sense of the heroism of the mellat would also be Shuster's. And there was, indeed, a good bit of justification for that view. The Majles was as representative of the nation as such a body could reasonably be. There were a few wealthy landowners and members of the Qajar nobility in that body but, Shuster found, most of the deputies were "nearer to the people," men who had studied law or medicine or had been lower-level officials or clerks under the Qajars. Several were members of the clergy but whatever their background, Shuster discovered, nearly all of them sincerely believed that the salvation of their country depended on putting their government on a firm and lasting basis.[215]

The Cabinet ministers that he would meet, on the other hand, would often be grandees left over from the Qajar period and interested in change but, as Shuster would discover to his vast chagrin, only up to a point. And only if they could see some personal advantage in the change.

He would also make another disquieting discovery. Several weeks after their arrival, he discovered that a rumor was going around that the Americans were Baha'is[216] and had come not to reform the finances but to proselytize. So the Minister of Finance suggested to Shuster that he should discharge the servants at Atabak as "they were all Baha'is." Since Shuster had never thought to put his personal servants to a religious test and it was against American principles anyhow, he told the minister that the Americans were *not* (Shuster's emphasis) Baha'is and he was not going to have the Persian government or anybody else pass "on the religious faith of ourselves, or our servants, or the color of our neckties, and that if the Government had not something more important than that to think about, it should find something." As far as he knew, that was the end of it.

It wasn't. About that same time, he began to hear about "intrigues" everywhere. "The Cabinet is making intrigues against you," he was told. And "Persia is the land of blague [sic] and intrigues." So, in self-defense, he finally declared that Americans thrived on intrigues and rather liked to see them going on.[217]

Not all of the intrigues he would face, however, could be so cavalierly dismissed.

Sir George Barclay
British Minister to Tehran

Stanislaw Poklewski-Koziell
Russian Minister to Tehran

IX

The June 13 Law

> *"I might say that the Persian finances were tangled—very tangled—had there been any to tangle."*
>
> —Morgan Shuster

About a week and a half after his arrival, Shuster met Mr. Lecoffre, a British subject of French extraction who had been in Persia a number of years, hated the Russians, and who now occupied the post of Controller in the Ministry of Finance. He welcomed Shuster with a rather disarming salutation: "I am glad, Mr. Shuster, that you have come," he said, "because *between us* we shall be able to straighten the miserable finances of these people." Shuster thanked him for "the encouraging thought."[218]

Apart from Mr. Lecoffre, there was not much about the Ministry of Finance that would give Shuster any "encouraging" thoughts. The Ministry was a haphazard collection of offices through which the internal tax, the *maliat*, was supposed to be collected. There was no civil service nor were there any specific qualifications, either ethical or professional, for positions in the Ministry. In a practice that had endured for generations and had unfortunately survived the Constitutional Revolution, places were granted to those who had sufficient family or political influence. A post in the Ministry required no knowledge of finance, accounting, banking, or even knowledge of the actual resources of the country. As a result, the Ministry was inefficient, wasteful, disorganized, susceptible to all kinds of fraud, larceny, deceit, and general corruption. If there had been any system, one could say that it didn't work. Or rather, it worked very nicely but only for those who held a sinecure within its domain.

There was no budget. Lecoffre had tried to produce one but from the day he had started to work on it, he had been viewed with suspicion by every minister of finance and tax collector.[219] There was not a single penny in cash; 400,000 tomans were due on a banking overdraft, and there were unknown sums due on a variety of outstanding checks, drafts, promissory notes, and various other notes drawn up by previous finance ministers. Central and provincial administrators had not been paid for several months, diplomatic representatives had not been paid for years, and Shuster would soon be receiving "pathetic" appeals from officials stranded in Europe who were unable to get back to Persia because their living expenses had left them in such debt that they were protected from arrest only by diplomatic immunity.[220]

When the Shuster team arrived, Persia's annual deficit was six million tomans assuming that all the internal taxes, the maliat, were paid.[221] But there was nothing to indicate that any more than about a fifth of that sum would actually be received by the central government. Moreover, with ballooning expenses, it could be expected that the minimum annual deficit of six million would grow to eleven million unless they could collect a much larger share of the maliat.[222]

The most secure source of revenue came not from the maliat but from Customs duties collected at various posts on the frontiers. That revenue was considerable. In 1910, it amounted to about three and a half million tomans. Unfortunately, every bit of it was mortgaged primarily to the British and Russians. Under a series of loans and agreements with the two Powers, the total minimum annual payments amounted to about 2,832,000 tomans. The remaining 568,000 had to be kept at the Banque d'Escompte in Tehran (the branch of the Russian State Bank) for a period of six months and placed to the credit of the Russian government twice a year. Moreover, the interest and amortization on the Russian loan had to be paid in rubles, not tomans.[223]

The Customs Department, under the Belgian administrator, Joseph Mornard, was the most efficiently run branch of the entire Persian government—efficient in that its revenues had been used to guarantee the considerable loans which Persia then had outstanding. It had its own books and records which, when Shuster arrived, there was no way of getting into. In other departments of the Finance Ministry, there were no records or statistics at all nor was there much help from the Persian gentlemen in the Ministry who were as eloquent of facts, according to Shuster, as the desks and chairs.[224] Even if, in the highly unlikely event that the anticipated revenues had actually arrived in Tehran, Persia's debts would have almost entirely swallowed them. The largest portion of the debt was to foreign governments and companies in the form of loans and interest on those loans. In addition, there was a so-called "Indian Government" loan made to the shahs by the British from the funds of the Indian Empire. And lastly, there was the so-called "Imperial Bank" loan of 1911 which had been made and ratified just before Shuster got there.

However, the chronic deficit was not entirely the fault of foreigners. Bloated army accounts, pensions, and the costs of maintaining the Court placed an enormous demand on government revenue. According to the "loosely kept" records at the various ministries, by the time Shuster arrived, nearly 100,000 people throughout the Empire were receiving a sum of about three million tomans every year in money and grain. Most of this "strange burden" had been inherited from the Qajar shahs but some had been decreed by the Majles to men who had served the Constitutionalist movement, and to relatives of men who had been killed fighting for the Constitution. To his chagrin, Shuster would discover that fully nine-tenths of the pensions allotted were for "pure graft."[225]

The June 13 Law

On May 22, the *chef de ceremonie* of the Ministry of Foreign Affairs conducted the Shuster team to some temporary offices in the Ministry. There, the Vice-minister of Finance and the chiefs of the various offices within the Ministry were presented, and there was more tea and more cigarettes. Each chief wanted a private interview with Shuster in order to properly explain the organization of his office and his own "thorough grasp of the needs of the situation." This usually included a complaint about the failure of the government to provide the chief or his employees with "sufficient pecuniary lubricant to grease the wheels of his department."[226]

What was necessary, Shuster decided, was to adopt a program of rigid economy in all branches of the government, central and as well as provincial, in order to reduce the chasm between the revenues actually received and the public expenditures that were actually necessary.[227]

But it also became obvious that no headway at all could be made unless full power to deal with the chaos rested solely with Shuster himself and his team. Acting merely in an advisory capacity to the ministers and Cabinet officials he felt would be futile because, as he pointed out, they were "neither equipped by experience and training, nor suited by character and disposition, to undertake the somewhat thankless task of stamping out the corruption and venality which marked the administration of Persian finances..." not only at Tehran but throughout the country.[228]

So, Shuster did what neither Bizot nor Lecoffre had done. He drew up a bill creating a new office, Treasurer-General, whose parameters roughly resembled those of Amir Kabir sixty years previously. The most important provisions were these: (1) The Treasurer-General would have direct control of all financial and fiscal operations of the Persian government, including the collection of all receipts and the control of all government expenditures. (2) The Treasurer-General would

151

have custody of the Treasury Department, and no government expenditure could be made without his signature or authorization. (3) The Treasurer-General would have authority over the personnel of the services under his control. What this would have meant was that Shuster would have been able to ignore the claims for office or preferment of anyone, regardless of personal, tribal, religious, or any other connections, that he did not consider qualified. That, in itself, was revolutionary.

Three offices were established under the Ministry of Finance: one was for the collection of the maliat, other taxes, and all other government revenues of *every* description; the second was for the inspection and control of all receipts and approved expenditures, and the keeping of accounts; the third office was for a Chief Officer, namely Shuster himself, to oversee all fiscal operations. All transactions of the government, whether it was a matter of revenue, expenditure, or any other financial obligation, thus had to pass through Shuster's office. All accounts would show on one set of books.[229] This was sensible and done in most Western countries. But not necessarily in Persia.

While he was engaged in drafting the law—and lobbying individual Cabinet members and Majles deputies to support it—Shuster was also working with A.O. Wood at the Imperial Bank to secure loans that would place Persia in a position to begin recovery. On June 9, at Shuster's request, Wood wired his London office to place the equivalent of 500,000 tomans into the Treasurer-General's account to be guaranteed out of Persia's general revenues. A week later the London office approved the loan. About the same time, Shuster learned that another 1,250,000 tomans would "probably" be put on the market around June 15, 16, and 17th.[230] The Cabinet approved Shuster's bill on June 8, and it was passed by the Majles on June 13 by a vote of 62 out of 69 members.[231] As Peter Avery points out, by giving Shuster control of Persia's entire financial machinery, the bill effectively made him the master, rather than the servant of the Majles, "a fact which was later to work to the detriment of his mission."[232]

Nonetheless, in its conception of a structure that would have placed real constitutional governance on a sturdy financial foundation, that law itself was arguably the crux of the Revolution. Indeed, it truly *was* the Revolution in that it essentially undermined a generations-old system upon which men had depended not only for their livelihoods but also for power, status, and influence. Had the June 13 law operated as Shuster envisioned it, it would have been able to breathe the kind of vitality into the Constitutional government of Persia that Alexander Hamilton's financial program had given the infant United States.

Like the Constitution itself, however, the effective implementation of the June 13 law was not guaranteed. Or, as Shuster gently put it, "There was already a very decent respect for money... but absolutely none for the laws as being the embodiment of the rights of the public."[233]

The chasm between a respect for law, especially a new law, and a respect for money and the privileges adhering to office became particularly apparent in the situation of the seven or eight senior tax overseers, the mostafis, in the Bureau of Mostafis within the Ministry of Finance. The men who held that office regarded it and the secret ketabche notebooks that went with it, as hereditary, personal possessions in which the government—any government—had no right to interfere. Indeed, because they were the only ones who had any notion of the complicated taxation of the country, it would have been unlikely that anyone could have interfered with it.

Even before the June 13 law was announced, Shuster circulated a telegram, signed by the prime minister and the Cabinet, that completely overturned that system. Thereafter, everyone from the tax overseers to the local tax collectors on down would receive all their directions, and communicate directly with the newly created Treasury. Even though a number of useless departments would be abolished, the mostafis would remain in their office in the Ministry of Finance because Shuster intended to use them "when they arrived at a proper frame of mind" to devise a plan for redistricting and making a rough tax survey of the empire in order to prepare a single, simple internal tax law.[234]

The encounter with Hormuz Khan, the Shuster party's loquacious guide from Rasht to Tehran, had been a harbinger of the resistance Shuster's efforts at financial reform would meet. Hormuz Khan knew English; he had tried very hard to entertain the party on the journey to Tehran and show them the beauties of his native land. Among his gifts, however, a knowledge of finance was not included. Nonetheless, he expected Shuster to hand him the office of Assistant Treasurer-General or Chief Tax Collector, posts to which emoluments were attached but which often bore little, if any, resemblance to any service actually performed by its occupant. But it was expected and when it was withheld, there was a sense of being wronged, of being cheated. Under Shuster's new regime, several men, far more powerful than Hormuz Khan, more powerful even than the mostafis, men like the Sepahdar, were likely to find that their own monetary claims for services rendered "but not satisfactorily recognized by an ungrateful nation"[235] would remain "not satisfactorily recognized." And they were not inclined to take that neglect lightly.

X

Creating a Respect for Law

"...the so-called Treasurer General."

From the Persians

Before the Cabinet had even approved the Finance Law, it had become clear that the concept of reform held by many of the people in the government was radically different from that held by Shuster. As he ruefully observed, "Laws, in Persia, and more especially financial laws, were lightly regarded."[236]

The Persian resistance came from two directions: the Court which, not surprisingly, was holding out for the restoration of power to the monarchy and had no interest in allowing the Majles to govern with any kind of efficiency, and from the Cabinet itself.

The first sign of resistance from the Court came even before the bill was passed. About May 28, Shuster learned that the Regent, Nasr al-Mulk, had decided to leave Persia because, he alleged, the Majles had passed a budget that greatly reduced the allowances for the Court without consulting him. Shuster was summoned to the private residence of the Regent and for three hours was subjected to a litany of the Regent's troubles. Shuster finally convinced him that even the rumor of his departure would not only embarrass the financial work he was trying to do but also throw the entire government into disorder. The Regent gave up the idea but only after Shuster took the matter up with the Sir George Barclay with the suggestion that Sir Edward Grey, the Regent's Oxford classmate, urge him to remain in Tehran.[237] Consequently, a few days later, on June 3, in an hour-and-a-half interview, the Regent told Shuster that he "heartily approved" Shuster's plan to make the Treasurer-General's control of Persia's finances "very large" and agreed that the finances should be taken "entirely out of politics."[238]

Nevertheless, that old Court habits would render financial reform difficult was made laughably clear to Shuster almost immediately. Two French citizens passing through Persia on a world tour stopped to pay their respects to the Regent. The next day, Shuster received a request from the Ministry of Foreign Affairs asking that these two "enterprising gentlemen" each be paid a hundred tomans "as a token of the royal esteem." Shuster, "not desiring...to raise an international question with the great French Republic," paid the sum but with a warning to the Minister that under the new law there had to be some legal justification for such an expenditure.[239]

About the same time, another request came from the Minister of the Court for two requisitions. One was for the purchase of oil for the royal camels and the other for straw for the royal automobile service. "This," Shuster admitted, "was too much for my official gravity." It turned out that the requests were perfectly legitimate. A certain kind of oil was needed to rub on camels to keep their skin lubricated, and the employees at the royal garage received their pensions in the form of straw. Shuster honored both requisitions.[240]

As with the Court, the difficulties with the Cabinet had appeared before it officially approved of the bill. The Cabinet had been organized in March and was composed largely of former Qajar bureaucrats whose intentions were probably honorable but whose ideas of reform did not include curtailing the prerogatives to which they felt entitled. This was particularly problematic in the Ministry of Finance.

Shuster and the Minister of Finance, Mumtaz ad-Dowla, had just reached a tentative basis for beginning their work when, on May 23, there was a "Cabinet crisis" and Mumtaz resigned, giving as the reason that his health would not be able to bear the extra work load required to deal with the new system. Apparently, the prime minister/ Minister of War, Sepahdar-i Azam, felt that Mumtaz had now become less willing to sign checks and warrants with the "freedom and abandon" which the Sepahdar felt he had a right to expect.[241] As Shuster quickly learned, "resignation" was simply a figure of speech meaning that someone was irritated about something. He would continue to perform his duties or simply move to a new position within the government. Nonetheless, the resignations were an unfortunate omen so early in Shuster's work. Mumtaz ad-Dowla was replaced by Mu'avin ad- Dowla.

In light of the continued Russian presence in the country, the ministry most vulnerable to Shuster's proposed cuts was the War Department which, according to Shuster, "was the roosting place for the most brilliant galaxy of uniformed loafers, masquerading as generals, commissaries, and chiefs of staffs, of petty grafters, amiable cutthroats and all-round scoundrels which it has ever been my fortune to encounter...."[242] As Lady Mary Sheil had observed over half a century earlier, the Constitutional Revolution notwithstanding, officer rank was sold and merit was no qualification for promotion. The gendarmes and police in Tehran, numbering no more than 1800, were poorly armed and equipped, and that force was necessary just to maintain order in Tehran. Shuster had estimated the cost of maintaining an efficient army of 15,000 men at two million tomans. Yet the annual amount demanded by the Ministry of War which "could not muster 5000 ragged, underfed troops in the entire empire was seven million tomans."[243] During the six and a half months Shuster was there, he never encountered the Persian regular army "in appreciable quantities" except upon requisition for their pay at the end of each month or in the form of bills for large orders of uniforms and other equipment.²⁴⁴

The Cossack Brigade, however, which was firmly under the command and control of Russian officers, cost the Persian government a bit over 230,000 tomans (£46,000) a year.²⁴⁵ While almost laughably insignificant in comparison with the seven million required by the ragged Persian army, the Constitutional government had never been able to pay that sum or even a significant portion of it.

On several occasions during those first days, the Sepahdar had assured Shuster of his support and full cooperation in stamping out abuses in government and had admitted "that while he was a natural military genius, there might be some things which he did not know about the organization of the War Department..." and would gladly, he pledged, welcome Shuster's advice.²⁴⁶ However, like many others, he found that Shuster's reforms had the potential to cause him more than a little discomfort.

On June 4, the Sepahdar came to Shuster wanting to know when Shuster was going to be able to raise ready cash at the Imperial Bank. It was only by his great personal influence and prestige, he told Shuster, that he was able to keep the governmental fabric from completely falling apart until "a little pecuniary assistance could be furnished for the gallant men of the regular army."²⁴⁷

Shuster had already arranged with A.O. Wood for a temporary advance of 250,000 tomans to be secured against the new loan. That evening, he was summoned to the Sepahdar's residence where, three days earlier, he had met Sir George Barclay and Poklewski-Koziell. Now, at the same place, Shuster would also meet with the new Minister of Finance, Mu'avin al-Dowla.

He arrived just before dusk and was escorted to the rear of the beautiful grounds to a small "out-residence" where he found Mu'avin ad-Dowla pacing "nervously" up and down.

Lamps were lighted and the inevitable tea and cigarettes served. Presently, the prime minister himself arrived amid "hoarse commands, the grounding of arms, [and] much salaaming by the double row of servants." But before any conversation began, "a venerable priest of Islam" came forward to ask a favor. The Sepahdar called a nearby officer and the poor cleric was summarily escorted out. The "solemn-visaged" Mu'avin ad-Dowla shook his head and, in French, told Shuster that the prisoner on whose behalf the mullah had tried to unsuccessfully appeal to the prime minister was to be hanged the next morning.[248]

With that inauspicious beginning, Shuster began the conversation, which was in French, with Mu'avin ad-Dowla translating for the Sepahdar since that worthy knew very little French and no English. Shuster described the financial crisis and then asked what sum was absolutely the minimum with which "the raging troops" could be temporarily "put in check." Warning that if the money were not forthcoming, "even our own lives will not be safe," the Sepahdar pulled a slip of paper from his pocket and handed it to Mu'avin ad-Dowla to read to Shuster. Then he stepped out of the room. The "trifling" sum of 406,000 tomans was the *sine qua non*, but of this, nearly half was for stores, uniforms, artillery horses, and "incidentals." What was left over was designated for the unpaid "raging" troops.

Shuster made no comment. The Sepahdar returned to the room "with a busy but anxious look." Mu'avin al-Dowla then spoke. "His Excellency requests your answer as to this important matter."

Shuster threw up his right hand and replied, "C'est impossible, Excellence."

To that, the Sepahdar replied with "volley after volley of eloquent persuasion and martial imprecation...." The "amiable" Mu'avin ad-Dowla paled and advised Shuster that he was making a mistake, but when Shuster asked if he knew of any successful method of withdrawing blood from a stone, he had nothing to suggest. Three hours later, the sum of 100,000 tomans was agreed upon.[249]

Eleven days passed. On every one, Shuster received a call from the man he referred to as "the Amir", Amir Azam, the Vice Minister of War, whose predictions of the horrors of mutiny, rapine, and bloodshed that would result from Shuster's unwillingness to produce the "modest" sums demanded by "that great patriot," the Sepahdar, were such that "nothing but a heart of flint coupled with an empty coffer" could have resisted his "pathetic appeals."[250]

On June 15, two days after the Finance Law had passed, the Sepahdar rose in the Majles and voiced his displeasure at the "arbitrary restraint" being placed upon him in the performance of his duties as prime minister and Minister of War. As he faced the unsympathetic faces before him, his anger increased and finally, having lost control of Persia's coffers as well as its Majles—and his own equanimity—he strode from the chamber, climbed into his carriage and ordered his coachman to drive him to "farhangistan," a term which meant, loosely, "Europe." Although he would announce that he needed to go to Europe "for his health," "farhangistan" could have also have been construed to mean Russia or, as some thought, he meant to join the ex-shah's brother, Salaru ad-Dowla, who, according to rumor, had recently captured Tabriz, roughly 250 miles from Rasht, the Sepahdar's home base, and had announced to the people that if they would set him upon the throne, he would need no taxes from them except for his "personal expenses." The question, as Shuster saw it, was whether the Sepahdar was going to join Salaru-ad Dowla or whether he was making for Anzeli in order to "skip out."[251]

The Sepahdar arrived in Rasht on June 18 whence, five

days later, he telegraphed the Regent stating that he would return to Tehran and resume his duties but only if the Finance Law of June 13 were modified so as to allow him a greater participation in deciding upon the disposition to be made of the public revenues. "There was loud mirth in the Majles when this statement was reported."[252]

The Sepahdar neither resigned nor returned until July 9, when he reappeared under the escort of the two stalwarts of the defense of Tabriz in 1909, Sattar Khan and Baqer Khan.[253] During that period, Shuster was in almost daily talks with the Regent, Nasr al-Mulk, as well as attending the sessions of the Cabinet trying to get the ministers to realize the seriousness of the financial situation and persuade them to stop making demands for "impossible sums of money." Some of the loudest demands continued to come from Amir Azam, the Vice-minister of War, who claimed that unless a "mere" 42,000 tomans were not immediately made available for pay and rations, there would be a general rising of the "Army of Tehran."[254] Ten days previously, Shuster had given him a similar sum for a month's arrears, and inquired what had become of that. "Gone," replied the excellency, "all disbursed to the poor, starving troops of the army." At that, Shuster pulled out a private memorandum showing that his abundant excellency had deposited the last month's pay plus several other sums for military purposes, in all amounting to 83,000 tomans, with a native banker "with whom it rested …while the predicted rising of the troops was being staged by the Amir's gallant officers of the line."

After reading the dates and amounts of the deposits, Shuster asked the Amir if they were not correct. The excellency then "lifted his two hundred and forty pounds of brain and adipose tissue to his full height of six feet, five" and, looking proudly at his colleagues on the Council, demanded to know whether his honor was being aspersed. If there were 83,000 tomans to his credit, he stated, he did not know of it. The other members of the Council, thinking that was perhaps improbable, suggested that the Amir's personal accountant be summoned. This was done and the Amir stepped out of the room, had a hurried conversation with the accountant, and returned wearing "a metallic smile of joy and friendship upon his countenance." He assured the Council that Shuster had, after all, been correct. The Amir had just learned, to his surprise, that the preceding month's payment had indeed not been made to the troops "(although His Excellency had so directed some time ago)" and it was that sum for which the troops were clamoring. Thus, the rising of the troops was "successfully postponed."[255]

While most people don't like to pay taxes, those who object most strongly are often those who are not accustomed to paying them in the first place. At one point, Shuster discovered that the Sepahdar, who owned immense estates in northern Persia, owed the government 72,000 tomans in addition to which he claimed a million more tomans for his "patriotic services" and expenses in relieving the city of Tehran from royalist control in 1909. He was also certain that both he and his descendants for ten generations should be exempt from all taxation. Another Qajar grandee, Prince Farman Farma, had "saved" several millions of dollars in the posts of provincial governor, general of the army, and a Cabinet officer. When he discovered that Shuster was serious about collecting what the prince owed, he went before the Council of Ministers in tears, recounting his valiant services to the Constitutional government. The members of the Council were so overcome with pity that they wrote Shuster a "polite" letter stating that the prince would not have to pay any taxes until they could "look into the question." The distraught prince brought the letter to Shuster who gave him the choice of either paying his overdue taxes the next day or having his grain warehouses seized. Most of his taxes were paid the next day.

Quite simply, without the June 13 law, Shuster would not have been able to check the corruption among the Cabinet members nor the extortions that were yet to come. The Regent would tell Shuster more than once that his work had saved the government two million tomans and had enabled it to keep forces in the field against the imminent invasion of the ex-shah.[256] Yet, the Regent would also be unable to separate his own financial interests from those of the government.

The dissatisfaction in the Cabinet, however, was deeper than simply at the top. Strikes by employees of several ministries were engineered almost every day and, although Shuster found that they provided "some excitement, but no trouble," he finally had to announce that any employee refusing duty would be permanently dropped from the payroll.[257] Among the mostafis, too, there was such unhappiness as to lead to rumors of the formation of an Anti-American Society.[258]

From the Foreign Interests

It might have been expected that Shuster's efforts to create a "respect for law" would have been difficult among the Persians, where "law" had either been custom or whatever the most powerful man in the room had decided it was. Yet, the most vociferous criticism came from the foreign diplomatic community whose governments were more than a little sensitive about their "interests" or "prerogatives" or whatever they chose to call them.

Although Shuster took pains to show that the Finance Law would actually increase the general security for their loans,[259] howls of protest rained down on the Persian Foreign Office from the French, German, Austro-Hungarian, and Italian legations, "many of them couched in the most undiplomatic, impolite, and insulting language."[260] Count Quadt, the German Minister, sarcastically referring to Shuster as "a certain Mr. Shuster," protested against the infringement of German interests which, he alleged, would result from the curtailment of two payments of 6000 tomans ($5400) to two German subjects, namely a hospital and a school, being signed by the Treasurer-General rather than by Joseph Mornard as had previously been the case. He did not, obviously, mention that the Kaiser's imperial ambitions would also have been threatened by an independent Persia. The Italians, whose interest in Persia was even less than the Germans, referred to Shuster contemptuously as the "so-called Treasurer-General."[261] The American Legation obviously stayed clear but so did the Dutch, the Turkish, and even, at least for the time being, the British. The entire Belgian force in the Customs Office, not surprisingly, threatened to resign if they were placed under the control of the new Treasurer-General.

The most serious difficulty came, as might have been expected, from the Russians. The focus of their vexation was the fact that the Belgian Customs Office, which had always been friendly to them under the management of Joseph Naus and then Joseph Mornard, would now come under the control of the American Treasurer-General. Moreover, the transfer of funds from Mornard's control to Shuster's had been accomplished without a prior notification to them. It seemed high-handed.

There may have been more to it than that, however. Later, in early August, Poklewski-Koziell would tell Barclay that Russia desired "a reasonably tranquil Persia" and, to that end, he recognized that "the Treasurer-General must be supreme in all revenue and financial matters." While he had full confidence that all obligations would be paid by Mr. Shuster, Poklewski-Koziell feared what would happen when Shuster left. If checks could not be signed by Mornard, they would have to be signed by a European who would have to then be trained in the office of Treasurer-General, an attitude that Barclay thought was "strongly indicative" of Poklewski-Koziell's desire to "arrange matters."[262]

The Customs Department was technically under the Ministry of Finance. But precisely because that office and its occupants, including the Administrator-General, had been foisted on Persia, and because Persians saw little benefit from the duties collected by that office, Mornard had become just as distasteful to the Persians as Naus had been. And like Naus, Mornard was strongly, and rightly, suspected of having Russian sympathies.

Even though the law had been openly discussed in several sessions in the Majles, the very day the law was passed, the Russian legation, in Shuster's words, "openly declared war upon it." And they threatened to have Russian troops seize the Customs houses in the north and put Russian officials in charge.[263]

The showdown came about a week after the Finance Law was passed.

There were five banks, including the Banque d'Escompte and the Imperial Bank, doing business in Tehran, and Shuster informed them in writing that no checks, drafts, warrants, orders of payment or government obligations of any kind were valid or payable without the signature of the Treasurer-General. The banks were also told that all balances or accounts standing to the credit of any government department or official were to be turned over to the credit of the Treasurer-General and were to be disposed of only upon his order.

On June 21, Mornard tried to put several checks through the Imperial Bank. The principal one was to be for a payment of 300,000 rubles to the Russian Government for a shipment of second-hand rifles which that "natural military genius," the now-absent Sepahdar, had purchased on behalf of the Persian government. The price was about three times that for which the same rifles could have been purchased on the market in Europe, and even though the purchase had been made several months previously, the rifles had not yet appeared at Anzeli. The Chief Director of the Imperial Bank, in accordance with the June 13 law, refused to honor the check, and informed the Russian Minister, Poklewski-Koziell—as Shuster had authorized him to do—that the sum would be paid only upon delivery of the rifles.[264]

Mornard protested to the manager of the Bank that such a procedure was illegal, and apparently immediately notified both the Belgian and Russian ministers. Shuster then notified Mornard and Poklewski-Koziell directly that, according to the June 13 Law, no expenditures could be made without the Treasurer-General's authorization. And he asked that all the receipts of the Customs be deposited to his credit at both the Imperial and Russian banks.

The dispute went back and forth and on June 29, the Cabinet adopted a resolution calling upon Mornard to obey the law of June 13. Shuster himself wrote the acting premier Mutashamu as-Saltaneh that if immediate action were not taken to secure Mornard's recognition of the authority of the Majles and its laws, he "would be compelled to lay the case before that body direct."[265]

Two days later, on July 1, because Mornard still had not turned over his bank balance, Shuster both wrote and wired him at his summer residence outside Tehran, telling him that if he [Shuster] did not hear that all the Customs balances had been transferred to Shuster's credit in the banks by four o'clock that afternoon, he would be compelled to report his refusal to do so to the Majles, and to consider his action as a breach of faith. After sending the telegram and before the written message, which he dispatched by a mounted gendarme, could reach Mornard, Mornard himself wired Shuster to take possession of the Customs funds in the bank.[266] So

Creating a Respect for Law

Shuster had won a battle but Mornard had yet to concede that authority over the entire spectrum of Persian finance now lay with Shuster and with no one else.

At this point, Shuster and the June 13 Finance Law had the support of the British. Sir George Barclay, with the backing of the Foreign Office in London, had let it be known that he wasn't taking any part in the controversy, indicating, however, that he favored the financial plans and reorganization that Shuster was trying to effect.[267]

However, hated though Mornard might be, the Cabinet had to be concerned that toppling him would almost certainly bring about some Russian reprisal. Thus, on July 7, it asked both Shuster and Mornard to attend a meeting the next day. At 10 o'clock the next morning, Mornard appeared and "showed himself extremely polite and attentive." He recounted the work the Belgian Customs officials had been doing, emphasizing the difficulties that would arise from making any changes in their existing method of conducting business—difficulties which were no doubt real and which Shuster, as an accountant, would have appreciated. Mornard promised to send a list of all the Government funds deposited in the different banks. He would also submit the usual requisitions for expenses which had been prescribed by Shuster's office. Mornard added that he had never had any other intention than that of obeying the law, an assertion which Shuster may have thought disingenuous at best. However, he replied that, since Mornard did intend to obey the law,[268] there appeared to be no need for further discussion.

There were "ample" funds in the Customs receipts to pay the interest and amortization charges on the Russian debt which were due on July 13. That morning, fearing that the Banque d'Escompte might try to discredit his new administration by not transferring the funds, Shuster went to the bank and saw the acting manager, a Mr. Diamantopoulos, to verify that the transfer had indeed been made. It had.[269]

If there was the beginning of some civility and formal cooperation with Mornard, however, the Russians were not going to accept the fact that they had "lost." Nor was Mornard.

Four days later, on July 17, the ex-shah Mohammad Ali arrived on the southeast coast of the Caspian Sea with the objective of regaining the throne he had lost two years earlier. That same day, Sir George Barclay informed Shuster that he had received a dispatch from Sir Edward Grey stating that the British Legation, rather than remaining neutral in the dispute over the control of the Customs funds, would side with the Russian Government, thus putting Barclay who had been supportive of Shuster's plan, into "a terrible state of mind."[270] With British support thereby guaranteed, about two weeks later, on July 31, on directions from St. Petersburg, Poklewski-Koziell demanded "that the interests on the Russian consolidated debt and various other fixed charges on Customs... be paid by M. Mornard, the Belgian Administrator General of Customs, instead of Mr. Shuster...."[271]

Shuster dismissed the directive. By then, he had already secured control of the finances. However, he had also added a large wrinkle to the question of who was in charge of things.

XI

The Stokes Affair

"...without a well-trained, well-equipped force to assist the tax-collectors, and...to maintain a certain degree of order in the provinces and distant districts, there was no possible hope of getting in the revenues."

—Morgan Shuster

By the time Shuster had reached a resolution with Mornard, he had decided to form a special gendarmerie which would assist the civilian officers in the collection of the different kinds of taxes throughout Persia. He hoped that, within a year, he would be able to enlist and train several thousand men and, in the course of several years, he would be able to enlarge the force to 10,000 to 12,000.[272]

The idea of creating a special Treasury Gendarmerie was not new. It had been on the agendas of various Cabinets since 1909, and the first steps to actually bring one into existence had been taken about the time Shuster had been hired.[273] But Shuster had found on his arrival that the gendarmerie was almost as mythical a body as the Persian regular army and, outside Tehran, was as likely to make away with the taxes as they were to assist in their collection. They were under the orders of the Minister of the Interior and commanded by some officers who, as Shuster so carefully put it, "did not belong to the elements desirous of seeing the finances of the country put upon a solid basis."[274]

In addition to Tehran, he would place this Treasury Gendarmerie in two or three of the larger cities such as Tabriz, Persia's second most important city, as well as Isfahan, Shiraz, or Qazvin—all of which except for Shiraz were in the Russian

169

zone demarcated in the Anglo-Russian Convention of 1907. Nonetheless, the Majles, under the impression that it was the governing body of a sovereign nation, passed Shuster's proposal to create a Treasury Gendarmerie on July 6. To organize and instruct the men and officers who would make up this Gendarmerie, Shuster selected Major Claude Bayfield Stokes, then the military attaché at the British legation in Tehran.

Arguably, a more competent individual than Major Stokes could not have been found. Previous to his station in Tehran, he had served on the Northwest Frontier in India and then, having joined the Indian Army, he served with the fabled Third Skinner's Horse in 1900. In 1907, he had been posted to Persia, had quickly learned the language, and had familiarized himself with the country. Like E.G. Browne, to whom he was supplying intelligence on the course of events in Persia, Stokes was deeply sympathetic to the democratic aspirations of the Majles. He was scheduled to end his tour of duty in Persia in October of 1911 but, as Shuster learned, "was loath to leave Persia."[275]

The choice of that particular officer was simultaneously prudent, naïve, and typically American. To get a job done, an American will look for someone with the expertise and the will to get it done. Unless one is plagued with some sort of racial or gender bias, concerns about nationality, accent, social class, and other extraneous considerations don't matter. In view of the urgency of the situation, and based on his experiences in Cuba and the Philippines, Shuster must have recognized he could not afford any kind of bias. Unfortunately, not everyone in Tehran thought like Shuster. Efficiency, competency, a knowledge of Persia and her language and, above all perhaps, a sympathy with her aspirations, were not, by any means, qualities that most of the parties interested in the situation valued.

Shuster could have secured the services of any number of

retired officers of the United States army to organize and train a gendarmerie, but none would have been nearly as qualified as Stokes. And, as he pointed out to Barclay, he chose Stokes for the task not because he was a British subject but "solely in the belief that he was the most efficient and capable man for the important work which was to be done, and because the prompt and thorough execution of this task was vital to my whole scheme of financial reform in Persia."[276] He emphasized that Stokes' nationality played no part at all in his decision. Had it done so, he remarked with no small logic, it would have been "natural to presume" that he would have sought assistance from an American. He also pointed out that one of the great handicaps from which any foreigner would suffer was ignorance of the language and customs of Persia—a defect, he argued, that would become even more serious for one called upon to deal with the large number of men who would make up the gendarmerie.[277]

In mid-July, Shuster wrote to Barclay again, stating that upon the termination of Stokes' services as military attaché in the Indian army, he "would be pleased" to hire him to organize the Treasury Gendarmerie.[278] About a week later, on July 22, after a second inquiry from Shuster, Barclay informed him that the British Foreign Office had decided that before Stokes could accept command of the gendarmerie, he would have to resign his commission in the Indian Army.

Thus, on July 28, the Majles under the impression that it had every right to hire officials who might contribute to its defense, passed a contract with Stokes at a salary of 5000 U.S. dollars to be paid in twelve monthly installments. It was signed in duplicate and a copy delivered to Stokes.[279] That contract enabled Shuster to purchase a sufficient amount of money from the Imperial Bank to provide for Major Stokes' pension following the acceptance of his resignation from the Indian Army. Stokes immediately cabled his resignation and both he and Shuster assumed that the resignation would be accepted.[280]

But...no.

Initially, the response of neither the Russian nor British governments to the proposed appointment was entirely negative. An undersecretary in the British Foreign Office, a Mr. Norman, thought that while the choice of Stokes was, from the Russian view, "unfortunate" since Stokes was known to be "fanatically anti-Russian," the Foreign Office should acquiesce in the appointment since "to throw obstacles in its way would look like opposing the efforts of the Majles...to reform Persia." However, if Stokes were to be appointed, thought Grey, "...he should be cautioned to suppress all anti-Russian feeling." It would be essential, he added "that no employee in Shuster's administration should show anything but complete impartiality between nations."[281]

While not completely hostile to the appointment initially, the Russian Foreign Ministry was not completely happy with it either. And the reason had less to do with Stokes himself than with a personnel change in St. Petersburg.

That spring, Sergei Dimitrovich Sazanov, the Russian Foreign Minister who had replaced Izvolsky, had contracted a severe respiratory ailment and had offered his resignation to the tsar, but the tsar refused to accept it and ordered him instead to take a leave of absence until he recovered. Sazanov had then gone to Davos, Switzerland, for surgery to remove a lung abscess. Sazanov's replacement was his assistant, A.A. Neratov, whose position vis à vis the Council of Ministers was obviously weaker than Sazanov's had been. And it will be remembered that there were elements on that Council who had had reservations about the 1907 Convention on the grounds that Russia had gained nothing by it. Sensing the insecurity of his position and unwilling to show any sign of weakness, Neratov tended to be far more aggressive about

The Stokes Affair

defending Russia's interests than Sazanov had been.

Initially, Neratov had no objection to the idea of a Treasury Gendarmerie as such but preferred that, if possible, the command be split between British and Russian officers—a suggestion Grey was willing to accept; but Grey also instructed Barclay to suggest to Shuster that he appoint a Swede instead of an Englishman.

Shuster refused both suggestions. A two-command solution was out of the question, especially if one of the commanders were to be Russian. Nor was a Swede, who would have had no knowledge of Persia, its people, or its language, be acceptable either.[282]

And the more it thought about it, the less the Foreign Office in London was now liking the Stokes appointment. Mr. Norman received a visit from an official of the Anglo-Persian Oil Company named Charles Greenway who claimed that Stokes not only held strong anti-Russian views, but that he had also joined a Persian revolutionary anjeman and had "lost no chance of denouncing the iniquity of British policy in Persia…." Sir George Barclay too, had to admit to Grey that, although he had never heard of Stokes joining any anjemans, he had been known to be in touch with "extreme nationalists."[283]

Poklewski-Koziell, although he could not permit an English officer to command a Persian force in the north, was still not entirely opposed to Stokes. As he telegraphed home in early July, "…we could agree to the appointment of Mr. Stokes only if a Russian officer is given the same position in our sphere of influence, or if the organization of Persian military forces is entrusted to our instructors."[284]

But the official Russian position now began to harden. The Russian press, notably the semi-official *Novoe Vremya*, had begun to "bluster" (Shuster's word) about the appointment.[285] As the Russians saw it, even if Stokes resigned his commission, he would still be acting as a British officer, and the gendarmerie would then be figuratively a tool of British policy—and never mind that the Cossack Brigade had for some time been a tool of Russian policy. Coming on the heels of the Mornard affair, it was perhaps logical that the Russians would suspect that Shuster's insistence on Stokes was indicative of anti-Russian designs.

And poor, honest, straightforward Shuster would shortly find that a new phrase related to the 1907 Convention had entered the diplomatic lexicon. The appointment of Major Stokes, he learned, would violate something called the "spirit of the Convention" by which each of the Powers "might interpret *any* [my italics] action which the Persian Government contemplated taking as an infringement of their self-created interests, mentioned but never defined...in that famous document."[286]

And therein was the rub. As Shuster pointed out to Barclay, the suggestion of Russia's "interests" in northern Persia was a tacit affirmation of the division of the country into "spheres of influence"—a claim that the Persian government and Shuster steadfastly refused to recognize. Indeed, Shuster noted that one of the difficulties he had encountered in even getting the Majles to approve the contract with Stokes was its fear that he was to be sent *only* into the south, that is, the British, "sphere of influence" thereby tacitly recognizing that the Anglo-Russian Convention had some legitimacy.[287]

Both the British and Russian delegations recognized that the appointment of Stokes would amount to a diplomatic victory for the British. Yet, if either side objected too much, it would give the appearance of opposing Shuster's work; and the political opposition in Britain would pounce if it appeared that Grey opposed serious attempts at reform in Persia. But shadowing everything was Grey's "craven dread" that Germany might take advantage of even the appearance of a rupture in the relationship between Britain and Russia.[288]

Thus, on August 8, Grey authorized Barclay to warn the Persian government that it could employ Stokes only if his activities did not spread to the Russian "sphere of influence."[289] In other words, the Persian government was perfectly free to employ Stokes so long as he operated only in the narrow southern zone.

Shuster was baffled. What had happened? Why the abrupt *volte face*? That evening, he wrote Barclay a personal note expressing anger, frustration and disappointment. "No one knows better than yourself," he wrote, "that the choice of Major Stokes was actuated by no political motive." If anyone could suspect him of "political jobbery," Shuster said, that would only make him [Shuster] look ridiculous and "spell absolute ruin for my work." The attitude taken by Barclay's government, he claimed, "amounts to a virtual veto of my efforts and a nullification of my chances of success." He criticized the "totally uncalled for interference" in the purely routine internal affairs of the organization he was trying to establish. Did the British Foreign office not realize, he wondered, that it was "inevitably giving the Persian people the impression that it was opposed to the successful accomplishment of his work on their behalf, as well as leading Shuster himself to assume that he could count on "no friendly moral assistance"?[290]

Barclay, "greatly wrought up," replied two days later admitting that Shuster's feelings on the matter were justified.[291]

Up to a point, Grey agreed with Barclay. Although he had repudiated Stokes, Grey was not yet willing to oppose Shuster. On August 15, in a note to Sir George Buchanan, the British Minister in St. Petersburg, Grey's exasperation was clearly evident when he wrote that Neratov must realize that the sole reason the appointment of Stokes had not been made was to coax the British public to be patient with the continued presence of Russian troops in northern Persia. "I have had to defend these matters several times, and if I had been as

175

exacting over them as Russia is now, the good understanding between Great Britain and Russia would have come to an end long ago." However, as Firuz Kazemzadeh elegantly puts it, "Grey's fortitude vis à vis Russia was exceedingly limited." The very next day, August 16, Grey "blustered," and the day after that he gave in and told Russia's ambassador to Britain, Count Alexander Benckendorff, that Stokes would not be allowed to resign his commission in the Indian army at all, thereby preventing him from accepting the appointment as the commander of Shuster's gendarmerie.[292]

With Grey sufficiently supine, two days later, on August 19, a memorandum from the Russian Legation to the Persian Foreign Office warned that "…The Imperial Government of Russia…considers the engagement…of Major Stokes as chief of the armed forces—called gendarmerie—for the collection of taxes as incompatible with its interests, and…protest[s] that appointment." Failing satisfaction, the note further warned, Russia would "take such measures as it might judge to be necessary for the safeguarding of its interests in the North of Persia."[293]

Barclay's statement the next day reinforced that. "His Majesty's government cannot accept Major Stokes resignation in view of the well-founded Russian objections to his appointment."[294]

The question here is why had the British Foreign Office gone from a lukewarm, possibly even positive, reception of the idea of the Stokes appointment to an outright rejection?

The answer lay not with any circumstance in Persia but with the Great Game being played out in Europe. And while the summer of 1911 would not be the worst in Sir Edward Grey's career as Foreign Secretary—he would remain in office through the first half of World War I—even his favorite hobby of fly-fishing would provide him with faint respite in 1911.

In April, with the usual pretext of protecting European

lives and property, a French force had entered Morocco ostensibly to put down a rebellion against the sultan. Since the resolution of the First Moroccan Crisis in 1905-06, French pre-eminence in Morocco had been recognized as a given, so there should have been little reaction. But on July 1, a German gunboat, the *Panther*, pulled into the port of Agadir, followed a few days later by a larger cruiser presumably in order to protect German trade interests. Britain was obligated to take France's side since, along with Russia, France was Britain's partner in the Triple Entente of which the Anglo-Russian Convention was a part. Moreover, a German presence at Agadir would directly threaten the British base on Gibraltar. The Agadir Crisis would ultimately be settled in early November with Germany recognizing France's interests in Morocco in return for territories in the central Congo. But in the summer of 1911, Agadir was not the only difficulty standing in the way of the Stokes appointment.

While negotiations concerning Agadir were ongoing, a potentially more alarming situation had begun to evolve the previous November, when Russia's Sazanov and Germany's Count Theobald van Bethmann-Hollweg had met in Potsdam to discuss their joint interests in Persia and Turkey. The center of the discussions was railroads.

Some of the most intricate diplomatic problems of the late nineteenth and early twentieth centuries involved railroads. The construction of railroads in Persia had been considered as early as the 1860s, but the confluence of British, Russian, German, French, Turkish, and Persian interests had resulted in a tangle of diplomatic agreements and balances which left Persia with no railroads at all. In 1903, Germany had embarked on the construction of a rail line that would run from Berlin across southeastern Turkey to Baghdad—the famous Berlin-to-Baghdad Railroad. According to the agreement settled on August 19, 1911, in return for Russia's promise not to interfere with the building of that railway, Germany acknowledged Russia's "special interests" in Persia. She also agreed that German capital would be provided to assist in the construction of a railway from Tehran to Khanikin on the Turco-Persian frontier which would ultimately link up with the Berlin to Baghdad line. That line would be financed partly by German and partly by Russian capital but be under the control of Russian concessionaries.[295]

Grey understandably saw the Potsdam accord, roughly coinciding as it did with the Agadir affair, as yet another example of Germany's desire to sabotage the Anglo-Russian friendship. On the same day the Potsdam Accord was signed, the Persian Foreign Office received the Russian warning against hiring Major Stokes and, still on that same day, Barclay had to affirm Britain's acquiescence in Russia's "well-founded objections" to the appointment.

That might have ended things, but Shuster did not give up. Whether one wants to view his further actions in the Stokes matter—which would drag on for several more months—as a kind of noble tenacity or plain stubbornness, or a combination of the two, is a matter of no small interest. He would later be accused of being unwilling to compromise on any number of matters; but his behavior in this affair belies that judgment. In early August, he had offered to limit Stokes' tenure in Tehran to six months. After that, he would accept a British officer in the south and an officer either from a "second-tier" power or even from Russia itself to command in the north. The offer had been rejected by the Russians.[296]

Again, on August 20, he visited Poklewski-Koziell and repeated the proposal. Poklewski-Koziell was willing to actually consider accepting Shuster's offer. So was Count Benckendorff who also suggested the acceptance of the compromise to his government.[297] Over the next few weeks, the conversations between Shuster and Poklewski-Koziell continued, and something like a middle ground was almost reached. "Would it be possible," Poklewski-Koziell wondered to his government in early September, "to arrange that, after six months, one of the Swedish officers could be put in command of the whole Gendarmerie and that Major Stokes should then work nominally under him and outside the so-called Russian zone?"[298]

The compromise was rejected out of hand. In the margin of the telegram that Poklewski-Koziell sent home with that request, the tsar wrote "No yielding." That was on August 26. The issue was permanently closed.[299] For almost everyone. But not for Morgan Shuster.

The debate over the Stokes appointment would drag on until the Major left Persia in mid-December and Shuster never would win the case. Nonetheless, he managed to create an 1100-man force that one scholar calls "the most effective arm of the new government."[300] Shuster himself supervised the selection of officers drawing recruits from "the pick of the Young Persia patriots who really desired to serve their country." Trained by four "brave and skillful" American officers supervised by Colonel J. N. Merrill and then commanded by thirty-five Persian officers, the Treasury Gendarmerie was well-trained, well-equipped and well-armed. The high pay, obviously, may have augmented their patriotism, but it clearly was not their only motivation. Later, when the Majles was overthrown, the Persian officers of the Gendarmerie came to Shuster to beg permission to fight for their country in what would have been a suicidal mission.[301]

In any case, the center of focus had now shifted. Since the middle of July, the Persian government had been dealing with a crisis far graver than the appointment of Stokes.

Major Claude B. Stokes
British officer whom Shuster wanted
to head his Treasury Gendarmerie

XII

Mohammad Ali Invades

"I am more than willing to sell my own life, if I could thus rid my country of that cruel tyrant."

—Samsam al-Saltaneh

The Persian Response

Spared the searing, dry heat of the two great central deserts, the Dasht-e Lut and the Dasht-e Kavir, as well as the humid and, at times, unbearable heat of the Persian Gulf, Tehran in the summer is merely miserable. Adding to the discomfort, early morning traffic on unpaved streets in 1911 would send up clouds of thick, suffocating dust which would not settle until late at night. Beyond the capital, the summer of 1911 also saw a crippling drought.

Then, as now, those who could afford to do so escaped to the suburbs that dot the nearby foothills of the Alborz Mountains. To these refuges, the foreign legations retreated. But, since he had just started the work of reorganizing the Treasury, Shuster remained in Tehran but moved his headquarters from the Ministry of Finance to Atabak Palace. The palace, like many large houses in the city, contained cool underground chambers that roughly duplicated the first floor. It was in that underground sanctuary that Shuster established his offices.

Late on the night of July 18, news came by telegraph that the deposed shah, Mohammad Ali, and about a half dozen followers, including his brother, Shu'a al-Saltaneh, had landed at the tiny village of Gomesh Tapeh on the southeastern coast of the Caspian Sea. Two days later, he set out for Astarabad (now Gorgon), reaching that city on July 22 where they were "greeted with a great deal of enthusiasm."³⁰²

Since his ouster in September 1909, the ex-shah had been busy. He had stayed for about a year in Odessa; but then, in October 1910, he had gone to Vienna, where he had gotten in touch with other Persian exiles. He had then returned to Odessa in early 1911 and stayed there until June 11, when he again left for Vienna. There, he had rented a house as "Khalil," a merchant from Baghdad. All of these movements, the Russians would argue, were accomplished without their knowledge.

During the following weeks, there had been a lot of coming and going from "Khalil's" house. In early July, 1911, "Khalil" and some of his closest adherents met with N.G. de Hartwig, who had been Russian minister at Tehran from 1906-08, and who was one of those who believed that the 1907 Anglo-Russian Convention had deprived Russia of the "ripe fruit" which should have fallen into her lap. Hartwig also thought that the only way in which that "ripe fruit" could be harvested was by Mohammad Ali Shah retaking the Persian throne.³⁰³ Hartwig now traveled from Belgrade, where he was Russia's minister, to Vienna, to talk "unofficially" about a "project."

One might surmise that, given Mohammad Ali's previous proven hostility to the Constitutional Government, the "project" under discussion would not have been favorable to that body. The unofficial reports of that meeting indicated that Hartwig told Mohammad Ali that the Russian government could give him no *direct* support. He was free to return to Persia if he thought he could succeed in regaining the throne; but if he failed, Russia would disclaim any responsibility.

Until "Khalil," wearing a false beard, actually landed at Gomesh Tapeh, it might have been possible to give the subsequent Russian denials of collusion the benefit of the doubt and to assume that the "escape" of the ex-shah was purely accidental and that the Russian Cabinet had not been advised by its diplomatic representatives in either Belgrade or Vienna of Mohammad Ali's intentions to recover the Persian throne.[304]

Russia's attitude was articulated a few days before Mohammad Ali's arrival in Mazandaran in a telegram from the Ministry of Foreign Affairs in St. Petersburg to the viceroy of the Caucasus. It was important, he stated, that no proofs of the ex-shah's direct intrigues should fall into the hands of the Persian government since, under the terms of the 1909 Protocol, Persia would then have a basis for depriving him of his pension and "we would have to take care of him."[305]

Although Hartwig had refused to grant Mohammad Ali money, arms, or men, there had apparently been some kind of assurances given, since they were able to transport three Austrian cannon, several guns, and ammunition packed in crates marked "mineral water" from Vienna through Russia all the way down to Baku without being detained or, presumably, without Russian knowledge. From Baku, "Khalil" was transported on board the Russian steamer *Christoforos* to Gomesh Tapeh—still, incredibly, without being recognized or detained.

The welcome the ex-shah received on his landing was enthusiastic and fairly widespread. Well before his landing, and for reasons largely unrelated to any particular cause, administrative connections between Tehran and western Persia had never really taken root. Most tribal leaders had always viewed any central government with distrust. Thus, most of the tribes were already in revolt. Kurds to the north of Kermanshah and south of Lake Urmiyeh joined with another of the ex-shah's brothers, Salaru ad-Dowla, as did Lurs to the south of Kermanshah. That put western Persia from Azerbaijan in the north to Fars in the south if not in royalist control, then at least beyond the control of the central government. In provincial towns, too, the inability of the government to provide security had weakened whatever fragile support it had been able to garner. And indeed, many Persians, not just the tribes, viewed government as the *man* who headed it, not the abstraction represented by the Majles. Thus, although Mohammad Ali might have been hated, he did at least seem to provide a promise of stability.

It was only in Tehran that there was any hope of unified resistance to the ex-shah. There, the Majles had been able to maintain relative peace and general stability most of the time since 1909. Also, sympathizers with the Constitutionalists would be in a most unhappy position should Mohammad Ali return and actually succeed in recovering the throne.[306] Moreover, while mistrust of Russia was deep and widespread among Persians and, although there had been rumors of the ex-shah's return, Shuster noted that, "few people in Tehran believed that Russia would have the face to violate so openly the solemn stipulation which she had signed with Great Britain and with Persia less than two years before."[307]

Financially and militarily, the Persian government was sorely underprepared to face this new crisis which it had every reason to fear would be a repeat of the bloodbaths of 1907 and 1909. The only disciplined and well-equipped force in Tehran was the Cossack Brigade, which would be loyal to the ex-shah—and to his Russian backers. The Brigade's commander, Prince Vadbolskii, took his orders from St. Petersburg, not from Tehran. What there was of a Persian army obviously was hardly worth the paper upon which its existence largely rested.

As for the government itself, so fragile was its coherence—and prestige—that, within a single week, two different Cabinets would be formed. Despite this weakness, however, the government met the landing at Gomesh Tapeh with a decisive and unified (albeit short-lived) response.

On July 19, the day after news of the shah's return reached Tehran, a coalition Cabinet, with the Sepahdar as prime minister, was presented to the Majles and approved. At the same time, martial law was declared and a price of 100,000 tomans placed upon the head of Mohammad Ali and 25,000 tomans each on the heads of his brothers, Salaru ad-Dowla and Shu'a al-Saltaneh.[308]

On the face of it, the most baffling appointment to the Cabinet would seem to have been that of the Sepahdar. Since his abrupt departure a month earlier for "farhangistan," he had neither resigned nor returned to Tehran. The government was technically without a prime minister. Moreover, rumors that he was supportive of the ex-shah seemed to be confirmed by the fact that when he had returned on July 9, it was not to Tehran but to his personal residence at Shemiran just outside Tehran *and* within the jurisdiction of the Russian summer legation where, it was said, his food was being served to him in sealed covers.[309] He also made no move to resume the duties of prime minister and was soon joined by a number of known reactionaries who would continue to plot against the Constitutional Government throughout the ensuing military campaign. Nonetheless, the majority of the Majles, although suspicious of anyone with suspected links to either Russia or to the ex-shah, was willing to back the Sepahdar. Initially, at least.

Interestingly, Shuster does not speculate on the strangeness of the choice of the Sepahdar. There may have been more to it than a simple revolving door, however. The Sepahdar would have been remembered for the prominent role he had played in 1909 in the recapture of Tehran and the deposition of the shah. With an army title and possibly with his considerable wealth (he had vast estates in two or three provinces, owned hundreds of villages, and was thought to be the richest man in the country), he might have seemed the only one fit to be in charge of the only army the government possessed, shabby though it was. In addition, it became known that

Mohammad Ali had indeed sent a telegram to the Sepahdar confirming him in office and instructing him to maintain order until he arrived. However, to that telegram the Sepahdar had replied, "The people will never endure your yoke," and he had done nothing to prepare a reception for the presumed forthcoming arrival of Mohammad Ali.[310] Moreover, despite the various rumors circulating about Russian backing for the shah—and the remarkably hollow denials—a Russian military presence was still not physically in the neighborhood of the capital at that point.

It will be remembered that on June 4 Shuster had reluctantly agreed with the Sepahdar to allow the sum of 100,000 tomans for the total expenses of the War Ministry. Now, although the Sepahdar was named prime minister, he was not allowed the War portfolio that he had held previously.

Ultimately, however, the defense of the Constitutional Government came to depend, not on the Sepahdar, but on three other men, Samsam al-Saltaneh, a tall, erect Bakhtiari khan in his early sixties who would shortly replace the Sepahdar as prime minister and Minister of War; Ephraim Khan, the Tehran Chief of Police; and, in the Majles, the leader of the Constitutionalists, Hussein Quli Khan.

The Bakhtiari Samsam al-Saltaneh had played a key role in dispersing royalist forces in Isfahan in 1909. Shuster found him to be a man "of great personal pride and with a very simple, almost childish mind." At one point, Samsam offered to go directly to Mohammad Ali, ostensibly as the Regent's envoy and, once in the ex-shah's presence, "to put a pistol to his chest and kill him." "I am an old man," he said, "and I am more than willing to sell my own life, if I could thus rid my country of that cruel tyrant." Nasr al-Mulk wisely rejected the plan.[311]

Samsam then asked Shuster whether, as War Minister, he had the authority to direct expenditures for the public defense.

On Shuster assuring him that he did, Samsam then asked for up to 100,000 tomans to send envoys to kill Mohammad Ali and his brothers. Shuster did not ask for an explanation of the high sum nor does he say whether he bit his tongue or merely winced—or both—at the suggestion. Rather, he mildly suggested that such steps might best be taken by the police and military authority.[312]

At least for the time being, Samsam's hatred of the ex-shah was cold and uncomplicated. Four months later, however, Shuster would have reason to wonder if Samsam's hostility to the ex-shah indicated loyalty to the Constitution and to the idea of a truly independent Persian nation. Or were his loyalties conditioned by the profits he could garner?

The second major figure was the Turkish-Armenian Christian, Ephraim Khan who had been on the verge of capturing the bandit Rahim Khan in 1909 before the Russians rescued him. Since the capture of Tehran and the restoration of the Constitutional Government in 1909, Ephraim Khan had held the post of chief of the Tehran police, a post that, as Shuster would later point out, carried with it a great deal more responsibility and dignity than it would have in a Western city. Ephraim Khan had built up and held together the only organized and decently equipped force the government possessed. Like Samsam, he had little formal education, but despite that and his status as a *kafir*, he had the capacity to draw men to him and to hold their loyalty. It would be primarily upon this man's shoulders that the safety not only of the city of Tehran, but, as Shuster pointed out, the salvation of the Constitutional Government itself ultimately rested.[313]

The third figure who would play a significant role in dealing with the crisis was Hussein Quli Khan, who had served as Minister of Foreign Affairs. He was then about fifty-five years old and, unlike Ephraim Khan and Samsam, possessed a European education, spoke English, French, and Persian with equal fluency and, "what is most remarkable of all," according to Shuster, "he had the reputation of being absolutely honest in both his official and personal affairs."[314]

The renewed relationship with the Sepahdar and the fragile unity both between the Majles and the Cabinet and among the different elements within the Majles lasted less than an eventful week. The official fabric quickly gave way, and what was left was not a government but a small group of men "determined to uphold the Constitution and to take all steps necessary to repel the rebels who threatened it."[315]

The most prominent focus of that disunity, not surprisingly, was the Sepahdar himself.

On July 22, the same day the coalition Cabinet had been approved and the Sepahdar appointed prime minister, the Council of Ministers ordered Ephraim Khan to arrest twenty "reactionaries" who had claimed to be organizing a volunteer force on behalf of the ex-shah. But an hour later, and before the order could be executed, the Sepahdar telephoned Ephraim Khan directing that the order be suspended. About the same time, one of Ephraim's men reported that the "reactionaries" had expected that Ephraim would get an order for their release since they were acting under orders from the Sepahdar himself. Ephraim himself was undecided whether the Sepahdar should be hanged or shot. Short of either choice, he thought he should at least be arrested but for obvious reasons hesitated to take that step. He was *kafir* and the Sepahdar was in good standing with the clergy. So, defying his orders was out of the question.[316]

The next day, however, Samsam and Arbab Kaikhosro, came to Atabak Park. If Shuster had had any misgivings about the appointment of the Sepahdar as prime minister four days earlier, the meeting with these two men would have confirmed them. The two men complained "bitterly" that the Sepahdar was a traitor, and the Regent, Nasr al-Mulk, was weak. When

Samsam had presented to the Cabinet the announcement of rewards for the capture of Mohammad Ali and his brothers, he had discovered that the ministers had been afraid to send it to the Majles for a vote, arguing that it was "so unusual." Nor was the Cabinet willing to put before the Majles Shuster's own bill granting Major Stokes the pension he would have been required to forfeit on resigning his commission in the British-Indian army.[317] Since his return to the capital, it had become clear that, even if the Sepahdar's full loyalties did not lie with the ex-shah, neither he nor several other members of the Cabinet really had their hearts into preparing definitive resistance to him unless they could be assured of deriving some personal benefit.

Despite the early decisiveness in the government, in the capital itself there was widespread fear that the Russians would restore the ex-shah to power and then stand by while the city was pillaged by Turkoman tribesmen. Nonetheless, while sentiment in favor of the ex-shah was growing in some quarters, the people of Tehran were growing more and more suspicious of the Sepahdar's loyalty. There had been no attempt to arrest well-known supporters of the ex-shah, and the Sepahdar controlled enough deputies in the Majles to prevent any decisive action being taken against him personally or against those allied with him.[318]

Thus, less than a week after it had been formed, the coalition Cabinet began to splinter. Three ministers, the Sepahdar, Mu'avin ad-Dowla, the Minister of Finance, and Mutashamu as-Saltaneh, the Minister of Foreign Affairs, became openly antagonistic to their four democratic colleagues. On July 25, by a large majority, the Majles voted to get rid of the Sepahdar and Mutashamu as-Saltaneh, and the second coalition Cabinet within a week was formed, headed by Samsam as both prime minister and Minister of War.[319]

Meanwhile, a consignment of 7000 rifles and 4 million

cartridges for which the Sepahdar had contracted and paid Poklewski-Koziell 360,000 tomans had arrived at Anzeli and was on its way over the Rasht road to Tehran.[320] Whether the Sepahdar had deliberately timed this to coincide with Mohammad Ali's arrival on the chance that the consignment could be intercepted and redirected to the ex-shah's use is not known. In any case, the greater part of the shipment did arrive safely in Tehran. There, in order to make them available to his Treasury Gendarmerie, Shuster took 1500 rifles and 600,000 cartridges to the basement of Atabak Palace for safe keeping because firearms "have a strange and mysterious way of evaporating in Persia...so if one really expects to need them, they should be kept in sight all the time."[321]

As much as he would have liked to remain aloof from the internal workings of the government, the pressures put upon it by the return of the ex-shah inevitably involved Shuster. On July 21, three days before the Cabinet reshuffling, Samsam had informed Shuster that 2000 Bakhtiari tribesmen had assembled at Isfahan ready to march to Tehran, a journey that would take ten days. Shuster immediately wired funds to the Bakhtiari khan who was then Isfahan's governor, to cover preliminary expenses.

Nonetheless, he was growing anxious. "Situation [in] Tehran grows daily worse," he wrote in his diary the next day. Reactionary sentiment was increasing while the Cabinet did nothing to punish "well-known" reactionaries. The new Cabinet was "squarely split" between moderates and democrats, and the Sepahdar refused to leave *bast* in the Russian legation and come to Tehran. "Distrust prevails everywhere," he wrote, and nobody appeared ready to save the situation. Because of the increased disorders and systematic breakdown of provincial governments under the Sepahdar's former ministry, the financial situation was "now practically helpless" and, to worsen matters, there were rumors that officers of the

Cossack Brigade were planning to provoke disorder in Tehran in order to create general panic in the city.[322]

By early August, the Bakhtiari contingent had begun to arrive in Tehran. That might have been reassuring but it was here that Shuster came into open conflict with Samsam's Cabinet—just as he had come into a similar conflict with the Sepahdar's Cabinet a few weeks earlier. To his dismay, Shuster would learn that the campaign against the ex-shah provided abundant opportunities for what he would call "official plundering."[323]

On July 30, a large man "of imposing presence" wearing long, bright yellow boots walked into Shuster's office. In addition to the yellow boots, his costume included a brace of automatic pistols and a garland of about 300 cartridges in belts draped across his shoulders, waist, and chest. For obvious reasons, Shuster christened this paragon of military couture "the walking arsenal." He introduced himself as Sardar-i Muhiy, a Bakhtiari khan, who had acquired a reputation for bravery in the government's expedition against the ex-shah in 1909.

Charged by the government with leading the first expedition against the ex-shah, Sardar-i Muhiy had agreed to lead several hundred volunteer cavalry against the Turkoman supporters of the ex-shah at Shahrud, some 250 miles northeast of Tehran. Given that task, he presented Shuster with a requisition authorized by Samsam for about 26,000 tomans. That amount, he said, he would need for his salary as a military commander and also as governor of Astarabad, a post to which the government had just appointed him. Since Astarabad at that moment was firmly in the hands of the ex-shah's forces, there was no probability of his even reaching, let alone governing the place. He would also need, he said, a large "contingent fund" for his own personal expenses. This colorful gentleman had already been paid 6000 tomans in advance as governor of the district of Kerman, a destination to which he had not yet started.[324]

Following "some rather warm correspondence" with the Cabinet, Shuster did pay the sum demanded but he ruefully, precisely—and briefly—named the problem that would bedevil his efforts to accomplish the task for which he had been employed, and very nearly cripple his efforts to save the government itself. "In truth…the efforts of the Cabinet to defeat the ex-Shah were tinged with a decided desire to see their favorites generously compensated." The demands for money, in fact, "were so preposterous" that he threatened to resign if the Cabinet continued to sanction "such wholesale attempts at looting the Treasury." Even the Minister of Finance, Hakim al-Mulk, expressed shame at the demands of the khans and also threatened to resign if the Cabinet supported them.[325]

About mid-August, after long debates, Shuster persuaded the Cabinet to agree that the troops of the central army should be paid directly by the Treasury instead of by the Ministry of War, a measure that gave Shuster the freedom to "effect decided economies."[326] That made sense, but it also did little to smooth relations with the Cabinet. Indeed, in an ominous sign of the difficulties Shuster would face later, Samsam reneged on an earlier promise to assist in the organization and training of the Treasury Gendarmerie by refusing Shuster the use of the Bagh-e Shah military barracks and stables at Tehran.[327]

Meanwhile, Ephraim Khan confided to Shuster that he had a plan for an expedition against the ex-shah, but he dared not confide it to any of the ministers "as he did not trust them." Nor was Ephraim Khan happy with the Majles, who had not yet voted the small pension (800 tomans per annum)[328] he had requested for Major Haase, a German gun expert whose services were urgently needed in the expedition to Astarabad but who was disgruntled at the treatment he had received. Shuster arranged for the pension and Haase then agreed to accompany Ephraim Khan.³²⁹ Besides assistance from Haase, whose services would soon prove to be critical, Ephraim Khan also had 500 gendarmes stationed at Qazvin under one of his own lieutenants, and some 200 Armenian volunteers or "professional fighting-men" as they were called.³³⁰

Nonetheless, it was now becoming apparent that, as preposterous as many of the demands for money were, Shuster's reluctance or outright refusal to acquiesce in them was losing him the support of many in the government. Called to a meeting of the Council of Ministers in early August, Shuster felt compelled to speak "very strongly about [the] general pillaging of the government" and told the ministers that he refused to pay out any more for "alleged" military operations until some results and less private gain could be shown.³³¹

A few days later, on August 6, that is, less than three months after most of them had pledged their full support for whatever financial reforms Shuster might inaugurate, the Council summoned eighteen Majles deputies and presented them with a list of seven complaints against Shuster. He had too much power, they claimed and was entering into politics as shown by the "frequent visits" he was getting from "certain deputies," and he maintained a "press bureau" which, of course, he did not. He had refused to pay monies ordered by members of the Council paying some requisitions and not others, and they wanted the Treasury Gendarmerie suspended for some months. Most ominously, as events in the next months would reveal, they wanted the Majles to adopt a "ligne de conduit" toward Russia. The meeting, noted Shuster, "broke up in a wrangle without result."³³²

Even more than the obvious self-aggrandizement, however, what was crippling Shuster's efforts to deal with the emergency was the lack of experience in constitutional government. Tragically, ministers who had been accustomed to regarding their offices as private domains and who viewed cooperation with each other as a humiliating concession, regarded Shuster's attempts at centralized control of the finances as a simple, and most unwelcome, interference with prerogatives they regarded as a legitimate right. And in the contest to protect those prerogatives, self-interest did not manifestly dictate defending a government so fragile and so beleaguered.

The Foreign Reaction

Mohammad Ali's landing surprised practically nobody in Tehran's foreign community. Hence, on July 23, when the Persian government addressed a note to all the foreign legations informing them that a state of siege had been declared, most of their occupants figuratively yawned.

Not surprisingly, the British and Russians were notable exceptions.

Months before, when rumors of the ex-shah's movements had reached Tehran, the Persian government had several times asked those two governments to restrain him in accordance with the 1909 Protocol. Russian denials of any complicity in Mohammad Ali's movements in Europe or in Russia or in Persia arose, of course, not from fear of offending the Persians, but for fear of difficulty with Britain.

The British were locked into the same box. The day after the ex-shah's landing, Shuster told the Regent that he was "absolutely sure" that England would lodge a protest.[333] He was wrong. While the British never had much confidence in Russia's denials of complicity in Mohammad Ali's plots, they also were not willing to risk their agreement with Russia on a matter of internal Persian politics, especially since it looked like many Persians were willing to welcome Mohammad Ali.

News of the ex-shah's landing was received by Russian

consular representatives, Shuster says, "with unconcealed joy." And he might have added that the news was not entirely a surprise to them. Ten days before Mohammad Ali had landed on Persian soil, at the dinner party where Poklewski-Koziell had offered the job of treasurer to Shuster under the presumably restored government of the shah, Poklewski-Koziell had asserted, according to Shuster, that within a few weeks the Persian Constitutional Government would cease to exist.[334] With what must have been a feat of prodigious self-control, Shuster did not ask the Russian minister how he knew this.

Sir George Barclay agreed that Russian elation over the ex-shah's return was due to the existence of a parliamentary regime in Tehran which, given the "unparalleled disorders" in the provinces, had proven its failure. But Barclay also lay some of the blame at Shuster's feet. In a note of July 21, he wrote, "No doubt Shuster's determined disregard of Russian susceptibilities which my Russian colleague [Poklewski-Koziell] feels bitterly is the determining force if the Russian Government prove resolved not to oppose ex-Shah's restoration."[335]

Clearly, after barely two months, Shuster had already become a critical factor in shaping the behavior of the Powers with regard to Persia. His creation of the Treasury Gendarmerie and his insistence on the appointment of Major Stokes to head it, his centralization of the finances and the defeat of Mornard, and perhaps the clear signs that he held the confidence of the Majles, all pointed to the fact that if constitutional government were to be defeated in Persia, Shuster might have to be defeated, too.

On July 31, a scant two weeks after Mohammad Ali had set foot in the country, the British and Russian governments addressed a joint communiqué to the Persian government that read in part:

> Seeing that the ex-Shah, contrary to the advice frequently given him by the Governments of England and Russia, in effect that he should forbear from any agitation whatever in Persia, has now landed in Persia, the British (Russian) Government declares that the ex-shah has now forfeited his right to the pension fixed by the Protocol. But, on the other hand...as the ex-shah is now in Persian territory, the British (Russian) Government cannot intervene. Therefore...in the conflict that has unfortunately arisen in Persia *they will in no way interfere.*"³³⁶

The interference, however, had already begun. The Russian Legation claimed the right to arrest directly at any time "illegal Russian subjects" defined in the note as anyone "who might take part in the events actually going on in the country." The intent clearly was to give the Russians throughout Persia an excuse to arrest any Persian fighting men who might take the side of the government against Mohammad Ali on the pretext that they were a kind of Russian subject. As Shuster noted, however, somewhat tongue in cheek, if that threat had actually been carried out, most of the Russian Consuls and the consular employees themselves would have been arrested.³³⁷

The threat was no laughing matter, however. The Russian Consul in Rasht informed the Persian Government of his intention to arrest anyone at all on suspicion of being a Russian subject, to investigate the matter "at his leisure" and hold that person until the end of the troubles.³³⁸

In Isfahan (within the Russian zone of the 1907 Convention), the clergy, nobles, and other prominent citizens and merchants decided to meet in order to frame a telegram to the representatives of the "foreign powers" protesting Mohammad Ali's arrival in their country. The Russian Acting Consul at Isfahan heard about the planned meeting and wrote to the Persian Foreign Office: "You must not uselessly give trouble in the matter of Mohammad Ali Shah...it is the duty of...the [Persian] Government to restrain and prevent any such incidents and they must fulfill it."[339]

About the same time, Rashid al-Mulk, a former governor of Ardabil on the southeastern coast of Azerbaijan, who had been placed in command of government forces, fled before an inferior force of tribesmen who had remained loyal to the ex-shah. He was then accused of treason, arrested, and confined at Tabriz. But on July 27, the Russian Consul-General at Tabriz sent 300 armed Russian soldiers to the governor's palace. They beat off the Persian guards, insulted the acting governor, and liberated Rashid al-Mulk who then, not surprisingly, joined the royalist forces who were threatening Tabriz. The justification for this was that the government of Russia had accorded "a certain protection" to Rashid al-Mulk.[340]

The threat was also becoming personal for Shuster. On July 28, the day the Cabinet ministers had signed the bill providing for Major Stokes' contract, a Majles deputy brought to Shuster a *feda'i,* a volunteer willing to risk his life, who had confessed to the deputy that a certain Russian vice-consul at Tehran had urged him, as a means of gaining Russian protection and good-will, to shoot or poison Shuster as he was "balking Russia's plans in Persia."[341] On a later occasion, a certain Farajoolah Khan was heard claiming to be a member of a band formed for the purpose of killing Shuster. Ephraim's police agents were informed, and the "valiant gentleman" was flogged and put in chains.[342]

The withdrawal of the Bakhtiari tribesmen from the south in order to fight the ex-shah's invasion brought with it a rather droll encounter between Shuster and Sir George Barclay. After weeks of frustrating negotiation, prevarication, hedging, quibbling, evasion, and what Shuster called "this pussy footed policy"[343] over the appointment of Major Stokes, Shuster had apparently had enough. The subject of the meeting was the rapidly deteriorating security situation in the south. The khans had long managed to provide a measure of security in the area that the besieged government in Tehran could not provide.[344] In early June, Barclay had asked Shuster to provide 80,000 tomans for the gendarmerie at Shiraz and Shuster had replied that he "would do what he could."[345] Now, in late August, Barclay complained to Shuster that the absence of the khans who were now fighting the ex-shah had left many portions of the trade routes in the British sphere unprotected. As a result, the Foreign Office was being attacked in the House of Commons for its failure to properly look after British commercial interests in that part of Persia. It would relieve his government of much embarrassment if he—Barclay—could cable his government that Shuster would undertake the policing of the area or at least furnish from the new Treasury Gendarmerie a force sufficient to restore order there.

Shuster replied that if the British government would assist in the formation of the Gendarmerie, he would be "entirely willing," with the approval of the Persian cabinet, to undertake the task; but, he added, the main factor in such an organization would be securing the services of Major Stokes. Without him, Shuster could not help. In the course of the conversation, Shuster also referred to the "unjustifiable" attitude of the British government in breaking its promise with regard to Major Stokes' services and siding openly with the Russian government in interfering with Persia's most elementary sovereign rights. He then "laughingly" suggested that in view of the hostility of both the Russians and the British to Persia's welfare, Sir George's government might offer certain concessions to German interests who had, for some time, been seeking entré into western Persia and who might be persuaded to provide the required services.

The look of horror on Barclay's face, given the recent crisis over Morocco, induced Shuster to quickly change the subject.[346]

XIII

Mohammad Ali Invades: The Military Campaign

"Mohammad Ali Shah has no other like me and indeed, it was with hope in me that he returned to Iran...."
—Rashid al-Saltan

The short campaign against Mohammad Ali was, in many respects, interesting less for what happened in the field than for the stresses it put upon the government. Fortunately, as weak as the government's own defenses were, Mohammad Ali's chances of regaining the throne on his own were never good. Despite Russia's machinations to help him retake the throne, including warning the Persian government not to oppose him, Russia denied any responsibility for the success or failure of the operation.

Two problems hindered the ex-shah. First, the demonstrations of support in the north and west of Persia were probably misleading, as they occurred largely among tribes already in rebellion against the government but not necessarily in support of the ex-shah. He was forced to rely primarily on Turkomans who were neither well-armed nor disciplined. And even among them, the support was uneven and inconsistent. Second, the two machine guns that he had brought from Russia might have been useful if they had ever been uncrated. Even if they had been, however, the ex-shah had no one who knew how to operate them.[347]

Not surprisingly, Persia's government was denied the service of the Cossack Brigade, whose Russian officers made excuses to refuse orders from the Ministry of War to confront the ex-shah. However, the government not only had a machine gun but the services of the German officer, Major Haase, who knew how to operate it. Its biggest assets, however, were Ephraim Khan and the Bakhtiari khans, one of whose leaders, Samsam al-Saltaneh, was the prime minister and Minister of War. Ephraim Khan commanded a force of about 1200 police and 600 gendarmes, but these were needed just to maintain order in Tehran. An additional force of about 600 Bakhtiari fighters, along with a few hundred students and other volunteers raised by Shuster, formed the nucleus of the government's defense.[348]

The royalist offensive involved a three-pronged assault targeted at Tehran. The first prong under the command of the ex-shah himself and one of his brothers, Shu'a al-Saltaneh, was to move south from Astarabad to just above Firuzkuh, about eighty-five miles northeast of Tehran. His army consisted of about a thousand Turkomans of questionable reliability and a few mountain guns. The second prong, commanded by Sardar Arshad ad-Dowla, who had accompanied the ex-shah into exile in 1909 and had been with him in Vienna, was to head toward Tehran along the southern side of the Alborz mountain range. The third prong, consisting of Kurdish tribesmen led by another of the ex-shah's brothers, Salaru ad-Dowla, was to come up from the southwest. The three prongs then would join in an assault on the capital.

On August 3, Salaru ad-Dowla, reached Kermanshah in western Persia where he ordered the merchants to stop paying Customs taxes and demanded a "loan" of 50,000 tomans. He also had the temerity to make a similar demand on the branch of the Imperial Bank, but this was refused.[349] He dallied there until August 23, when he headed for Hamadan which, although it was in the hands of Mohammad Ali's supporters, wasn't happy about the prospect of 10,000 Kurds suddenly appearing on its doorstep. The citizens sent a bribe to Salaru ad-Dowla asking him to avoid the city.[350] And so he did.

To oppose Salaru ad-Dowla, the Bakhtiari chief, Amir-i Mufakhkham, had located his force near Hamadan. Without orders from Tehran, however, he was unable to move. His force had already been paid; but the Bakhtiari chieftains at Tehran, especially one of Samsam al-Saltaneh's brothers, Sardar-i Jang, demanded the payment of another 60,000 tomans before they would give orders for Mufakhkham to take the field. So flagrant was this attempt to gouge the bankrupt government that Shuster informed the press of it and soon all of Tehran knew of it "to the great discomfiture of the Bakhtiari chieftains."[351]

Mufakhkham's own loyalty was also suspect, however. Two years earlier, in 1909, he had sided with the ex-shah against the Nationalist forces, and he had remained loyal to the ex-shah until his abdication. Thus, there was reason to fear that he might desert the government and ally himself with Salaru ad-Dowla in the march on Tehran. Later, that fear was realized when his "cowardly actions" in an engagement between a portion of Salaru ad-Dowla's troops and the Bakhtiaris under his command resulted in a complete rout of government troops who fled without offering any resistance.[352]

Meanwhile, the second prong of the royalist force, consisting of a large number of Turkomans under Sardar Arshad ad-Dowla, proved to be more dangerous. On August 8, news came that he had defeated a government force at Damghan, a bit southwest of Shahrud and thus closer to Tehran. The Sepahdar, when he had been Minister of War, had stationed 1200 government troops there, but they now fled, leaving behind two cannons along with other supplies and ammunition which fell into the hands of Arshad's troops, who promptly pillaged the town.

That victory for the royalist cause, however, was offset the next day at a narrow mountain pass at Firuzkuh, when a young Bakhtiari chieftain, Mu'in-i Humayun, who had been one of the first khans to reach Tehran at the end of July, defeated a royalist force under Rashid al-Saltan. Rashid was killed along with sixty of his men. Rashid had led a rebellion in Mazandaran against the government the previous year and had been fully aware of his value to the royalist cause. His last words, characterized by neither regret nor humility, were reported to have been, "Mohammad Ali Shah has no other like me and indeed, it was with hope in me that he returned to Iran...."[353]

The battle at Firuzkuh, although not decisive, was perhaps the most significant of the campaign. As McDaniel points out, had Rashid al-Saltan won, he would have been able to link up with Sardar Arshad's army now moving south along the southern flank of the Alborz toward Tehran. Moreover, a victory for the ex-shah might have emboldened the resistance to the government in the capital.[354]

Meanwhile, following his victory at Damghan, Arshad ad-Dowla and his force of Turkomans reached the town of Aiwan-I Kaif (Aradan) about fifty-six miles from the capital, on August 28. There, they met and defeated a small force of government irregulars, but the mountainous terrain prevented communication with Salaru ad-Dowla and his Kurds. Salaru ad-Dowla, following his rout of the Bakhtiari forces under Mufakhkham, had almost reached Saltanabad, and might well have linked up with Arshad if they weren't checked.

Meanwhile, Ephraim Khan had been dispatching small forces to guard the mountain passes leading into Tehran and was hoping to place a force in Mohammad Ali's rear in order to cut off any retreat toward the Caspian Sea. He had decided not to confront the ex-shah's forces directly until they were within striking distance of the capital.[355] In view of the turmoil and uncertain loyalties in Tehran, that was not an unwise decision.

On September 4, word came that Arshad had reached the vicinity of the town of Imamzadeh-Jafar, about forty miles southeast of Tehran. Ephraim Khan now took 350 picked men, along with Major Haase, his Maxim gun and three cannons, and marched out to meet him. The government forces also included about 500 mounted Bakhtiaris under Sardar-i Buhadur and 180 Armenian volunteers and gendarmes.

The next morning, Arshad, whose forces consisted of about 2000 Turkoman horsemen along with four cannons, posted himself on a hill about half a mile square roughly two miles south of Imamzadeh-Jafar. There, he faced about 400 more Bakhtiaris and a few gendarmes.

At 11 o'clock in the morning, the government forces attacked Arshad's Turkoman army.

Ephraim sent Major Haase with the Maxim gun and Sardar-i Buhadur and his cavalry to an open elevation to the right of Arshad's forces. Unobserved, they opened fire with the Maxim gun and the cannons on the Turkomans. According to Arshad, who was later captured, the firing of the Maxim frightened the Turkomans, and when the Bakhtiari cavalry charged them, they broke and fled in confusion. Arshad himself was wounded in the foot and, unable to escape, was captured and brought to Ephraim's headquarters where his wound was treated, and he was given food, drink, and cigarettes.[356]

During the night, he was asked about the ex-shah's movements in Vienna and thereafter. It was Arshad who revealed the ex-shah's treachery, including his talks in Vienna with Hartwig. The night passed quietly. Arshad pleaded for his life "very strongly, though not in so many words." The next morning, about twenty Persian gendarmes, led him "unbandaged" up against a wall and fired. He threw up his hands, but only one bullet had hit him. He was left on the ground for a few minutes while a file of Armenian volunteers was marched up

Mohammad Ali Invades: The Military Campaign

to replace the Persians who had apparently proven to be poor marksmen. A donkey strolling between the target and the marksmen had to be driven off, giving Arshad the chance to fall on his knees and call out "Long live Shah Mohammad Ali!" The second volley hit him, and he was instantly killed.[357]

The next day, Arshad's body, as he had requested, was taken to Tehran for burial with a golden locket and necklace he had worn. The body was propped up against an ordinary cart in the main *maidan* where it was viewed by a large crowd. As macabre as this seems, there was a purpose in it. In light of the rumors flying around that very tense city, the government rightly was concerned that it had to convince people that this well-known general had actually been killed and his Turkoman supporters defeated.

Arshad is one of those failures that suggests that sometimes the servant is greater than the master. The fact that his body was not violated when it was exposed in Tehran suggests one of two things: grief among the ex-shah's supporters, since his death dispelled any hope that Mohammad Ali's drive on Tehran from the northeast would succeed; or genuine admiration for a truly great man. Or possibly both.

Shuster rarely conceals his judgments of the people with whom he deals. The care with which he tells of Arshad's conduct in the battle, of his capture, of his last night, and the dignity with which he faced his death likely reflect the respect of Ephraim Khan from whom Shuster heard the story. Possibly also reflecting Ephraim Khan's judgment, Shuster calls Arshad the ex-shah's "bravest and most skillful general" and praises his "very remarkable and courageous dash" to within forty miles of the capital.[358] But Shuster may also have been revealing some small envy in that Arshad's fidelity to his prince stood in sharp contrast to the limp fidelity of several of the government's own commanders.

Meanwhile, the Turkomans had left behind between

sixty and seventy dead and between 300 and 400 prisoners or wounded. The prisoners, "many of them old men with white beards," were brought to Tehran a few days later along with four captured cannon and a "considerable number" of rifles.[359]

The main body of the Turkomans fled to the south to reach the Mashhad road and return to their home in the northeast. The Bakhtiaris, exhausted by the long ride of the previous night and by the battle itself, did not pursue them; but the Turkomans were kept unaware of that. A British employee of the Indo-European Telegraph at Tehran, George New, wired his operators along the route to warn the Turkomans that the Bakhtiaris were "just behind them" in order to prevent them from pillaging the countryside and villages along the way.[360] Despite the fabricated warning, which succeeded in hastening the retreat, a group of the Turkomans were attacked and killed as they passed by Shahrud, a city they had pillaged only a month earlier.

With Arshad's defeat and death, the only remaining force upon which the ex-shah could rely was that of his brother, Salaru ad-Dowla in the district of Hamadan where, with questionable fraternal loyalty, he issued proclamations calling himself king and referring to "my Majles" and "my Council of Ministers." In early September, near the town of Malyer, he defeated government forces under the command of Amir-i Mufakhkham. Two hundred Bakhtiaris were killed or captured and a number of rifles, cannon, and cartridges were lost. Mufakhkham also claimed to have lost 15,000 tomans which he had received from the Imperial Bank at Hamadan. Under what Shuster calls "suspicious circumstances," another government general, Amir Nizam, surrendered to Salaru ad-Dowla several big guns that had been entrusted to him for the defense of Hamadan.[361]

On September 8, two days after Arshad's execution, a combined force from the north commanded by Sardar-i

Muhiy, the "walking arsenal," and another contingent of Bakhtiaris, commanded by the young Mu'in-i Humayun, attacked and completely routed a motley band of Turkomans and Mazandaranis still loyal to Mohammad Ali. Under cover of dense fog, the ex-shah escaped capture. Accompanied by only seven followers, he reached Gomesh Tapeh where he had landed only a month and a half earlier.

Royalist forces were still in the field, however. About a week later, on September 27, Bakhtiari forces joined by Ephraim Khan's volunteers and artillery met and defeated Salaru ad-Dowla at the village of Bagh-i Shah (the shah's garden), less than eighty miles southwest of Tehran. The prince's forces numbered about 6000 men. He lost 500 killed and wounded, and 200 were taken prisoner. In addition, six cannons and "a large quantity" of ammunition were captured. Ephraim Khan, with a force of about 2000 men, lost two men and six wounded.[362]

Shuster gave full credit to Ephraim Khan for this victory as well as for the victory at Imamzadeh-Jafar. On his return to Tehran, the Majles presented Ephraim Kahn with a gem-studded sword, gave him the title "Commander of the Army of the North," and granted him a pension of three hundred tomans a month. The pension was a trifling sum compared with the exorbitant sums that had been demanded by the Bakhtiari khans for far less worthy service.[363]

Major Haase, however, received much less. Denied his request for more men as well as the money to purchase a new Maxim battery, Major Haase had also seen the War Ministry pay no attention to his reports. He was disgusted at his low pay and the failure to receive "proper" recognition for his efforts. He was tired and told Shuster he would leave Persia in October. Shuster did arrange for the purchase of two batteries of Maxim guns, 400,000 cartridges for them, as well as 5000 rifles with three million cartridges. Nonetheless, Haase left

Persia on September 30 for a five-month vacation.[364]

In an interesting coda, in late October, Sardar-i-Muhiy, the "walking arsenal," who had been the first to request war funds, was defeated by Turkomans at Bandar Djez on the Caspian coast not far from Gomesh Tapeh. At the same time, Russian troops were assembling at Bandar Anzeli and a larger force was gathering at Baku. where they would continue to threaten the Constitutionalist cause.[365]

Nonetheless, the royalist assault was fairly well extinguished. Following his defeat at Bagh-e Shah, Prince Salaru ad-Dowla fled to the southwest while Mohammad Ali left Gomesh Tapeh for Baku on March 10, 1912. With both him and the ex-shah now in full flight, the royalist threat to the Constitutionalist government evaporated. Pockets of the ex-shah's followers remained near Astarabad but about October 8, Mu'in-i Humayun was dispatched to the area with 500 government troops to oppose them. They were routed.

For a time, the ex-shah continued to be a threat to Persia, albeit a receding one. In 1920, he went to Istanbul and finally to Italy where he died at San Remo in April, 1925. His death was not greatly mourned.

Ephraim Khan
Revolutionary Constitutionalist active in Tehran 1909~1912

XIV

September

"I...adopted an arbitrary and total monthly expense for... each Ministry...."

—Morgan Shuster

Despite the fact that the victory over Mohammad Ali could not have been accomplished without the financial reforms Shuster had put in place, for him, that victory would prove to have been pyrrhic. For some weeks, Shuster had been developing a strategy to put Persian finances permanently on the road to recovery. Buoyed by the successes against Mohammad Ali, he unveiled that plan on September 11.

Essentially, it was an elaboration of the June 13 Law. That law had been designed largely to prevent the further hemorrhaging of Persia's finances. The September plan was far more elaborate and ambitious. In order to enhance revenue, Shuster would hire new assistants and invest large sums in a variety of revenue-producing projects. In addition to taxes on opium, wine, and liquors—all of which were, in any case, prohibited by Muslim law and thus, as in the Qajar era, amenable to relatively high taxation—as well as taxes on tobacco which would have produced considerable revenue, he recommended seeking the consent of the foreign powers to a revision of the Customs schedule in order to eliminate the levying of internal taxes on any imported goods.[366]

Shuster also envisioned a rough census of the population for taxation purposes; a survey of the forests and mines; a survey of the public domains; the building of barracks and the purchase of equipment for the Treasury Gendarmerie; the repair and improvement of existing roads and the building of certain new roads; and the construction of irrigation systems at various points in Persia. Finally, he recommended building or granting concessions to build a nationwide rail network of eight lines, several of which would have cut across the boundaries designated in the Anglo-Russian Convention.

He estimated that his plan would generate a net increased revenue of about five million tomans a year. Critical to Shuster's program, however, was securing a loan of four million pounds from the Seligman Brothers firm which continued to show a willingness to grant such a loan.[367] About £1,100,000 of the loan was to be used for the redemption of a Russian bank loan. The floating debt at the Banque d'Escompte had been converted in January 1911 to a fixed sum that was to be paid off by the Persian government with 7% interest. Thus, by paying down the loan the Persian government would save a considerable sum in interest payments each year.[368]

Although he took pains to point out—as he had with the June 13 Law—that his proposal would have no effect on foreign creditors except to increase the general security of their loans, the Russians did see a flaw. As they had when the Seligman firm had been proposed a year earlier, the Russians saw that if the Persian government defaulted on its payment, the Seligmans, and through them the British government, would have acquired economic and thus political power in northern Persia. That was intolerable to the Russians, who had recently found something more to worry about from Britain in the south.

Since late summer, it had become clear that the Persian government was unable to deal with what amounted to a civil war in the south. It might be remembered that the absence of the Bakhtiari khans during the fight against the ex-shah had left many portions of the trade routes in the British sphere unprotected. In late August, Barclay had suggested to Shuster that the Persian government undertake the policing of the

211

area or at least furnish from the new Treasury Gendarmerie a force sufficient to restore order there. Given the opposition to the appointment of Major Stokes, Shuster had refused.[369]

Policing the roads in the area had therefore fallen into the hands of mostly military men from India who had become increasingly irritated by diplomatic attempts to deal with the deteriorating conditions. As the disorders continued to extract a heavy financial toll on British companies doing business there, consular officials had begged the Foreign Office to increase the consular guards in the region. Then a British woman doctor was attacked, beaten, and robbed on her way to Isfahan. It may have been that outrage that brought the British Foreign Office to its final decision to send troops into Persia.

So, on September 25, the British government asked the Russian government if they had any objection to establishing a consulate at Bam and increasing consular guards throughout southern Persia. It took the Russians ten days to answer. The reason for the delay was understandable. At the same time they were being asked to consider the Seligman loan they were now also being asked to approve an increase in British forces in Persia. It did not require too much of a stretch to imagine that those "consular guards" could go from protecting British interests in the south to preying on Russian interests in the center and north of Persia. The Russian Council of Ministers finally did decide that it could not turn down the British request for the consulate, so they replied that it had no objections, noting that they were "equally concerned at the general state of insecurity" and, if the disturbances continued to spread, they would also probably have to reinforce the "escorts" of some of their consulates in northern Persia.[370] In other words, the threat of force by one of the allies was being met by the threat of force from the other ally. Approval of the Seligman loan, however, was now utterly out of the question.

Shuster's proposal to build a railroad network was also a non-starter. Less than a month earlier, the Russians and the Germans had signed the Potsdam Agreement.[371] Then, suddenly, Shuster was proposing building not one line but an entire railway system. Railroads would have replaced the donkeys that carried the maliat to Tehran, but railroads could also obviously carry information, intelligence, and a wide variety of commodities including weapons and soldiers. Moreover, it did not take a master strategist to point out that railroads would have given the central government the means to unite the country economically and thus politically as well. Quite simply, a system of railroads in Persian hands and existing outside the control of Russia or Britain would have been intolerable to both Powers.

The most significant opposition to the September 11 Law came not from Russia or Britain, however, but from the Persian Cabinet. Throughout the summer, Shuster had been working to get the different ministers to prepare simple budgets to serve as a guide in approving or disapproving requisitions of funds made on the Treasury. The ministers agreed, and then uniformly failed to do so. Shuster finally gave up and adopted a completely "arbitrary total monthly expense for the regular needs of each Ministry" and made it clear that he would then refuse to grant anything above the amounts he had fixed "no matter how great the complaint or pressure."[372]

The Ministry of War had been and still was the department of government that was the most resistant to any reform at all. When Shuster presented overwhelming evidence of corruption and waste in the War Ministry to the Council of Ministers, the Council readily approved his budget for that Ministry. Approval was one thing; acting upon that approval, however, was quite another; and on that point, the budget ran into difficulty from Samsam al-Saltaneh, who, as both prime minister and Minister of War, was influenced by the powerful

Bakhtiari khans who were, after all, his own kinsmen, and by Amir Azam, (the "fat, oily giant") who was still Vice-Minister of War.

In late August, Shuster had had a long visit with Hakim al-Mulk, the Finance Minister, during which Shuster had complained that the Council of Ministers, particularly Samsam al-Saltaneh was "playing fast and loose" with him. Despite repeated promises to do so, and his statement to the Council in early September that Shuster "was working harder for Persia than any Persian,"[373] Samsam refused to give the necessary orders for putting Shuster's budget into effect. So, Shuster refused to pay the central administration of the War Ministry at all. However, he did see to it that the troops in the Tehran barracks were paid by the Treasury paymaster directly, thus bypassing the Ministry. Shuster also scratched the names of about a hundred "rascals" from the military rolls who not only attempted to collect tens of thousands of tomans from the government in salaries but were, according to Shuster, "the chief manipulators of graft" throughout the entire department.[374]

Such measures obviously did nothing to endear Shuster either to Samsam and the officials in the War Ministry or to the other "chief manipulators" of the graft. His plan also called for the gradual redemption of the pensions, many of which were embedded in the Qajar era. This proposal was almost certain to offend the nearly 100,000 holders of those pensions, many of whom were in positions of considerable power and influence. Consequently, there were oaths to take Shuster's life and there were threats of mutiny, but the fact that the troops had been actually paid without any deductions prevented any serious disturbance.[375]

By the end of September, Shuster's tight control of the purse strings had so frustrated and angered members of the Cabinet that they now began to oppose him at almost every turn. On September 23, Shuster learned from Colonel Beddoes that Barclay had been doing whatever he could to clear a loan of four million pounds from his government but that it was Vosuq ad-Dowla "and others" in the Cabinet who were doing their best to discourage it.[376]

That month, the contract of George New, the British official who had telegraphed the flight of the Turkoman forces along the Mashhad road following the battle at Imamzadeh-Jafar and had been hired by the Persian government to reorganize the Ministry of Posts and Telegraph, came up for renewal. Although New had worked for the Persian Telegraph Administration before, his close association with Shuster tarnished him for the Cabinet—as his nationality tarnished him for the Russians. Thus, when the appointment reached the floor of the Majles, Hakim al-Mulk suggested referring it to committee. It turned out to be too late to send the bill back to committee, however, and the vote was put off until the next morning. By then, Shuster's weight had been felt and the Majles approved the contract, whereupon Hakim al-Mulk who had earlier expressed shame at the demands individuals were placing on the treasury, resigned. As McDaniel nicely puts it, "Thereafter, the Cabinet was nearly as interested in curtailing the powers of the Treasurer-General as they were in running the country."[377]

The Cabinet's indifference to Shuster's plans had become apparent earlier, when Shuster had asked the Foreign Minister, Vosuq ad-Dowla, to write to both the British and the Russian ministers at Tehran to ask for their good offices on behalf of the Seligman loan. Not only had Vosuq ad-Dowla not written such a letter but he also often indicated in conversation with Barclay that the Seligman loan was Shuster's affair and he wasn't concerned about it.[378]

In any case, it wouldn't matter. It might be remembered that a year earlier, the Majles had sought financial assistance from the Seligman Brothers, and that firm had been perfectly willing to comply with the request. Then, it had been Russian resistance that had caused the failure of the overture.[379] This time, however, as Shuster linked the loan to the entire spectrum of Persian finance and included cuts affecting many of the officials running the government, the Russians were not alone in causing the failure. Even though the loan would have gone a long way toward making Persia economically viable, powerful Persians were no longer interested in it either.

By the end of September, Shuster's efforts to reform Persia's finances, which had been so crucial to the defeat of the ex-shah, should have resulted in praise and enthusiastic support from the government he served. And from the Majles, indeed, there was still very strong backing. From the Cabinet, however, he was becoming increasingly isolated. And that isolation would prove dangerous.

XV

The Shu'a al-Saltaneh Incident

"Mon unique dette, à cette date, consiste en une obligation de 46,000 tumans envers ma mère ["My only debt, at this date, consists of an obligation of 46,000 tomans to my mother]...."

—From the will of Shu'a al-Saltaneh

By the beginning of October, Shuster had been in Tehran four and a half months. Those months had been, to say the least, tumultuous. With Ephraim Khan's defeat of Salaru ad-Dowla at Bagh-i Shah, and with the cooling breezes finally making Tehran almost comfortable, October should have been pleasant. Yet it would prove to be Shuster's worst month yet.

The entrance into Persia of the princes Shu'a al-Saltaneh and Salaru ad-Dowla with their brother, the ex-shah, at the head of armed forces in July had not only been a violation of the 1909 Protocol; it had also been an act of open rebellion against Persia's legitimate government. The government had, therefore, declared their pensions and properties forfeit.

On October 4, the Council of Ministers gave Shuster an order for the confiscation and seizure of the estates of the princes and the transfer of them into the Persian treasury. At the same time, however, as a gesture of courtesy, the government sent an official from the Ministry of Foreign Affairs to both the British and Russian legations to notify them of the action they were considering, taking care to point out that the rights of foreigners were to be fully respected.[380]

Neither legation offered any objections, so on the morning

of October 9, Shuster, anticipating no difficulty, gave the order to proceed with the seizure of the estates. He sent out six small parties, each composed of one civilian official of the Treasury Ministry, an officer of the Treasury Gendarmerie and five gendarmes. They were to seize, in the name of the government, the properties of the two princes in and around Tehran. They were to act with discretion and patience, and under no circumstances use violence without further instructions from Shuster himself.[381]

Prince Shu'a al-Saltaneh had fled to Turkey. One of his properties was not far from Shuster's own residence at Atabak. A "magnificent building" containing priceless tapestries, carpets, and furniture, it was surrounded by a large garden and enclosed by the usual wall. The place also housed the prince's wives, his children, and his mother.

At the gate to the compound, the little party, led by an officer of the Treasury Gendarmerie named Mirza Ali Asghar Khan, was met by Persian Cossacks, who forbade them to enter. When they explained that they had been ordered to seize the property, the Cossack guard allowed them to enter the garden. After placing a gendarme at the gate, they entered the palace property, opened the rooms, and began making an inventory of the furnishings.

While they were about their work, two Russian officers, having been notified by the Persian Cossacks, also entered the apartments, insisting that they had no right to enter the park and must depart immediately. When Mirza Ali Asghar, who spoke Russian, protested that they were acting under orders from the government, the Russians declared that if they did not leave immediately, they would be beaten by the Cossacks. The threat was not idle. Mirza Ali Asghar was able to see about a dozen Cossacks apparently waiting for an order to attack them. Because they had been ordered by Shuster to refrain from any kind of violence, they left the garden, followed by Russian officers and Cossacks who kept threatening them if they did not hasten their departure.[382]

Upon receiving the report, Shuster immediately sent a note to Poklewski-Koziell telling him what had happened and requested, "in this friendly manner," that the Russian Consulate withdraw its force from Shu'a al-Saltaneh's compound. He added that he would send his representatives the next morning to take possession of the garden and expressed his "personal regret that any misunderstanding should have arisen" on the matter.[383]

Poklewski-Koziell did not respond until about 11 o'clock that evening, and then the response was a bit puzzling. He replied that Dowlatabad was a property rented by two Russian subjects, and he protested that no measures should have been taken against the property without an assurance that the rights of Russian subjects would be safeguarded "and their contract not interfered with." But the affair had not happened at Dowlatabad, which lay outside the city of Tehran. And the "contract" to which Poklewski-Koziell referred was also a mystery. In any case, Shuster replied that since he had received no response to the prior notification of his intention to seize the properties, he had felt justified in pursuing their confiscation.[384]

At 10 o'clock the next morning, Shuster sent out Frank Cairns, his Director of Taxation, with a force of fifty Treasury gendarmes commanded by five Persian officers along with fifty gendarmes of the city police, commanded by three officers who would be under the orders of Colonel J.N. Merrill, the American who had arrived in Tehran about a month and a half earlier to supervise the training of the Treasury Gendarmerie. They were to take possession of the garden "peaceably, if possible." If they met with opposition, they were, under no circumstances, to fire the first shot.

Shuster's cadre arrived at the garden and after leaving

their gendarmes outside the compound, Cairns and Merrill, along with an officer of the Treasury Gendarmerie, went to the Russian Consulate, which was nearby.[385]

There, they were met, not by Poklewski-Koziell, who was in his summer quarters in Zargundeh several miles from the city, but by his subordinate, Ivan Fedorovich Pokhitanof who, as consul-general in Tabriz in 1909, had supervised the siege of that unhappy city.

The presence of Pokhitanof at this particular point is one of the most unfortunate features of this unfortunate story. This man had had a long career in Persia where he had established a pattern of acting on his own apart from directives either from Tehran or St. Petersburg. Having arrived in Tehran in September, Pokhitanof had set up an establishment apart from the Russian legation, complete with his own staff, including a Cossack escort.[386] The lines of authority between him and Poklewski-Koziell had never been clearly drawn. They could and often did report separately to St. Petersburg. In addition, Pokhitanof was held in such low esteem by both Poklewski-Koziell, his superior, and by Sir George Barclay, that the latter would not even receive him socially and would declare his actions in this affair to be those of "a crazy man."[387]

Unfortunately, it was to Pokhitanof that Cairns had to explain the purpose of the order for confiscation while, yet again, giving assurances that the rights of foreigners would be respected. Cairns then asked that the Russian force at the garden be withdrawn. Pokhitanof adamantly refused to withdraw it. Having arrived at a rather unfortunate impasse, Cairns responded that he then would take possession of the garden "by force."[388] The government gendarmes then returned to the iron gate of the garden and saw, inside, six or seven Persian Cossacks armed with rifles. They were ordered to open the gate and warned that if they refused to allow the government gendarmes to enter peacefully, force would

The Shu'a al-Saltaneh Incident

be used. The Cossacks, however, did not have the key to the gate, so the gendarmes entered the garden by another gate a short distance away. They disarmed the Cossacks who then withdrew. Now, in complete possession of the garden, the gendarmes returned to the work of taking an inventory of the furnishings, being careful, in accordance with Shuster's orders, not to disturb the women living within.

While they were engaged in that task, about 2:30 in the afternoon, the Persian officer who had been left in charge of the garden phoned Shuster that three armed officers had driven up before the gate. What happened next is not entirely clear.

Two of the officers "seemed to be" from the Russian Consulate. Apparently, these were two of Pokhitanof's subordinates. The third was a Persian officer of the Cossack Brigade. The Russians began to insult and harangue the government gendarmes, apparently with the purpose of goading them into opening fire. Fortunately, the gendarmes kept their composure and the encounter ended with the appearance at least of civility.[389] In short, nothing significant really happened at all. The report Pokhitanof sent to St. Petersburg, however, indicated quite the opposite. Without notifying Poklewski-Koziell, he sent a dispatch to Neratov claiming that Persian gendarmes had aimed their rifles at the officials of the Russian consulate and publicly insulted them.[390]

On two other properties, however, affairs turned out less amicably. At Dowlatabad, the property Poklewski-Koziell had referenced in his note to Shuster the night before, and at another property, Mansuriabad, the government contingents, having read the order of confiscation, peacefully took possession and, after posting sentries, entered the houses. That should have been the end of it. But it wasn't.

Sometime later, two officers of the Russian Consulate arrived at Dowlatabad with fourteen or fifteen Russian (not

Persian) Cossacks, who entered the house. One of them seized the officer of the Treasury Gendarmerie by one arm while another Cossack seized the other arm. After searching him, the Cossacks took the weapons of all the Treasury gendarmes and locked them in a room under the guard of three Cossacks.[391]

The Cossack detachment then went to Mansuriabad, about two kilometers away, and repeated their action but with a little more humiliation. After assembling their prisoners, the Russian Consular officials ordered the officers of the Gendarmerie to enter the carriages with them, then ordered them to mount donkeys and conducted them, under arrest, to the Russian Consulate in Tehran. There, they were warned not to repeat their actions regarding the properties of Shu'a al-Saltaneh and Salaru ad-Dowla who, they claimed, were Russian subjects. Having been thus humiliated and intimidated, the gendarmes were then given back their arms and cartridges and allowed to leave.

The afternoon of October 10, when Pokhitanof's Cossacks drove the Treasury gendarmes from Shu'a's garden, Poklewski-Koziell called Pokhitanof, demanding to know why he had interfered in the matter. A heated argument took place between the two men in which Poklewski-Koziell demanded to know what justification Pokhitanof had for his action and told him that if he had no excuse, he "had better find one shortly" since Poklewski-Koziell had filed a complaint with St. Petersburg.

Pokhitanof replied that he would "send up some papers"[392] and immediately sent a messenger to the Banque d'Escompte to get a "certain document" that Shu'a al-Saltaneh had apparently executed to the bank in 1908 when the ex-shah's deposition had been arranged. Hoping to protect his property, Shu'a al-Saltaneh had given a document mortgaging his Tehran estate, hoping that, in collusion with the Banque, he would be able to collect about 225,000 tomans from the government on the grounds that he was indebted to the Banque for that amount. The document had no validity, as everyone connected with the transaction knew.

From what corner of the stratosphere Pokhitanof had retrieved the notion that the Russian government had any legal or moral right to the estate is unclear. Equally unclear is why, without consulting either Poklewski-Koziell or St. Petersburg, he took it upon himself to declare any of Shu'a's assets the property of Russia.

Interestingly, almost immediately, Shuster came into possession of Shu'a al-Saltaneh's will. He received it through one of his principal Persian assistants, who obtained it from his sister, one of Shu'a's wives. She had delivered it, "though at enormous risk to the lives and property rights of herself and her children" because, she said, "she believed it was her duty to her country."[393]

The will "executed...in compliance with all the ceremony and formality required by law and the Muhammedan religion..."[394] contained full lists and inventories of all the Prince's lands and properties—in other words, a full account of all debts owed by and to him. As far as the Banque was concerned, rather than owing it 225,000 tomans, he was its *creditor*. He had 38,000 tomans in his account which "d'une certain difference" had not been paid out to him and, indeed, was now being "injustement" retained in his credit balance. His only debt, it turned out, was to his mother, to whom he owed 43,000 tomans.[395]

Whether Poklewski-Koziell knew of the will or not is unclear, but in three separate telegrams on October 12 and 13, he pointed out that not only was Shu'a al-Saltaneh *not* in debt to any bank, including the Russian one, but that, since he was a Turkish subject,[396] he was not under Russian protection. Persian officials, he pointed out, had given the legation notice of their intention to confiscate the properties, Pokhitanof's intervention was "unauthorized," and he had been given "categorical orders" not to meddle.[397]

The next day, Shuster's gendarmes took over Shu'a's properties and removed the five Persian Cossacks who had been stationed there by Pokhitanof. And when Pokhitanof asked the commander of the Cossack Brigade, Prince Vadbolskii, to send a detachment to restore Cossack occupation, Vadbolskii refused, saying, "I find that the action of the Consul General [sic] constitutes not only a rude and inexplicable insult to the Persian Government, but also a grave offense against the Legation..."[398]

The Persian government asked that Pokhitanof and several other officials be recalled. That was an insult the Russian government could not accept, even though it had been considering his recall. Poklewski-Koziell, who also asked that Pokhitanof either be recalled or stationed to a posting closer to home, did promise to investigate the matter, and the Persian note was returned.[399]

The Russian government never presented—never was able to present—any evidence in support of the Pokhitanof claim. So flagrant was the attempt to defraud the Persian government that Sir George Barclay had no choice but to support the Persians. But, by then, neither that support nor the text of Shu'a's will mattered.

Beginning with this incident, Shuster's mission in Persia began to quickly unravel. In St. Petersburg, Neratov knew Pokhitanof's claim of Shua's indebtedness was a fabrication, but he wrote, "it is entirely clear that we would never admit that this document is fictitious." All the blame had to be placed on the Persians.[400] Caught in the middle was Poklewski-Koziell, whose efforts to resign were rejected by Tsar Nicholas.

What is interesting about this whole affair is not only Pokhitanof's crude brutality and St. Petersburg's willingness to condone that behavior but also, as Shuster said, "the truly remarkable absence of all discipline or coordination in the Russian Ministry of Foreign affairs."[401] Grey concurred. The Russian government, he acknowledged was:

> ...a despotism without discipline. Different Ministers and different diplomatic agents pursued different politics. Russian agents were of all sorts, some were able and clever; some were not; ...some meant well, some did not, and some meant nothing at all.[402]

Russia was trying Grey's patience, but his enthusiasm for the American accountant was also waning.

What did remain a constant was that Poklewski-Koziell was the emissary of a government that had absolutely no interest in the financial independence of Persia. However, the prestige of Shuster and the Majles had been enhanced and that of Russia diminished. To be humiliated by another Asian nation only six years after being defeated by Japan was not something to be willingly endured. Russia would have to retaliate, and Poklewski-Koziell would be the unhappy instrument by which that retaliation was carried out.

Shu'a al-Saltaneh
Royalist brother of the deposed Mohammad Ali Shah

XVI

October. The *Times* Letter

"...a very mild statement of the facts"
—Morgan Shuster

The dispute over the estates of Shu'a al-Saltaneh was simply the prelude to the opera bouffé that would entirely unhinge Shuster's mission. Until the end of September or early October, there had been a decent attempt in most quarters, both Persian and foreign, to maintain at least the façade of favoring financial reform. But even that façade now began to crumble, and before the first snows had fallen in the Alborz, the stark reality had emerged that it was only Shuster and a few democrats in the Majles who were committed to it.

But if Shuster was becoming a problem for the Cabinet, he was an even bigger headache for Russia, and a headache for Russia was a migraine for Sir Edward Grey. It was the Stokes appointment that again became the focal point of the problem.

Since August 8, when the British and Russian governments had warned the Persian government against pursuing the appointment of Major Stokes, Shuster had been carrying on informal negotiations with both Poklewski-Koziell and Barclay in which he had tried to persuade them to bring their governments to see that not only was the posture of their governments toward Persia unjust but that real benefits could accrue to them by withdrawing their opposition to the Stokes appointment.

It will be remembered that in late August, Shuster had offered to hire Stokes for a period of only six months. At the expiration of that time, Stokes would be sent to Shiraz in the neutral zone; or else, as Poklewski-Koziell had suggested, one of the Swedish officers could be put in command of the Gendarmerie and Major Stokes, nominally under that officer, could then work outside the so-called Russian zone.[403]

Early in October, when the Persian government again proposed Swedish officers to train the army, Neratov admitted that although the Russians had no legal right to protest, even that plan would be harmful to Russia. That admission was underlined when, in the margin of the dispatch he sent to Tsar Nicholas II, the tsar wrote, "Since it is harmful to Russia, it is therefore impermissible. We are the masters in the North of Persia."[404]

Barclay was still not entirely opposed to the appointment of Stokes to a post at or near Isfahan, in the Russian zone, *provided* any portion of the force in the northern sphere be commanded by Persians or officers of another "minor power."[405] Scoffing at that idea as "child's play and ridiculous," Shuster's reply two days after receiving that note put the matter bluntly where it had always been "...when I said I wanted Stokes *here in Teheran to assist me* [his emphasis]...in the formation of a Treasury gendarmerie, I meant just that and nothing more." And he wondered if it was not about time that the two Powers stop playing at the matter and state plainly whether they intended to continue to oppose the appointment.[406]

Interestingly, in his response that same day, Barclay referred to the possibility of Stokes taking employment at Shiraz in the neutral zone, something Shuster had suggested earlier. By now, however, Shuster's own attitude had hardened, and he regarded such an appointment as no solution at all. In direct, straightforward terms, without diplomatic niceties, he nailed the heart of the issue—the appointment only to Shiraz would have been a tacit recognition of the hated "spheres of influence." As such, it would be a violation of the "independence and integrity of Persia" seemingly guaranteed in the 1907 accord.

It had now become clear to the British and Russians, however, that Stokes was not really the problem at all. It was Shuster himself. Any appointment Shuster tried to make, any financial reform he tried to construct had to meet with Russian approval, and the last thing Russia was willing to tolerate was the financial and, therefore, the political independence of Persia. And, as much as Sir George Barclay might personally sympathize with Shuster's efforts, his government, shadowed by the threat of a pugnacious Germany so recently unveiled in the Agadir crisis and with the agreement at Potsdam, would take great pains to maintain the delicate balance of the Anglo-Russian Convention—at Persia's expense. Without consulting the Russians or anyone else, which as the employee of a sovereign nation he had the right to do, Shuster would continue to choose for posts in the Finance Ministry people who were qualified for the tasks at hand. These appointments were made without political considerations on Shuster's part, but they happened usually to be either British or Americans, which for Russia was, in fact, a political consideration and thus unacceptable.

At this point, Shuster would have been justified in packing his bags and heading for home. And perhaps, in terms of realpolitik, he should have. If he had done that, he might have saved himself and Persia much of the anguish that was to come.

But he did no such thing. In what had now become a Sisyphean endeavor, he continued to try to do the work he had been engaged to do. However, about the early or middle part of October, he seems to have become concerned with something much larger than simply reforming Persia's finances or securing the appointment of Major Stokes. He had always been one of the very few who took the "independence and integrity of Persia" seriously. Indeed, he may have been wedded more closely to that ideal than some Persians in the government. "[T]he land of Cyrus has fallen upon evil times," he would write. "However, even the ragged misery of the beggar and his indifference to fate does not justify us in giving him a gratuitous kick."[407]

There may have been more to his decision to remain than simple aversion to gratuitous kicks, however. That he took his Christian faith seriously had already been demonstrated when he had "taken up the cudgel" for the Filipinos and Cubans. Although he would later claim to have no illusions about altruism in international affairs and found no excuse for "self-deception," he asked nonetheless, "what answer can the Christian world make to Muhammadanism today, if a question is put as to the value of the Ten Commandments, when the doctrine of 'Thou shalt not steal' is interpreted as it has been in the cases of Morocco, Tripoli, and Persia?"[408]

And so, Shuster stayed on.

On October 10, the same day that Shuster's gendarmes were ousting and being ousted from Shu'a's property, the British government notified the Persian government that it was increasing its consular guards in the south. The Persian government naturally protested; it was a direct intervention in its internal affairs. As usual, the protest was in vain.

Five days later, Poklewski-Koziell reiterated to Shuster his government's opposition to the Stokes appointment if he were to serve in northern Persia.[409] That, together with Pokhitanof's actions in the Shu'a al-Saltaneh incident—which St. Petersburg had not disavowed—Russia's opposition to the £4,000,000 Seligman loan, and the "only too apparent weakness of the British Foreign Office" regarding Persia, convinced both Shuster and the Majles that there was no longer any hope of accomplishing anything constructive.[410]

Realizing that he now had little to lose, Shuster allowed

his frustration to become public. Two days after receiving Poklewski-Koziell's letter, in an interview with W.A. Moore for the London *Times* as well as with a correspondent from the Reuters News Agency, Shuster remarked that British acquiescence in Russia's behavior plainly showed that there was no "genuine friendly feeling" on the part of those two governments toward the financial regeneration and general progress of Persia. The actions of the two Powers, he told them, stretched toward the "actual partition of Persia and the deliberate denial...of her sovereignty" and, he charged, they thwarted all progress "by which [Persia's] sovereignty might be maintained or exercised."[411] Whether he realized it or not, Shuster was charging the two Powers with, at the very least, deep hypocrisy. The moral justification for empire had long rested on the moral superiority of the ruling white Christian class. Calling that moral justification into question amounted to a mortal diplomatic sin.

Consequently, in its October 19 issue, in a tone that might politely be called smugly patronizing, the *Times* regretted Shuster's action and would be surprised "if before long he does not regret it himself." Although he had accomplished "much excellent work," his accusations of British and Russian hostility toward the regeneration of Persia were "unjust and unfounded" and his "indiscretion" would make the reorganization of the finances "more difficult than ever."[412]

With the unofficial sanction of the Cabinet, Shuster now threw down a moral gauntlet and sent a lengthy letter to the *Times*—a letter, and an action that marked a vital turning point in his mission to Persia. For him, something much larger than financial reform was at stake. Rather, it was for the sovereignty of Persia itself that Shuster was now taking up the cudgel.

The letter would be published in two parts on November 10 and 11. Relying on "the fair-mindedness of the British

231

public" and "with a slight regard for my own reputation," Shuster outlined the long list of the transgressions against Persia's sovereignty, dignity, and that independence which both Powers had bound themselves to respect both in the 1907 Convention and in the 1909 Protocol. Most of the transgressions he listed were Russian but, he made it clear, Britain had done little to stop them, and thereby shared in Russia's culpability. Citing the letter he had delivered to Barclay on August 8, Shuster wrote:

> Before accepting this work, I was given clearly to understand that neither of the two principal powers having interests here offered any objection to my undertaking it, and surely such a statement was something more than an empty pledge.

Then, addressing the tacit support Russia had given Mohammad Ali's recent incursion into Persia and its behavior in the Shu'a al Saltaneh affair—all with British acquiescence—he brought up the opposition to the Stokes appointment arguing that "...unless the Convention of 1907 is a farce or a deception...it has no bearing whatever on the proposed appointment of Major Stokes as a financial aide...."[413] Protesting yet again that he had had no political motive in pressing the issue, he declared that he was being forced to consider setting forth to his own government a formal public statement of what he had experienced since his arrival in Tehran. Such a course would be regrettable, he wrote—he did not point out that it might well have also been futile—but, he added, "there is such a thing as just dealing even between Government and individuals."[414]

Since its founding in 1785, the *Times* had been closely allied with the government and was widely viewed as the voice of the Foreign Office. Now, far from supporting him, the *Times* turned vehemently against Shuster. In an editorial, the paper accused him of having "thrown in his lot" with Persian nationalists, an insult almost on a level of ignominy with "going native" in the imperial lexicon. Instead of taking offense, Shuster wondered with whom he should have "thrown in his lot" while he was in the employ of their government.[415] The *Times* had to admit that there was no evidence for the Russian-owned Imperial Bank's claim to a lien on Shu'a's confiscated property and thus, it had to admit, the Russian consular staff had had no right to confiscate it. Nonetheless, on November 11, the *Times* "reluctantly" published the second segment of Shuster's letter, "not so much owing to any fear of its effect on informed public opinion as concern for its effect upon the Treasurer General's own position and influence in Tehran." Mr. Shuster, the *Times* pointed out, "ignores the fact that Persia is not really an independent country in the full meaning of the word." Some Russian authorities had, the *Times* admitted, connived at the ex-shah's return, but in doing so, "the F.O. in St. Petersburg acted most loyally towards Britain and Russia."[416]

The condemnation the *Times* gave the letter was not, however, universal. Grey's policy in Persia had never been without its critics, including most notably Lord Curzon. Another publication, notably hostile to the Grey government, *The Nation*, came to Shuster's defense. "If a little country may be invaded by a great Power because a foreign official in its service has ventured to write a reasoned and temperate letter to the *Times*," the article read, "...we must revise our conceptions of international discourse." "We have," the *Nation* further complained, "violated our natural instincts of chivalry, our Liberal principles of respect for nationality, and every sane calculation based on our Eastern interests."[417]

Nonetheless, as far as the British Foreign Office was concerned, that letter sealed the end of any support it might still have been inclined to give to Shuster's mission. By appealing to the British public, Shuster had broken an unspoken rule. In 1911, European diplomacy was a matter for "experts" to manage. Shuster had not played the game. By openly shredding the fiction of "protecting" Persia's independence and integrity, he had called the British and Russian bluff. He was not being a good sport. That was almost as unforgiveable as attacking Edward Grey's foreign policy just as it was being attacked by both Parliament and the public. Even worse, however, was the intimation that Britain's behavior not only with regard to Persia but throughout its empire could not be justified upon any claim to a superior morality.

The letter also somewhat cooled Shuster's relations with Barclay. The Shusters had been invited to dine with the Barclays at the British Legation on November 13. Sensing that the *Times* letter would make things a bit awkward, Shuster declined the invitation in a note to Sir George on November 2 in order to relieve Sir George and his wife of any possible embarrassment the letter had caused. He added, too, that he and Mrs. Shuster would be glad to dine with the Barclays informally at a later time. In a gentle response, Barclay thanked Shuster for his "friendly" note and agreed that it would be best to postpone the dinner "till times are better."[418]

Both the Russian and British governments now began to talk seriously about Shuster's removal. However, since he still had support in the Majles, it would be almost impossible to get the Persian government to dismiss Shuster without outright intervention. The difficulty was that, as one writer put it, "By obstructing his work…the two Powers expose themselves to the inevitable suspicion that they desire the decay of Persia in order to justify partition."[419] So obvious had that been for some time that the observation might have been laughable had it not been so tragic.

October. The Times Letter

Then, unwittingly, Shuster gave the Powers an opening. On October 28, that is, about two weeks before the *Times* published his letter, Shuster made two more appointments: E.C. Haycock, an Englishman who had lived for twenty years in Persia and had a Persian wife, as well as Alexander Schindler, a former employee of the Imperial (British) Bank. Schindler was to serve in Shiraz in the neutral zone. Haycock, however, was to serve in Isfahan in the Russian zone—whereat the Russian consul in Isfahan expressed "surprise" at the appointment.[420] By this time, the Russians had received more than adequate evidence—most significantly the British refusal to accept Stokes' resignation—that the Foreign Office in London was deeply invested in making the 1907 Convention hold at any cost. Shuster's appointment of Haycock made it clear, therefore, that the difficulty in "managing" Persia lay, not with the British, or even with the Majles, but with "managing" Mr. Shuster.

Major Stokes, who was living at the Atabak Palace and deeply but unofficially involved in the organization of the Treasury Gendarmerie, disagreed. He was one of the very few willing to openly admit that the heart of the problem lay not with Shuster at all. The success of Shuster's mission was, he charged, incompatible with Russia's attitude, and no reconciliation was possible.[421]

By the end of October, roughly 4000 Russian troops had landed at Anzeli and a larger force was being assembled at Baku. Once in a supine Persia, those troops could edge toward the Persian Gulf, thus threatening India. The 1907 Convention was proving to be useful only when it served the goals of one or the other of its signatories. At the same time, two squadrons of Indian *sowar* cavalry were landing at Bushehr on the Gulf from whence they would proceed to Shiraz as "Consular Guards."[422] The rationale, as usual, was to quell the anarchy which the Persian government was unable to subdue. However, there would have been no need to send those troops there, charged *The Nation*, "…if Mr. Shuster had been allowed to re-organise the finances and if Russia had not connived at the ex-Shah's invasion." And, *The Nation* added, "If this is anarchy, it is because Persia has not been free to repress it."[423]

The nightmare of the British-Russian rivalry breaking out into the open now seemed imminent. And if open hostilities broke out, Persia would become the battlefield. Keeping the fragile British-Russian alliance from falling apart worried not only Sir Edward Grey, but also his friend, the Regent, Nasr al-Mulk, who complained that Shuster "completely failed to appreciate that Persia is a country *protected* [my emphasis] by Russia and Britain." Nasr al-Mulk too had concluded that "the only way to preserve the Entente…is to get rid of Shuster."[424]

XVII

November. Demands and an Ultimatum

"...if the Cabinet was going to stand at all on the rights of Persia, this seemed a very strong case for them."

In his recounting of the events leading up to the end of his mission, Shuster gives no particular significance to the date November 2, 1911, perhaps because there were many worse days to follow. Nonetheless, two events of that day converged to set the stage not only for the failure of his task but also for his departure from Persia. The first incident was a sequel to the Shu'a al-Saltaneh incident. The second involved taxes.

On that day, Poklewski-Koziell called at the Persian Foreign Office to deliver a verbal message. It had two parts: (1) the Treasury Gendarmerie stationed at Shu'a al-Saltaneh's compound should be immediately withdrawn and Persian Cossacks installed instead; and (2) his government demanded an apology for the "insult" which, his government alleged, had been offered to its consular officers. Poklewski-Koziell's instructions were to obtain an immediate "yes" or "no" from the Persian Cabinet—a demand that was impossible to meet since Vosuq ad-Dowla, the Minister of Foreign Affairs, could not take any action without consulting his colleagues.[425]

The first demand was a clear interference in Persia's internal affairs and thus a violation of her sovereignty. The second was patently absurd. As Poklewski-Koziell himself knew, if any "insult" had been cast by Persians in that confrontation, it would have paled in significance compared with the shabby behavior of Poklewski-Koziell's own colleague, Pokhanitof, about which he had already complained to Neratov. Moreover, with Russian troops landing at Anzeli and another force assembling at Baku, the last thing Neratov wanted or expected was that the Persian government would accede to the demands.

To add insult to injury, the Persians' written protest to the verbal demands was summarily returned although, as Shuster pointed out, "[Poklewski-Koziell]...received and acknowledged the same."[426]

The timing, as with so many events in this story, was most unfortunate. Even if the Russian government had been willing to compromise on its two demands (and according to Robert McDaniel there were indications that they might have been), Shuster himself had just made it impossible for the Russians to retreat from them.[427]

The question is why it took two weeks after the confrontation at Shu'a's compound for the Russian government to react and to react in the way that it did.

It will be remembered that a few days after his arrival in May, Shuster had met a M. Lecoffre who had assured Shuster that between the two of them they would be able to straighten out Persia's finances. At some point on or around November 2, only a few days after his appointment of E.C. Haycock to Isfahan, Shuster announced the appointment of Lecoffre to Azerbaijan to investigate the misappropriation of about a million tomans of the taxes of the preceding two years.

To the appointment of Haycock, the Russian consul at Isfahan simply expressed "surprise."[428] The Lecoffre appointment was another matter entirely, however. On the face of it, there should have been no difficulty with it since, although Lecoffre was a British citizen, he was simply being transferred from one post within the Russian sphere of influence, Tehran, to another, Tabriz. Moreover, the appointment was to *investigate*, not to *collect* taxes.

Unlike the Haycock appointment, however, the appointment of Lecoffre ran into opposition not only from the Russians but also from members of the Persian Cabinet. To the Russians, it was yet another sign that Shuster had no intention of playing the game the way it was supposed to be played. He had—again—not notified or consulted them before making the appointment. And Lecoffre's hostility to the Russians, like that of Major Stokes, was no secret. Once again, Shuster was ignoring Russia's "interests."

The problem for the individual members of the Cabinet, however, was more personal. Many of them had fallen victim to Shuster's own rigid honesty. The appointment of Lecoffre was a particularly difficult pill to swallow for two of the ministers, Vosuq ad-Dowla, and his brother, Qavam al-Saltaneh, who held the post of Interior Minister. Their father, Muta'midu al-Saltaneh, was a pishkar in Azerbaijan.

Whether the Cabinet would accept or reject either or both of the Russian demands would have been difficult to predict. The demands really were not about which troops were at Shu'a's compound or about any "insult"—given or contrived. Indeed, the demands which, in themselves, were almost trivial, shadowed the real issue, the one that mattered. And that was who held the reins to Persia's sovereignty? Put bluntly, it was Russia, backed by Britain. But how much pressure could Russia place on that alliance without breaking it? And within the Persian government itself, was it the Cabinet or the Majles that controlled policy? And standing at the center of all these questions was W. Morgan Shuster.

On that same day, November 2, that Poklewsi-Koziell delivered his two demands and Shuster announced the appointment of Lecoffre to Tabriz, an incident inaugurated by Shuster brought his relationship with Persia's Cabinet nearly to the breaking point. It involved taxes.

There had been a number of futile attempts to get certain wealthy grandees in Tehran to pay their taxes, some of whom had not paid them in years. One of the most flagrant tax violators was Prince Alau ad-Dowla, the chief of police of Tehran who had ordered the bastinadoing of the bazaar sugar merchants in December 1905. By late October, Shuster's Treasury Gendarmerie already had become a well-organized force, and Shuster was ready to make use of it to enforce the collection not only of current taxes but also of their arrears.

Tax collectors had been sent to the prince's house several times to collect what he owed. They had been insulted and driven away. So, on November 4, two days after Poklewski-Koziell's demands had been presented, Shuster sent the collectors back, this time with several Treasury Gendarmes who posted themselves at the gates of the prince's compound and told the prince that his property was seized until the taxes got paid.

The prince thereupon fled through another gate and rushed to the house of Samsam al-Saltaneh, who lived nearby. Weeping, the distraught prince so played on the sympathies of the prime minister that the latter's brother, another Bakhtiari chieftain named Yousef Khan, Amir Mujahid, was sent to drive the Treasury gendarmes away. This man had already become Shuster's bitter enemy since Shuster had earlier refused to honor a heavy demand he had made for money, presumably for his forces. Amir Mujahid, along with several Bakhtiari guards, went to the estate of Alau ad-Dowla and, rushing upon the gendarmes, beat them with heavy sticks and had their guns taken from them.[429]

When Shuster heard of the affair, he demanded an apology from Samsam, the punishment of the guilty parties, and the full payment of the taxes due. The next day, in Council, Samsam made "a very manly" written apology. He was an excitable old man, he said, and "had gone quite out of his head" when the "great Prince," Alau ad-Dowla, had rushed in with tears in his eyes. The guns of the Treasury gendarmes were publicly restored to them and the taxes paid in full. In

Shuster's mind, the incident "greatly enhanced" the prestige of the Treasury, especially in the eyes of the princes and other grandees who had hoped to continue to evade paying taxes.[430] As far as he was concerned, the matter was closed.

But it was not closed. Tax collections were only a part of a web that united former Qajar bureaucrats, the formidable Bakhtiari khans, large landowners, pension holders, wealthier businessmen, and other notables—that is, a large part of the country's traditional leadership—with key members of the Cabinet in opposition to Shuster's agenda. Shuster's insistence on honesty had, as a German representative in Tehran put it, threatened "their most sacred possession: their freedom to steal and their freedom from taxes."[431] Worse, and far more dangerous, it made them vulnerable to Russian demands.

That same day, in the midst of the Alau ad-Dowla affair, with the Lecoffre appointment in the air, and with news coming in of Russian troops landing in the north, the Cabinet consulted Shuster on "their best course." While disclaiming any desire to enter into political affairs—a disclaimer which by this time was entirely disingenuous—Shuster was forced to do just that. He gave the opinion that "if the Cabinet was going to stand at all on the rights of Persia, this would seem a very strong case for them."[432]

Why the Cabinet, most of whose members had felt the sting of his honesty, now consulted Shuster, and whether or not they sought his advice in good faith, is a matter of serious conjecture. Worried as they were about the Russian presence, they still had some reason to hope that there might be room for a settlement with Russia. However, they also knew that the Majles, most of whose members still fully supported Shuster, would never accept the Russian demands. Therefore, on November 6, the Persian Foreign Office conveyed a carefully framed *verbal* reply to Poklewski-Koziell which amounted to a refusal to accede to the demands but with an offer to abide by "an impartial and complete investigation" into the Shu'a al-Saltaneh incident.[433]

In its leaning toward at least partial acceptance of the Russian demands, the Cabinet had support from a direction that might have been expected—London. With the Moroccan crisis barely resolved and the Potsdam Agreement freshly signed, Grey felt that he could ill afford to alienate Russia and allow a Russian-German entente. Thus, as unreasonable as Grey would have had to admit that the two demands were, he felt he had no choice but to acquiesce, yet again. Indeed, to Grey, those demands were of far less consequence than the Lecoffre appointment.[434]

So on November 8, Sir George Barclay called on Shuster, not to discuss the November 2 demands but to inform him that Sir Edward Grey, by telegram, had instructed him (Barclay) to inform Shuster that his assignment of Lecoffre to Tabriz would result in a protest from Russia and would "create the danger of her seizing Northern Persia." Grey had instructed Barclay to point out that "[Shuster] must be made to see that the Russians are sure to take measures for the protection of their own interests if administrative posts in their own sphere of interest are filled by British subjects." Further, he said, to deprecate such measures "would be contrary to the spirit of the convention of 1907."

Shuster replied that he had always been anxious to observe the "legitimate" interests of Russia and the other powers in Persia but neither was he ready "to allow all progress in Persian reforms to be nullified."[435] But that, precisely, was the rub. Neither Shuster nor the Persian government for which he worked recognized the "spheres of influence" as "legitimate."

Shuster understood from Barclay's manner that Russia had instigated Grey's action. Barclay had, Shuster noted, gone through the delivery of his message, "like a man taking medicine" and left without further argument.[436]

November. Demands and an Ultimatum

Barclay was not alone in his discomfort. The day before, on November 7, at a fully attended session of the House of Commons, a resolution, submitted by the London Persia Committee, had been passed unanimously to be sent to the Secretary of State. That resolution, which would receive "a somewhat curt acknowledgement," read, in part,

> This meeting of Members of Parliament and others invites the serious attention of His Majesty's Government to the difficulties placed by the Russian Government in the way of Mr. Shuster's efforts to reorganize Persian finance, and offers His Majesty's Government their support in any action His Majesty's Government may see fit to take, as signatories of the Anglo-Russian Convention, to support Mr. Shuster.[437]

Support for Mr. Shuster, however, would not be forthcoming. Fairly well assured of that, a few days later, on November 11, the day on which the *Times* published the second installment of Shuster's letter with its own stinging rebuke, the Russian line hardened further. That day, the Oriental Secretary of the Russian Legation, a Monsieur de Giers, delivered in writing the same demands that had been delivered orally on November 2. Now, however there was an additional warning: if the demands were not met within forty-eight hours, the Russians would break off relations with Persia[438] and, he added verbally, they would "take measures."[439] There was little doubt in anyone's mind what the "measures" would be.

The Cabinet now turned, not to Shuster as it had a week earlier, but instead asked the British government for advice on what course of action they ought to pursue. Grey cabled

243

back that the Cabinet should accept the Russian demands and apologize as was demanded. Would the fulfillment of their demands secure the withdrawal of Russian troops, asked the Cabinet? The British responded that "in all probability" the Russian troops would be withdrawn if the demands were met.[440]

Heeding Grey's advice, therefore, the Cabinet decided to yield to the Russian demands and that same day, Samsam al-Saltaneh sent Shuster a letter demanding the removal of the Treasury Gendarmes from Shu'a's compound. Shuster noticed, however, that the letter was signed only by Samsam rather than by the entire Council of Ministers as the original order for confiscation had been. Thus, he could not obey the order unless a document signed by the *entire* Council should be submitted to him. And, Shuster insisted, his agents should either be left in charge of the properties, or he, Shuster, should be relieved of all responsibility for them.

Shuster's demand for the signatures of the entire Cabinet had to have been made with tongue in cheek. One by one the ministers had resigned, and by November 11 the only ministers left were the prime minister, Samsam, and Vosuq ad-Dowla, the Foreign Minister. Resignations, as Shuster had learned, came and went, and those who "resigned" usually continued to fill their posts. Accordingly, the entire Cabinet sent Shuster a written order to hand over to the Russians the estates of Shu'a and recall the gendarmes. Shuster had the order executed being careful to get receipts for everything they had seized.[441]

While the unity of the Cabinet unraveled, and as the threat of Russian intervention became more real, the usually divided Majles started to come together, its support of Shuster still firm. Indeed, the same day, November 11, the Majles passed a law authorizing Shuster to contract with ten more American financial assistants.[442] And it was now that the

November. Demands and an Ultimatum

Majles became the protagonist in the drama.

Since the middle of summer, the Majles had occasionally debated a revision of the electoral law to replace the one of 1909. The new electoral law, passed on October 22, was much more democratic than the 1909 one and hence was viewed with skepticism if not real alarm by the more conservative elements of the government. Under this new electoral law, the existing assembly would adjourn in mid-November and a new Majles would be elected in the spring of 1912. Thus, there would have been no Majles to manage things for at least six months. The Russian demands with their threat changed all that. So, on November 13, the Majles voted by an overwhelming majority to extend the session.[443] It would continue to sit and the Cabinet, now truncating itself on a fairly routine basis, would not be free to work out a solution to the foreign problems without the Majles.

Unfortunately, as the factions in the Majles came together, so too did the views of the British and the Russians that the removal of Shuster was not only desirable but had now become urgent. Attempts to get the Majles to vote to cancel the Lecoffre appointment to Tabriz, hoping that such a setback would force Shuster to resign, would most certainly be met with failure. And his voluntary resignation on any terms except those that might be imposed by the Majles was not likely.

By mid-November, because Grey was reluctant to see Russian troops occupying Tehran, he was willing to support Russia's demands. With that assurance, on November 18 the Russian legation informed the Persian government that, since their demands had not been accepted, diplomatic relations were thereby broken off, but commercial matters would still be handled by the Russian Consuls.

Two days later, Samsam and Amir Mujahid quietly called at both the British and Russian legations to discuss a coup. Would those governments intervene if the Bakhtiaris forcibly brought the Majles to heel? They especially wanted to know what the Russians would do. A week later, they found out when dragomans of the two legations visited the Bakhtiari khans and assured them that there would be no interference from Russia if a coup were to take place. If there were to be a coup, it could not come from outside the government; it would have to come from within. Although several thousand Russian troops were scattered across northern Persia, there were only a few hundred Bakhtiaris in Tehran. The only other forces were those of Ephraim Khan, the chief of police, who seemed not to have been involved in the Bakhtiari plan.[444]

The Russian position in this instance resembled its attitude toward Mohammad Ali. While it could not take a visibly active role in overthrowing Persia's legitimate government without undoing the 1907 accord, it would not interfere with the attempts of other parties to do so. Besides the Bakhtiari plot, rumors of other plots, Russian-backed and otherwise, now had vigorous circulation in the capital.

On November 22, the Cabinet decided that, humiliating though it would be, an apology was necessary. Vosuq ad-Dowla, as the Foreign Minister, would be the one to make it. But he was sick. So, the apology was not made until two days later when Vosuq ad-Dowla, in full uniform, drove to the Russian Legation. There, he seized the hand of Poklewski-Koziell and said, "...I am instructed by my own Government to apologize in its name for the affront put upon the Consular officers of Your Excellency's Government in the Shu'a al-Saltaneh affair."[445]

That was not at all what the Russians had expected—or desired. Whether Grey and the Persian Cabinet had intended it or not, the Persians had actually called Russia's bluff. Grey had assured the Persian Government that if the demands were accepted and the apology given, Russian troops on their way to Persia would be withdrawn. The Russians could not now withdraw, however, without achieving something concrete. An outright occupation of northern Persia, however, would skewer Anglo-Russian relations. If the Russians took over the north, the British would have to take over the south, thus re-activating the rivalry in the East which had been presumably settled by the 1907 Convention.

For all of Russia's menacing gestures, the idea of occupying the north and installing a puppet government in Tehran—apart from jeopardizing the alliance with Britain—was insupportable. Since the puppet government would not be able to stand on its own without constant support, they would be stuck there indefinitely. And, in 1911, the continued stability of the government in Moscow itself was not guaranteed.

So, the Persian problem had now changed. Grey indeed wanted the movement of troops halted if the apology was received; but Shuster's letter to the *Times* had also given him a rationale for going along with the Russian demand for his dismissal.

By the time Poklewski-Koziell had accepted the apology and officially re-established relations with the Persian government, the Russian Council of Ministers had had time to come up with the bludgeon that would destroy Persia's Constitutional Revolution. It was an Ultimatum that contained three items. The first item was the dismissal of Shuster and Lecoffre. Secondly, the Persian government was to pledge itself not to hire foreigners without the consent of the British and Russian legations, and third, the Persian government was to pay an indemnity for the cost of the Russian military expedition then entering the country. Further, compliance was expected within forty-eight hours. During that period, Russian troops would remain at Rasht. If no reply or an "unsatisfactory" reply had been submitted by then, the troops would advance, and that would, of course, increase the indemnity to be paid by Persia to Russia. In other words, Persia would have to pay to be invaded. At the same time, the Persian government was informed that the mother of Shu'a al-Saltaneh and her property were placed under the "protection" of Their Imperial Majesties, the Tsar and Tsarina of All the Russians."[446] The lady in question was, of course, a Persian subject.

In a separate explanation by Poklewski-Koziell, the reason given for the first demand was that the Russian government had been forced to send troops to Persia "owing to the recent insulting acts of Mr. Shuster towards Russia."[447] In other words, a Russian army would be activated toward Persia because of the actions of a private American citizen who had no official diplomatic status.

The substance of this Ultimatum was communicated to the British government two days later, on November 26. The Foreign Office replied that it would be unable to object to its terms, even though it really did fear a full-scale Russian take-over of northern Persia. The only objection Grey could urge against it was the indemnity clause which, if it were paid, would cripple Persia's ability to police the southern trade. That would prejudice British commerce.[448]

The Ultimatum was presented to the Persians on November 29 at noon.[449]

Tehran was stunned. Up to that point, it still had been possible to think that the British, and possibly even the Russians, might at least give the appearance of adhering to the 1907 Convention's guarantee of Persia's integrity and independence. The two Powers had required the Persians themselves to live up to each and every requirement placed on them by the Convention. Persians had by this time become accustomed to Russia's autocratic interference in its affairs—and Britain's cynical acquiescence in that behavior. But this went beyond even what the country had experienced before.

That afternoon, Samsam went to the Majles to present, for its approval, another new Cabinet which he had formed.

Among the names was that of Mutashamu as-Saltaneh for Minister of Justice, a man who had served in the Cabinet of the Sepahdar. That Samsam put forward that particular name only an hour or two after the Ultimatum had been delivered was almost laughably indelicate, as Mutashamu's close relations with Russian emissaries and agents were well-known. And Samsam's own colleagues had strongly advised him against that nomination.[450]

The leader of the democrats in the Majles stood up and declared that, although the prime minister himself possessed the confidence of the deputies, Mutashamu was unacceptable. At that point, Samsam launched into a violent harangue against the democrats. He was called to order by the president of the Majles, but he then rushed from the chamber, threatening to call up his Bakhtiaris and kill all the democrats. In the melee, the chief mullah (Shuster calls him the chief "priest") of Tehran attacked the president and the democrats. The president thereupon called the mullah to order three times, the third time implying imprisonment for the offender. At that point, the entire assembly broke into an uproar.[451]

That rather undignified scene, together with news of the Ultimatum, threw Tehran into an uproar. It was quieted by Ephraim Khan's police and the Treasury Gendarmerie, now numbering about 800 men. But the damage had been done. There seemed little doubt that Samsam's attempt to get a known Russian sympathizer into the Cabinet, and his threats to use the Bakhtiaris against the Majles, signaled that the Constitutional Government was again threatened as it had been in 1909. And not only by foreigners. If the strangling of Persia were to be at the hands of Russians, it was several Persians themselves who would be supplying the rope.

XVIII

December

"...a desperate and down-trodden people who preferred a future of unknown terror to the voluntary sacrifice of their national dignity...."

—Morgan Shuster

On the morning of December 1, just a few hours before the Ultimatum was to be debated in the Majles, as he was leaving his house, Prince Alau ad-Dowla was shot and killed by three men who had been waiting on a neighboring balcony. It was rumored that the prince had been involved in one of the plots to ask the Russians to restore Mohammad Ali to his throne. When Samsam al-Saltaneh heard of the prince's death, he burst into tears and promptly vowed to kill twenty democrats. Yet another assassination was directed at Mushiru as-Saltan, a former prime minister under Mohammad Ali, while he was out riding. He was wounded in the leg, but his nephew who was riding with him was killed.[452]

The timing of the assassination—and Samsam's threat—could not have been worse. The coherence of the government which had been teetering for some time now utterly collapsed. The Majles saw itself as the representative of the Persian nation, the mellat, against Samsam's Cabinet and the Regent, the dolat. And it was the Cabinet that had decided to accept the humiliating Ultimatum.

Although the first item in the Ultimatum was his own dismissal, Shuster had some sympathy for the members of the Cabinet who, he admitted, saw the "naked steel" behind Russia's threats more clearly than the deputies in the Majles. And he thought, too, that perhaps "...they suffered from that abandon and tired feeling which comes from playing an unequal and always losing game."[453]

And Shuster himself may have been tired. He had been opposed on every single proposal that could have secured Persia's financial independence. He had not been able to secure the Stokes appointment or the Seligman loan, and Russia's opposition to the seizure of Shu'a's properties and to the Lecoffre appointment, coupled with British acquiescence, were convincing proof that his mission was fairly well finished. The *Times* letter had given Grey grounds, however flimsy, for refusing to block the implementation of the Ultimatum. What hopes Shuster had for Persia's future now were slender. The only thing left was her dignity. And the Cabinet support even for that was almost non-existent.

But what price dignity? Or honor? Or self-respect? Were these worth the expenditure of yet more Persian treasure? More Persian lives? One might be willing to pledge one's own life, property and sacred honor for such ideals. There is perhaps some glory in that. But there is more than a little moral ambiguity in choosing a course of action that will almost certainly cause the deaths of hundreds or even thousands of others for whom martyrdom is not at all glorious.

At 11 a.m., an hour before the expiration of the 48-hour limit imposed by the Russians, the seventy-six deputies of the Majles met to consider the Ultimatum. What must have been on their minds can only be imagined. Obviously, there would have been some apprehension arising from news of the assassination of the prince only a few hours previously. Then, too, the hostility between members of Majles and the Cabinet, and the feeble unity that existed even within the Majles, must have made the tension in that chamber almost palpable. Shuster's narrative movingly conveys not only the drama of the moment itself, but also the depth of his own sympathy for the actors in it.

Samsam arose from his chair and announced that, because of the ridiculously short period mandated by the Russians, there could be no time for real consideration or discussion. He then presented the Majles deputies with a resolution authorizing the Cabinet to accept Russia's demands.

A deep silence, Shuster says, fell upon the crowds within the Majles building and on the grounds outside as the proposal was read. Then a young cleric from Tabriz, Sheikh Mohammad Khiabani,[454] rose from his seat and, Shuster says:

> This servant of God spoke briefly and to the point: "It may be the will of Allah that our liberty and our sovereignty shall be taken from us by force, but let us not sign them away with our own hands!" One gesture of appeal with his trembling hands, and he resumed his seat. Simple words, these, yet wingéd ones. Easy to utter in academic discussions; hard, bitterly hard, to say under the eye of a cruel and overpowering tyrant whose emissaries watched the speaker from the galleries and mentally marked him down for future imprisonment, torture, exile, or worse.

Other deputies spoke in "dignified appeals"—brief, because the time was short. Just before noon, the vote was taken. As each name was called, the deputy rose in his place and gave his vote. There was no secret ballot. One or two deputies, Shuster noticed, "sought a craven's refuge and slunk quietly from the chamber."

> And when the roll call was ended every man, priest or layman, youth or octogenarian, had cast his own die of fate, had

staked the safety of himself and family, and hurled back into the teeth of the great Bear from the North the unanimous answer of a desperate and down-trodden people who preferred a future of unknown terror to the voluntary sacrifice of their national dignity and of their recently earned right to work out their own salvation. Amid tears and applause from the spectators, the crest-fallen and frightened members of the Cabinet withdrew....[455]

By that vote, the Cabinet, according to the Constitution, officially ceased to exist—a legality, however, which would have little meaning in the ensuing weeks.

That afternoon and in the days immediately following, the Majles' rejection of the Ultimatum seemed to have strong support. Crowds which included women and students thronged the Lalezar, one of the principal streets of Tehran, shouting death to the traitors in the Cabinet and calling on Allah to witness that they would give up their lives for their country. Protests denouncing the Regent and the Cabinet poured in from the provinces while members of the clergy called for a boycott of all Russian and British goods. Windows of shops displaying Russian goods were smashed and, in the south, the boycott of British goods became so severe that it became difficult to obtain basic food supplies for the British Indian troops stationed there.[456]

Support for the Majles' refusal, however, was anything but universal. In the days following the December 1 vote, the atmosphere of dread and anxiety in Tehran was so thick that, Shuster says, "...the snow-covered mountains themselves seemed afflicted with the mournful scenes through which the country was passing."[457]

There were threats against the Majles deputies, and Shuster himself became the target of anti-Majles sentiment. That very afternoon following the rejection of the Ultimatum, Shuster was informed that several Bakhtiari khans, having thrown their lot in with the Russians, had discussed attacking his residence and offices in Atabak Park with the object of seizing the Treasury, burning the records, and driving the Americans out. When he received this news, Shuster sent a Persian friend to tell the khans that if they attempted anything so foolish, "they had better think twice about it," and he had the guard at Atabak increased by fifty men, making a total of 150 on duty there. The Bakhtiaris never came.[458]

The day after the rejection of the Ultimatum, the Russian legation announced that if, within six days, the Ultimatum had not been complied with, the 4000 troops stationed at Qazvin would start for Tehran. A few days later, under cover of that army, 2000 Turkomans did begin advancing toward the city from Mazandaran. They got only as far as Damghan, where a tiny force of only 600 under the command of Ephraim Khan managed to keep them in check.[459]

Meanwhile, a group of Persian merchants, in a telegram to the British Chamber of Commerce on December 7, expressed the hope that British pressure might deter the Russians from enforcing the Ultimatum which "so flagrantly violates the integrity and independence of Persia."[460]

In a pattern that had now become brutally tiresome, the appeal was ignored. Shuster and, by extension the Majles itself, had become expendable.

As might have been expected, Shuster had no support from the Cabinet. For two of the ministers, Vosuq ad-Dowla, and his brother, Ghavamu as-Saltaneh, the chill had set in well before December 1 when Shuster had sent Lecoffre to look into the misappropriation of funds at Tabriz. Their father, the pishkar, Muta'midu as-Saltaneh, still had not remitted a single toman to the government and indeed, Shuster says, "he sneered at the Central Government at Tehran, including the Treasurer-General."[461] Since one of the demands in the Ultimatum was also the dismissal of Lecoffre, it required no leap of the imagination to understand the two ministers' willingness to accept it. And the dismissal of Lecoffre was inextricably linked to the dismissal of Shuster whose own life, as he himself quaintly put it, "did not seem…to be particularly healthful."[462]

Because a number of assassination plots had been discovered even before December 1, Shuster had not left Atabak since mid-November. The fact that Russia had sent a large army into Persia specifically to expel him was threatening enough, but there had also been attacks on him in the semi-official Russian press inviting various Persian "political renegades" to do him harm in the belief that they would thereby gain the Russian government's favor.

The Tehran police arrested two men who had been paid to "blow up" Shuster as he was driving. During the day, bullets whistled over the garden as he worked in his office, while every night he was presented with a Mauser pistol "serenade." One evening, as he and his wife were about to go out to a dinner party, they received word that three Caucasians were "on the watch" for him in a nearby street. Some of the Nationalists organized a personal bodyguard to protect Shuster. They never allowed Shuster out of their sight. One of these Nationalists was hanged shortly after Shuster's departure on the grounds that he was a feda'i.[463]

A newly arrived American assistant, Turin Boone, and his wife dined at Atabak on December 18. Mrs. Boone noted that the dinner was elegant and the room "interesting"—with bullet holes in the mirror.[464] Shuster was heavier, she noted, but looking well.

On December 14, under orders from Grey, Stokes left

Tehran to return to his regiment in India.[465]

About the same time, Grey announced in Parliament that although the 1907 Convention recognized Persian independence, it had placed the signatories under no obligation to *protect* it. He could not object to Russia's cardinal demand that Shuster be removed, he argued, because "Had I supported him...I should...have been breaking the spirit of the Anglo-Russian Agreement."[466]

Shuster, he said, had acted foolishly in appointing British officials. Grey accepted Russia's demand for a Russo-British veto on any foreign administrators appointed by Persia. The demand would not affect the appointment of Persian officials, he reassured the Majles deputies. What he did not say—did not have to say—was that any officials appointed by Persians would be subject to officials named by the two Powers. Ominously, he also declared that, once the present crisis was resolved, the Powers would pursue a "constructive policy" to put the Persian house in order.[467]

Meanwhile, messages of encouragement were coming in to the Majles from Muslim societies all over the world, including a telegram from the Persian Defense Society of Calcutta urging the Majles not to submit to the demands and to "Increase the relation with America." There was an exception, however, that inadvertently carried a touch of bleak humor. As Russian troops poured across Persia's borders, the Majles, in desperation, approached even the Ottomans to intervene to prevent the partitioning of the country. The Turkish Minister of Foreign Affairs suggested that Persia's independence could not possibly be in danger because it was guaranteed by the 1907 Anglo-Russian Convention.[468]

As the mood in Tehran darkened, several proposals were put forth to resolve the crisis. One idea was that the government would comply with Russia's demand for Shuster's dismissal as Treasurer-General but then he would be retained as "general advisor" to the Majles. Shuster rejected that idea.

Another idea, however, was fairly sophisticated. Several members of the Majles suggested that Shuster draft a short law granting a concession to build a number of railways. The name of the recipient of the concession was to be left blank and, once the law was passed, Shuster would fill in the name of an American capitalist, or group of capitalists, telegraph the concession to New York, and then have the concessionaires demand the protection of the American government.[469]

In light of the strained relationship between the governments of Iran and the United States in the twenty-first century, that suggestion has a poignant air about it. These men came not only to a stranger in their country, but one who was *kafir*, an infidel, an American. On the other hand, the appeal is also heartbreaking. In late November, when the Ultimatum had become public, the Foreign Minister, Vosuq ad-Dowla, had cabled the Persian envoy in Washington, Mirza Ali Quli Khan, asking him to find out what, in the opinion of the United States government, Persia ought to do. Pointing out that acceptance of the Ultimatum would destroy Persia's independence but that its rejection would cause "great misery and bloodshed," the cable pleaded for the United States government "in the name of Peace and Humanity, [to] use its great influence to assist an ancient Nation in this serious crisis...."

The American reply had been cold. The Secretary of State, Philander Knox, did not find it "appropriate to offer any suggestions." The response of Congress was even more callous. When the message was read in French (its original version), the translation was met with laughter.[470] Shuster does not mention this snub in his *Strangling of Persia*, and there is every possibility he did not know of it.

Some days after the Majles' rejection of the Ultimatum, in an effort to salvage some advantage, however small, from the deteriorating situation, a committee of twelve deputies informed the Regent, Nasr al-Mulk, that, since they had no confidence in the Cabinet ministers, the Majles was about to vote on a resolution authorizing him to enter negotiations with Russia and Britain in order to come to some settlement on Persia's behalf. The Regent paled, fled in a panic, and threatened to start for Anzeli if such an idea should be mentioned again.[471]

Although outright armed resistance to the Russian incursion was suicidal, all four parties in the Majles decided to do just that. Their total available defense amounted to about 2000 Bakhtiaris (whose loyalty to the Constitutionalists had already proven to be inconsistent at best), roughly 300 Armenian fighters with a few machine-guns, and perhaps 3000 feda'is who had sworn to uphold the Constitutional Government to the death. To that force could now be added the 1100 Treasury gendarmes who had been trained by the four American officers and who were under the immediate command of thirty-five Persian officers. Although vastly outnumbered, Shuster thought this force might have been able to hold off an advance of Russian troops through the mountain passes leading to Tehran. His reason for thinking so was that a few days earlier, a similar force, outnumbered five to one, had held out against Russian troops and artillery at Tabriz for six days.[472]

Late on the night that the decision was made to resist the Russian incursion, about a dozen men came to Shuster wondering whether they should take a step that, while heroic, would place not only their own lives but possibly the lives of thousands of their countrymen in jeopardy. The "strange, sad talk" lasted about three hours, during which Shuster gave the "reluctant" opinion that if a single hostile move were to be made against the Russian troops north of Tehran, by the time the snows melted in the spring, the last spark of Persian liberty would have been crushed "and leave, perhaps, not even widows and orphans to mourn at soldiers' graves." They decided, therefore, on a course of only passive resistance to the Russian demands—and "another humble chapter had been written among many which mean little to the world at large." [473]

The women of Tehran, however, had other ideas. While the Constitution had seemed to be in no danger, they had been fairly quiescent; but now, when it appeared that leading figures in the government itself were willing to sell the country to Russia, they sprang into action.

With rumors flying about that the government was about to cave in to Russian demands, the women acted. Shuster writes,

> Out from their walled courtyards and harems marched three hundred of that weak sex, with the flush of undying determination in their cheeks. They were clad in their plain black robes with the white nets of their veils dropped over their faces. Many held pistols under their skirts or in the folds of their sleeves. Straight to the Majles they went, and, gathered there, demanded of the President that he admit them all. What the grave deputies of the Land of the Lion and the Sun may have thought at this strange visitation is not recorded. The President consented to receive a delegation of them. In his reception-hall, they confronted him, and lest he and his colleagues should doubt their meaning, these cloistered Persian mothers, wives and daughters, exhibited threateningly their revolvers, tore aside their veils, and confessed their decision

> to kill their own husbands, and sons, and leave behind their own dead bodies, if the deputies wavered in their duty to uphold the liberty and dignity of the Persian people and nation....
>
> May we not exclaim: All honor to the veiled women of Persia!...Watched, guarded and rebuffed, they drank deep of the cup of freedom's desire and offered up their daily contribution to their country's cause, watching its servants each moment with a mother's jealous eyes, and...even in that grim, tragic hour when men's hearts grew weak and the palsying dread of the prison and its tortures, the noose and bullet had settled on the bravest in the land.[474]

Meanwhile, W.A. Moore reported on a large meeting of women held in the great mosque of Sepah Salar, where several female orators gave what were described as "eloquent" speeches. One woman announced that, even though the law of Islam forbade it, the women themselves would nonetheless take part in *jihad*. And a Persian source reported on armed women marching to the Majles ordering the deputies to "prefer death in honour to life in slavery."[475]

Less dramatic but more politically sophisticated, was the appeal of a Persian women's association, the *Anjeman-i Mokhadira't-i Vatan*, (Society of the Women of the Homeland) to the British Women's Social and Political Union (WSPU) urging British suffragette support for the cause of Persian freedom by exerting pressure on Grey. The response, signed by the leading British suffragettes, Emmeline Pankhurst and Emmeline Pethick-Lawrence, expressed sympathy for their

Persian "sisters" but admitted that their organization was unable to move the British government to grant political freedom even to them, their own country-women. A Persian women's organization in Hyderabad, India, the *Anjeman-i wifa'q-i Iranian* (Society of Iranian Alliance) also contacted various organizations and individuals in Britain on behalf of Persian independence. In a message to Queen Mary, George V's wife, the Society asked her to show her "great kindness of heart... by preventing the inroad of Russia in Persia."[476] The appeals fell not on deaf but on helpless ears.

The rejection of the Ultimatum raised objections not only from the Cabinet and its supporters, but also from what might have been unexpected quarters. From exile in Istanbul no less a radical democrat than Sayyid Hasan Taqizadeh wired leading figures in the government pleading with them to accept the Ultimatum and issue the required apology because "hostility and stubbornness would result in eternal damnation." The whole world, Taqizadeh pointed out, "would reproach us for showing such stubbornness over a mere apology."[477] The motherland was in danger, he warned, and it would be treason to insist on rejecting the Ultimatum.

In citing Taqizadeh, Homa Katouzian adds, "To say that Iran was right, is to state the obvious but miss the point." And the point, as he sees it, is whether what the Majles—and by extension, Shuster—did served the country's best possible interests." Perhaps it was right to resist, he says, if this could have been done without aggravating Russia's feelings. Was it right for the Majles leaders "merely to give vent to their emotions"? He sees the rejection of the Ultimatum as belonging to a tradition of mystical martyrdom "in the new garb of political action."[478]

Indeed, a "tradition of mystical martyrdom" may have played some role in the deputies' decision to reject the Ultimatum, but neither that nor "stubbornness over a mere apology" nor giving vent to emotions fully accounts for the real anguish that Shuster saw in these people. Taqizadeh may not have known that, despite the Cabinet's acceptance of the first two demands in early November, Russian attacks on Tabriz had not abated, Russian troops had not been withdrawn from Persian soil but were continuing to move southward and, most importantly, acceptance of the two demands in early November had simply led to the November 26 Ultimatum with its much harsher demands and without a word of reproof from the British Foreign Office. Acceptance or rejection of the Ultimatum made absolutely no difference to what the Russians had done before or were about to do in the future.

The rejection of the Ultimatum did matter to Persia, however. Rather than placing it in a tradition of martyrdom played out in political action, Shuster noted, "…the Persian people gave to the world an exhibition of temperance, of moderation, of stern self-restraint, the like of which probably no other civilized country could show under similar trying circumstances." Then he adds, "No one who knew these representatives of a stricken race in those dark days could fail to love the Persian people, or to sympathize with their just aspirations."[479]

XIX

Making Angels Weep

"It is enough to make the angels weep to see all Shuster's machinery fall into incapable hands....I really liked the man."
—Sir George Barclay

The end came on December 22, when a select "Commission" of the Majles and the deposed Cabinet met together and agreed to submit to the Russian demands. The next day that message was delivered orally to Poklewski-Koziell. It wasn't until two days later, however, that the Persian government agreed to the final wording of the note, and in those two days, Vosuq ad-Dowla tried to persuade the Russian government to commit itself firmly to pulling the troops out of Persia as soon as Persia agreed to the demands. The Russians would not make that commitment. Nonetheless, the Persians yielded and signed the agreement accepting the Ultimatum in all three of its demands.

Since this "Commission" had not been legally elected, the decision to accept it was of questionable legitimacy, a matter which, at this point, had little significance. With that decision, the Majles ceased to exist. As for the Cabinet, "It is impossible to say," wrote Shuster, "just what...proportions of fear and cupidity [or both] decided the members of the deposed Cabinet to take the aliens' side against their country."[480] For a small pile of cash and the promise of a title that would be hereditary, he says, these seven were willing to sell out to the Russian government.

His judgment may be a bit harsh. A good part of the reason for their capitulation indeed was simple venality, but there may have been more to it than that. We honor patriots who are willing to sacrifice their own lives for their country. But what credit do we give those who are faced with decisions that could result in the massacre of scores, even hundreds of others? These men, unlike Shuster, had seen Liakhov's shelling of the Majles in 1909, and they were aware of the massacres in Tabriz, as well as atrocities committed on individual citizens throughout the Russian zone. And if they thought that survival, their own and that of many of their countrymen, outweighed personal heroism, perhaps they should not be blamed.

Nonetheless, there was a cravenness about the end. That same day, the deposed Cabinet, with the acquiescence of the Regent, Nasr al-Mulk, and with a demonstration of Bakhtiari tribesmen and gendarmes, expelled all the deputies and employees then within the Majles grounds. The gates were locked and barred, and the deputies were threatened with death if they tried to meet there or in any other location.[481] There would be no further convening of a Persian Majles until December 1914.

That afternoon, several of the Majles deputies came to Shuster's office. They came in tears, Shuster says, torn by whether they ought to kill the former ministers and the Bakhtiaris who had made the destruction of the government possible—or kill themselves. Shuster did hesitate, wondering whether he should try to save the lives of "notorious betrayers," but he ultimately recommended restraint. To engage in any type of killing would give credence to Russian and British claims that the Persians were incapable of maintaining order without their help.

The deputies took his advice, but in his own bitterness, Shuster wrote that Persia had become the helpless victim of "the wretched game of cards which a few European powers... still play with weaker nations as the stake, and the lives, honor and progress of whole races as the forfeit."[482]

Shuster's grief was also felt by Turin Boone, who had been in Persia less than two weeks. He wrote in his diary, "This unhappy land torn by internal strife and menaced from without...." Boone did not finish that sentence.[483]

Samsam, along with another Bakhtiari chief, Sardar-i Mutashem, who called himself "Minister of War" now began the process of turning their country over to the Russians. The city of Tehran was placed under *de facto* military control under a self-constituted body of seven men supported by a force of 2000 Bakhtiari tribesmen who had remained in Tehran following the defeat of Mohammad Ali in September.

Even Ephraim Khan, who had just sent a small force to Mazandaran, briefly lost heart and fell in with the plans of the so-called Cabinet. That alliance, however, collapsed when Ephraim Khan learned that the khans were plotting to disarm his men and take charge of policing Tehran themselves—with the assistance of the Cossack Brigade under the Russian Colonel Vadbolskii. Rumors fly fast in Tehran, and when news of this got out, the threat of serious rioting and bloodshed arose. So, the Bakhtiaris and Ephraim patched up their differences, and the latter resumed control of the city.[484]

Although the Cabinet informed the Russian government that it had dismissed Shuster on December 22, it did not officially notify Shuster of that until two days later. Prior to December 24, the Cabinet had, through various emissaries, proposed to Shuster that he should resign rather than be removed. As inducements, they offered him the Order of the Lion and Sun plus compensation and a formal testimonial for his services, the privilege of naming his successor, and a couple of other honorariums.[485] It would have made things easier for them if Shuster himself had taken matters out of their hands, accepted the inducements, and simply resigned.

Resignation, however, was not something Shuster could easily do. As far as he and especially the majority of the deputies in the Majles were concerned, it would have been a usurpation of the right of the Majles, his erstwhile employer, to decide on a question that was integral to the sovereignty of the country. His answer was that unless he could get some authentic (even though unofficial) expression from the deputies of the Majles that they freely willed his resignation, he would not and indeed, could not, resign.

Nonetheless, with the destruction of the Majles, Shuster and his staff effectively had no employer unless they chose to recognize the legality of the de facto Cabinet which they obviously were not inclined to do. As for the proffered inducements, he was not interested. Nonetheless, as of that date, Shuster had to regard his task as finished.[486] And with that, any reasonable hope of an independent constitutional government in Persia ended as well.

With the Majles now destroyed but having accepted the Ultimatum's stipulation that Shuster must go, the burden of just how to make that happen now fell to the deposed Cabinet. On Christmas Day, Shuster was presented with a letter in Persian which informed him that the "Commission" had decided to accept the Russian Ultimatum. The letter read, in part, "Seeing that the stipulations of the aforesaid ultimatum necessitate the recall of your honorable person from the service of the Government and the severance of your connection with matters financial…." The letter was signed by Samsam al-Saltaneh, Vosuq ad-Dowla, and the other five former Cabinet ministers.[487]

That afternoon, officers of his Treasury Gendarmerie called upon Shuster to pay their respects. Shuster reminded them that they were officials of a purely financial administration and thus should refrain from any acts or public "dissensions" of a political nature. Nonetheless, the false news immediately spread that he had called the Gendarmerie to arms in order to use them to restore the Majles.

Accordingly, the next day, on December 26, realizing that Tehran might well erupt into worse rioting and bloodshed, Shuster sent word that he would accept the dismissal as soon as he was informed of the individual to whom he was to transfer the official responsibilities of his office. He also required a resolution to the question of the status of his (now) fourteen American assistants, most of whom had arrived in November and early December.[488]

An idea was circulated to have Shuster named as Minister to replace Charles Russell. As Minister, Turin Boone thought, Shuster would still be a thorn in the side of Russia and within recognized diplomatic limits still would try to prevent her from increasing her control over Persian affairs. "Wouldn't that be a good joke on the Russians?" Boone wrote in his diary.[489] In any case, Shuster was completely uninterested in the post.

The government's acceptance of the Ultimatum had made no difference in Tabriz which was now surrounded by two batteries of artillery and filled with about 4000 Russian troops. Additional troops were expected from Julfa. The slaughter had already begun. On Christmas Eve, a message arrived from the acting governor at Tabriz that Russian troops there had begun a massacre of the inhabitants. Women, children and other non-combatants were being killed. Poklewski-Koziell immediately telegraphed an order to the general in Tabriz to stop the killing since "matters were being arranged in the capital." The general responded that he took his orders from the viceroy of the Caucasus at Tbilisi, not from the minister in Tehran.[490] The state-run Russian newspaper, *Novoe Vremya*, justified the slaughter on the grounds that "true humanity requires cruelty" and the entire population must be held responsible and punished for the acts of the feda'in.[491]

The killing would go on. On Sunday, December 31, Russian troops in Tabriz executed a prominent Muslim cleric along with twelve other Persian nationalists in retaliation for opposing the Russian invasion.[492] On New Year's Day, 1912, the tenth day of the holy season of Muharram, the Russian military governor hoisted Russian flags over the government buildings in Tabriz and hanged the chief mullah and two other clerics as well as five others who had been officials of the Government. Nor was the terror confined to Tabriz. In Rasht and Anzeli anyone suspected of being a Constitutionalist was in danger of being hanged or shot.[493] All this, despite the acceptance of the Ultimatum.

On January 7, 1912, Shuster relinquished charge of the Treasury where there was a standing credit to the government in money and grain of over 600,000 tomans, including excess Customs revenues. All of Persia's debts, including the expenses incurred during the campaign against Mohammad Ali Shah, had been paid.[494] He designated Frank Cairns who had served as his Director of Taxation as his successor in the post of Treasurer-General.

The Russian-backed Belgian agent, Joseph Mornard, however, had not forgiven the slight he had suffered at Shuster's hands in June. The day after Shuster's departure, Mornard was named by the Cabinet as Acting Treasurer-General. He had Russian support, but Sir George Barclay was disappointed with the appointment. In early December, he had written a long dispatch which concluded, "It is enough to make the angels weep to see all Shuster's machinery fall into incapable hands…the latter is nothing but a pigmy compared to Shuster." And, he added, "I really liked that man."[495]

Mornard immediately approached Cairns with an order from the Cabinet threatening the American finance officials with dismissal and punishment if they did not immediately turn over the Treasury offices.[496] He also accused the Shuster team of leaving a deficit of two million francs in various banks in Tehran. In addition to the healthy balance which Shuster had left in the Treasury, he had also been working for some weeks to provide an orderly transfer of the Treasury offices to the government. Before his departure, he handed the offices to Cairns who was then ready to transfer them to the Persian government. Thus, Mornard's peremptory order was simply a gratuitous insult. As the order was being read, Cairns and the other members of his staff simply walked out. Cairns then sent written protests to both the Russian and British legations who now openly controlled the actions of the Cabinet. The legations informed the Cabinet that its action had been improper. The matter was easily rectified with a second letter which suddenly inexplicably appeared, similar to the first but containing no offensive or threatening language.[497]

In view of the appearance of the second "real" letter from the Cabinet, Cairns took up the matter of the status and departure of the remaining Americans—a matter which now became quite vexing. When the Russians asked the Americans to stay and help the Belgians, meaning Mornard, take over the Treasury, the Americans agreed, provided there was an equitable adjustment of their own contract rights, that is, full payment for the entire three-year period of their contracts, plus travel expenses, although ten of them had barely arrived and were not at all anxious to remain in what Boone called "this miserable country."[498]

There now occurred an ironic, indeed shabby, confluence of American, Russian, and British interests. The Americans were anxious to get out of Persia, and the Russians were even more eager to see the last of them. Poklewski-Koziell gave part of the reason in a conversation with Frank Cairns. "It was a monumental error to bring Americans to this country," he said. "I know them—I know for what they stand—the conditions under which they live—freedom, liberty, equality and democracy and you can't make them 'fit' in this country."[499]

But it wasn't only American ideas that Poklewski-Koziell

was considering. With Americans still in service to Persia, Russia's own plans for, as Boone put it, "exploiting the country," made it willing to get rid of them whatever the financial cost. With Americans out of the way, Russia could, Boone supposed, "get back all it cost her to pay us off and more besides by reprehensible methods which we would not be there to check."[500]

The question was, who would pay the Americans? So anxious were the Russians to get rid of the Americans that they were willing to pay off the Americans for the full three-year contract. Boone himself would have been only too glad to accept only six months' pay and get out.[501]

The block to the American departure, however, oddly became the American Minister, Charles Russell, who refused to accept the collapse of the Shuster mission. And he had the support of members of the erstwhile Majles who were also reluctant to see the end of things. Several leaders of the Majles met with Russell on January 4 and confided that they were all anxious that the Americans remain. "We know you do things, work hard and are unselfish," they told Russell. "We want you to teach us to develop the resources of our country and educate the people."[502]

So anxious was Russell to keep the Americans in Persia that he delayed their payment and departure against the orders of the Secretary of State, Philander Knox.[503] The matter was eventually resolved and, except for Colonel J.N. Merrill, who at the request of the legations had decided to remain as an instructor to the Gendarmerie, the Americans were gone by the end of March.[504]

In Persia, there was bitterness, a lashing out at the government. And poetry. Poet-laureate Bahar from Mashhad wrote a long poem, condemning Nasr al-Mulk, the Regent, calling him a "Europe worshipper," "gutless," and "duplicitous" and accusing him of plotting with the Russians to bring Mohammad Ali back. That was foiled, he argued, by the heroes who fought and defeated the shah. And because Shuster, "that highly esteemed Consultant," had gone to work against him, Nasr al-Mulk had arranged for his dismissal:

> Traitors have no shame of their deed,
> May they go blind and blind in speed,
> Slaves and agents of Russia are they,
> From the general to the colonel indeed....[505]

In London, meanwhile, Lord Curzon forwarded a motion in Parliament to censure Grey for his policy in Persia. In the face of this and other mounting protests, Grey warned the Russian ambassador that the formal Russian occupation of northern Persia would trigger a "revision" of the Anglo-Russian Convention. In March 1912, the Persian Cabinet accepted an Anglo-Russian note, providing a loan of £200,000. Assuming that Russian troops would be withdrawn, the Cabinet stated that it would conform to the principles of the 1907 Convention.

Russian troops were still in Persia when World War I began three years later.

Frank Cairns
Director of Taxation, Shuster's assistant

XX

Khoda Hafez (Good-bye)

"I had been ambitious to serve the Persian people."
—Morgan Shuster

On the morning of Thursday, January 11, 1912, surrounded by a circle of "gloomy" American and Persian friends, Morgan Shuster, his wife, their two little daughters, and a governess left Atabak Park in a "powerful fifty-horsepower car" placed at their disposal by the Regent. Their trunks had gone ahead.[506]

The day before, the young shah had received Shuster in a private audience, thanked him for his services and promised to send him a framed portrait of himself.[507] Shuster had also received farewell notes from both Poklewski-Koziell and Barclay wishing him well on his journey. Poklewski-Koziell assured him that he would "always keep the most pleasant recollection of our personal acquaintance"[508] and Barclay hoped they would meet again "in happier and less constrained circumstances."[509]

It was a beautiful, sunny morning. The mountains behind Tehran were snow-covered "and there was life tonic in the air...." When the inhabitants of Tehran learned of his leaving, a "great crowd of them wished to come and say farewell," but Shuster had asked that no demonstration should be made, and the police had also notified the leaders of the different societies that no farewell gathering would be permitted.[510]

The companies of the Treasury gendarmes were drilling at the Bagh-e Shah barracks as his car passed by. "They were a body of men not to be despised," he reflected, "and had the organization been allowed to develop many of Persia's most serious problems would have been promptly solved."[511]

As they left the busy streets of the city behind and came into a quieter neighborhood, memories of the last eight months crowded in upon him and he reflected: "One cannot leave forever the scene of a frustrated ambition without a pang at the mere physical realization that it is all over. I had been ambitious to serve the Persian people."[512]

They reached Qazvin about 3:30 that afternoon. Russian troops thronged the city's streets. A couple of them picked up stones; but if they threw them, none hit the car. Beyond that, they experienced no other discourtesy on the trip.

Nature, however, showed less restraint. About fifteen miles beyond Qazvin, a severe snowstorm stopped their progress and forced them to spend the night in a little stone hut at a tiny road station called Buinak. The next morning, they found that the snow had completely blocked the mountain passes. The car was half covered by snow and it took two hours to thaw out the engine. They got underway about 10:30 but found the highest pass blocked by about four feet of snow. With the assistance of road gangs and the skill of their driver, they got through the pass and that evening reached Manjil, about sixty miles from Qazvin. "A pleasant run" of five hours brought them to Anzeli the next afternoon.

A Russian cruiser was in the harbor and the city itself lay under the control of a Russian consul. The next day, January 14, the Russian new year, the cruiser and several gunboats exchanged salutes, and at 5:30 in the afternoon the Shusters embarked on a Russian steamer, ironically named *Tehran*, headed for Baku. The Caspian coast slowly disappeared from view and with that, "The brief and disappointing chapter of American financial administration in that ancient land had been written."[513]

The Shusters stopped in London, where he was honored

at a dinner given by the London Persia Committee at the Savoy Hotel on January 29, 1912. In a lengthy speech, H.F.B. Lynch, the Committee chair, while criticizing the behavior of the Grey government regarding Persia, praised Shuster's work and pointed out the real reason for his dismissal. A "countryman" residing in Persia, had put it bluntly, he said: "Mr. Shuster's mission was doomed at its inception, seeing that a prosperous Persia would have brought about a weakened Russian control."[514]

As one might expect in Persia, the loss of Shuster evoked poetry. Arif of Qazvin wrote:

> Shame upon a home when the guest leaves the table unfed,
> Give him your life and do not let him leave,
> If Shuster goes from Iran, Iran will go with the wind.
> O' young people do not let Iran leave.
> You are life to a dead body!
> You are life to the whole world!
> You are an immense treasure!
> You are life eternal!
> God let you stay, God let you stay![515]

From his own government, Shuster received neither poetry nor a warm welcome. By siding with the Persian Constitutionalists, Shuster had, like Howard Baskerville, inserted the United States into the arena of international politics and diplomacy, thus ignoring the American policy of non-intervention.

As for the public, however, Shuster allowed Americans the luxury of wallowing in sympathy for the underdog while ignoring racial and social injustices on their own shores. *The Nation*, admitted that Shuster lacked tact and wondered if an older man more skilled in the arts of diplomacy might have held his place. Nonetheless, that journal also hailed him as a Parsifal who had served a gallant young nation in "the spirit in which an ambitious and clean-cut young American businessman goes about his work."[516] And admiration for Shuster was often coupled with scorn for the decadent powers of the Old World. With just a touch of moral superiority, *The Nation*, put it more harshly. Shuster had no alternative between acting as he did, the journal argued, "and sinking to the parasitic level of the typical European administrator in Persia, whose functions would seem to consist chiefly in drawing a fat pension and doing nothing."[517]

The Shuster episode, by itself, was soon forgotten, but the impact was permanent because it brought Persia to the political consciousness of the American public. For the first time, it was not missionaries who were the dominant consideration. Along with admiration for Shuster and his heroic, albeit doomed struggle on behalf of a nascent democracy, there was also sympathy for Persia. *The Nation* praised the "nucleus of brave and enlightened men animated by unselfish motives, backed by the best sentiment of the country." Then, not neglecting those who may have thwarted Shuster's work, the journal commented that even though there were men, such as the Sepahdar, of "more doubtful, or rather, more mixed attributes, there were also men who did good service for the constitutional cause without quite forgetting their personal interests."[518]

Immediately upon his return home, Shuster wrote *The Strangling of Persia*, detailing his work in Persia. He dedicated the work "To the Persian People.... In order to repay in some slight measure the debt of gratitude imposed on me through their confidence in my purposes toward them and by their unwavering belief...in my desire to serve them for the regeneration of their nation...." Although he was disappointed that he had been unable to finish the "intensely interesting" task for which he had gone to Persia, "such rancor or bitterness as I may have felt...has certainly disappeared."[519] Indeed, his dry wit still intact, he was able to see something of a silver lining in that Russia "unwittingly paid us the compliment of fearing that we would succeed in our task."[520] The book was published in 1912 by the Century Company which had been founded in 1870 and of which Shuster soon became the president. He would then lead the company into a merger with the Appleton publishing company in 1933 and then a further merger in 1947 with Crofts to create the Appleton-Century-Crofts firm. He died May 26, 1960, at the age of 83. Greenwood republished the *Strangling* in 1968, and Mage published it in 1987 and again in 2005.

Meanwhile in London, on February 12, 1912, the Persia Committee sent a proposal to the Foreign Office for direction of future policy on Persia. Among its recommendations was finding a *qualified* replacement for Shuster, which suggested an unequivocal vote of no-confidence in Mornard.[521] That same day, Grey received the Order of the Garter (the highest honor of knighthood) becoming the only foreign secretary since Palmerston to receive that honor.

In August 1911, Britain and Russia had jointly declared to the Persian Government that Mohammad Ali, by entering Persia in an attempt to regain the throne had forfeited all right to the pension of 100,000 tomans which he had been receiving under the 1909 Agreement. On February 18, 1912, however, the two Powers forced the Persian government to restore that pension and grant his followers amnesty.[522] The force that had upheld the Constitution and defended Tabriz was disbanded and, in its place, Persia was compelled to establish a small professional army. Grey accepted the "necessity" of a Russian army on Persian soil. Ultimately, nothing was left of Persian independence.

A month later, on March 18, 1912, the British and Russian legations presented the Persian government with a joint note announcing that the Banque d'Escompte and the

Imperial Bank would each advance the Persian government the sum of 100,000 tomans. The advance would be in rubles, amounting to 947,750 rubles. The interest on the loan would be 7%. The advance would be under the control of Mornard, the Treasurer-General, and it was understood that a "considerable amount" would be assigned to the organization of the government gendarmerie with the assistance of Swedish officers.

The end of all this brought disillusion, pessimism, and self-denigration in Persia and not just about politics but about Persia's very culture. One newspaper in 1913 blamed the failure of the Constitutional Revolution on Persians themselves. After removing tyranny, the paper claimed, Persia did not reach its destination because "we were ignorant, and ignorance finally did its job."[523]

But the pessimism was not at all justified. The two Majleses had established schools, a fairly free press, civil courts administering secular law, and at least recognition of the urgent need for internal changes in fiscal management. Albeit fleeting and at times disorganized, there had been enough unity and steadiness of purpose in support of constitutionalism to manage two coups and withstand an attempted countercoup. Most important, while ethnic and tribal divisions would continue to play a discordant role, the Constitutional Revolution had sketched out the image of a Persia that embraced its discrete parts.

And Shuster had played a crucial role in that development. He was criticized then, and has been since, for a variety of things: his tactlessness, his stubborn insistence on Stokes to head the Treasury Gendarmerie, his appointment of Lecoffre in the face of Russian opposition, his letter to the *Times*, his failure to pay sufficient homage to the "interests" of Britain and Russia or to the traditional prerogatives of Persia's own grandees. But it was precisely those very actions, those

Khoda Hafez (Good-bye)

"failures," that refusal to allow Persia's integrity to be sold, that put flesh on the bones of the Constitution.

Shuster was the servant of the Majles, not a single tribe or ethnic group. Article 2 of the Constitution reads, "The National Consultative assembly represents the whole of the people of Persia...." Shuster took that more seriously than perhaps many of the Persians in government did. He didn't ignore but transcended those different parts. Although that Constitution would be perverted, neglected, ignored, and finally rejected in 1979, by the time he left, Persia had been permanently transformed from a rickety empire belonging to a king into a nation belonging to its citizens. As the American journal, *The Nation*, put it, "The submission of Persia to Russia's demand for the dismissal of W. Morgan Shuster... closes an episode, but not an epoch." Although Persia had been beaten to her knees, *The Nation* argued, Shuster's "bold stand" had served three purposes: first, Russia and Britain had been forced out of their "jungle diplomacy" to an open avowal of their "unhallowed" motives; second, it had aroused the conscience of other nations to protest against "co-partnership" in robbery with Russia; and third, it had brought forth the resources of the Persian people to the point of "venturing battle with Russia's millions." The journal put the Shuster mission in a much larger context, however, in suggesting that "...the stirring of the subject races the world over is warrant for the belief that Mr. Shuster's fight for the preservation of the rights of an ancient people will have its results in the future."[524]

There was a fourth result of Shuster's and the Majles' "bold stand" that Turin Boone noticed just before he left Persia in February, 1912. At the American mission, he encountered several hundred boys, aged 11 to 30, studying English, arithmetic, botany, and rhetoric. He asked one boy, an eleven-year-old from Rasht how long he had studied English. For four months, was the boy's reply. And when Boone asked him why he studied English, the lad replied, "I study English because I want to be educated...for my country."[525] What Boone failed to appreciate was what the boy saw, that without the outreach to the West, as challenging as that might be, his country's progress would be hampered. And at times imperiled.

There is another darker view. That nascent devotion to Persia was something that Boone himself dismissed. Shortly after encountering that lad, Boone wrote,

> Not a native in all Persia with perhaps one or two exceptions unselfishly devoted to country's good—looking for own interests—not ready for Constitutional Government...don't work together for common good—masses densely ignorant—steeped in moral and political degeneracy—necessary conditions of a healthy national life missing."[526]

Boone had been in Persia for only about three months, so his pessimism may have been the result of seeing Persia at its most troubled. Yet Abraham Yeselson points out that the Persian patriots who had defied the Russian invaders to protect their American benefactor were "disillusioned and embittered" by the failure of the United States government to oppose Russia. For Persians, the United States appeared to be the chief friend among the world's powers, and Shuster had kindled the hope that the United States would help overthrow any power that threatened Persia. Ironically, in 1953, nearly mimicking the Russian support for Mohammad Ali, the United States would itself be complicit in the overthrow of the democratically elected government of Mohammad Mosaddegh and the installation of an unpopular monarch.

Two and a half years after Shuster's departure, the two

Khoda Hafez (Good-bye)

parties to the 1907 Convention would be embroiled in the bloodiest war in modern human history. Ancient dynasties, including Russia's Romanovs, would be overthrown as horrifying new weapons slaughtered an entire generation of young men not just on one continent but around the world, and the world order on which the Anglo-Russian Convention had been based collapsed in monstrous ashes. Sadly, old shibboleths had not. In the aftermath of the First World War, the Powers, enfeebled though they were, would still assume that they knew best how to manage things. Nonetheless, the "Great Game" was over. There had been no winners.

For five months between 1919 and 1920, as Britain's ambassador, Grey would be in the United States urging the Congress to join the League of Nations. By then, his eyesight was failing, impeding his favorite pastime, fly-fishing. There is no evidence that he tried to contact Shuster while he was in the United States. Nor, if Shuster had been aware of his presence, was he apparently eager to visit him.

XXI

Conclusion

"We wanted to maintain our pride and dignity, only that."

—Foreign Minister Javad Zarif, 2019

Beginning with the complicity of the American CIA in the overthrow of Mohammad Mosaddegh in 1953, there began to be a reprise of the Great Game of 1907. Germany was replaced by the Soviet Union as the bogey man against which a bulwark would have to be maintained, and that bulwark was, again, Iran. As Russia and Britain had supported Mohammad Ali in his attempt to recapture his throne in 1911, now the United States and its allies, worried about the spread of Soviet influence, supported the recovery of that throne by Mohammad Reza Pahlavi. Unlike that earlier attempt, however, the 1953 effort was complicated by Iran's valuable oil reserves.

While Americans may not have seen the similarity between their continued support of an increasingly unpopular regime under the shah, the Iranian people did. To many of them, the shah became an American puppet much as Mohammad Ali had been the stooge in 1911. Thus, when the shah was overthrown in 1979, in what should have been a surprise to no one, the Islamic Revolution turned against the United States. The capture of fifty-two American hostages embittered Americans, and the American support for Saddam Hussein in the decade-long Iran-Iraq War embittered Iranians. Since then, relations between Iran and the United States have grown increasingly bitter as one hostile event after another has occurred.

Conclusion

Does the Shuster story change that narrative? Should it change that narrative? In the larger sense, does his story even matter?

In an uncanny foreshadowing of the Majles' December 1 refusal to accept the second Russian Ultimatum with its terrible consequences, the Greek historian Thucydides, in his history of the Peloponnesian Wars, relates a dialogue between a delegation from Athens and the citizens of the island of Melos. The Athenians offer the Melians a choice between subjugation to themselves or simple destruction. To the argument the Melians offer that they have done nothing to injure Athens, that they have as much right to their liberty as Athens does and that justice is on their side, the Athenians retort that the gods, like men, rule wherever they can. Justice, they say, matters only between equals. Otherwise, the strong do what they can and the weak suffer what they must. Rather than surrender their freedom and dignity, the Melians refuse to surrender to Athens and, predictably, are destroyed. The men are murdered and the women and children sent into slavery in Athens. The lesson is unambiguous; the decision of a weaker power to resist the stronger on the basis of honor, or justice, or love of freedom is to court its own destruction.

Since Thucydides, Western political theorists such as Machiavelli, Richelieu, Hobbes, Talleyrand, Bismarck, and Henry Kissinger, have made the argument that diplomats and politicians should operate always on the side of what is practical. Since, as Hobbes put it, in a state of nature, there is always war of everyone against everyone, it would be practical to view politics in terms of power blocs, of weighing what is realistic and possible rather than conducting diplomacy on the basis of moral principles. What matters in diplomatic discussions comes down to who has the most weapons, the most battleships, or the largest economy since, as the Roman orator Cicero once declared, "Money is the sinews of war."

The ability to wage war is ultimately at the root of what has come to be known as realpolitik.

There is much to be said in favor of realpolitik. A cool, careful, and complete assessment of one's own economic and military strength, of geographic and topographical realities as against those of one's potential friends or foes often is of more benefit than trying to "make the world safe for democracy" or promoting "regime change" or "civilizing missions." The gallons of blood that have been shed in religious wars and crusades or in the name of one ideology or another give ample proof of the wisdom of knowing when to set aside such things. Machiavelli might have been right, after all, that it is better—and less bloody in the long run—if a prince or a government or a policy is feared rather than loved.

With that in mind, then, should Shuster not have played the game? Should he not have recognized—and acted on the recognition—that, as Grey had pointed out, the "independence and integrity of Persia" did not, in fact, exist? Was he wrong to keep insisting on the appointment of Major Stokes? Should he not have consulted Russia at least, and perhaps Britain, before tasking the Majles with giving him sole power over Persia's finances in the June 13 Law? Should he not have made the calls on the foreign embassies as soon as he arrived? Of all the failings Shuster was accused of, naivete was not among them. Should he not, then, have anticipated that his letter to the *Times,* while it might have gained applause from Persia's friends in a few British circles, would surely gain him nothing from Grey's government—where it mattered? And should he not have known that sending Lecoffre to Tabriz would provoke a reaction not only from the Russians but also from Vosuq ad-Dowla's family?

As far as Persia was concerned, from E.G. Browne he had to have been aware that real power in Persia did not rest with the Majles alone, that it was diffuse, spread out among tribal khans, the ulema, Qajar autocrats, bazaar merchants, and even village kadkhodas. One can rant all one wants about Qajar "corruption" or Bakhtiari venality or official dishonesty, but that, after all, was the reality. Shuster's principles, lofty as they were, placed him and the Majles directly in opposition not only to Russia and Britain but also to the way politics had been practiced by the Persians themselves for generations. His hands already tied and his mission already in shambles, should Shuster not have resigned rather than forcing the Majles to vote on the Ultimatum which included his dismissal on December 1? Was what Shuster and that small cadre of democrats in the Majles believed in and labored for and what some of them would die for worth the game? His stiff honesty and his passion for justice had won him no plaudits for his work in the Philippines. Could he not then have "toned down" that honesty just a little bit? Should he not have bent his principles just a bit more and possibly been able to accomplish more? Should he not, as his fellow American, Turin Boone, argued, have been willing to sacrifice some of his American "directness" in deference to "Oriental diplomacy"[527]—an assumption, of course, that diplomacy was somehow different in the East than it was in the West. Should he not have come to terms with "two powerful and presumably enlightened Christian nations [who] played fast and loose with truth, honor, decency and law…"?[528]

To all of these questions, the answer in Thucydidean terms, is "yes, of course." When one views the carnage in the wake of the destruction of the second Majles, it is hard to justify Shuster's stubborn honesty.

Shuster's refusal to compromise was more than mere stubbornness, however, nor was it indifference to that ethical challenge. Neither he nor those members of the Majles who came to him in tears wondering if they should commit suicide were unaware of the terrible cost their decision would have not only for themselves but also for thousands of Persians who were given no choice in their fates. But Shuster's loyalty to his employer, the Majles, also entailed a loyalty to its Constitution, a document, which like that of his own country, enshrined rights which Americans claim to be "inalienable," rights therefore, that simply cannot be compromised.

When power becomes an end in itself, or rather, when "power" is understood solely in terms of economic or military force or strategic alliances based on self-aggrandizement, we get into trouble. And we miss a startling truth. In the twentieth century, the victories that made the greatest difference in human affairs were won not by military or economic power but by what Mahatma Gandhi called "satyagraha," that is, moral force. It was that moral force, not the Russian Empire that Britain had spent so much sweat worrying about, that brought about the end of the British Raj in India. Wielded by Nelson Mandela in South Africa, simple moral force broke the back of generations of apartheid, and in the United States Martin Luther King's non-violent protests brought about the Civil Rights Act of 1964 ending legal segregation based on race.

All diplomacy, all politics whether local or international is, at the root, not about power but about justice. And justice assumes honesty and a decent respect for the rights all human beings cherish. Ironically, it was a Persian statesman who, in the eleventh century, provided a counter to the Thucydidean argument that the strong do what they can and the weak suffer that as best they can. Faced with rebellions, disorders of all kinds, and threats of invasion, the eleventh century Seljuk sultan, Alp Arslan, turned for advice to his trusted prime minister, Nizam al-Mulk. The response was Nizam al-Mulk's *Siyasat Nameh (Book of Government)* in which he advised the sultan to seek not to overpower his people but to treat each class with justice, with special regard for the poor. And he warned that where there was disregard for the Divine law that requires justice, there would be discord, anarchy, and bloodshed. In other words, whatever carnage might result from carrying out the commands of justice, violating those commands brings about even greater disasters.

A centerpiece of the world's three monotheisms—Islam, Judaism, and Christianity—as well as any number of other belief systems and philosophies is the command that embraces justice. To love one's neighbor. Since, presumably, it emanates from very high Authority, one might assume that it is not a mere suggestion. Nor is about flowers, valentines, and "have a nice day." It most certainly is not about political, social or economic enthusiasms such as communism or capitalism or populism, and it has even less to do with mere religious fervor or some vapid idealism. It is not interested in "good guys" and "bad guys" or labels or who did what to whom twenty or thirty or five or two years ago, or last month. It is not about winning so much as helping others win.

The command to love shouts down ignorance and slogans and facile solutions to complex problems. It cries and pleads and insists, first of all and most fundamentally, that we make the effort to know each other, that we engage in conversation—a lovely word the first syllable of which, "con" meaning "with"—assumes a willingness to enter a relationship based on mutual respect, a willingness to be changed rather than forcing change on another. A willingness to talk honestly, openly and charitably *with* rather than *at* one another has no downside. Nor is it really even about some feeble altruism. Rather, it's a matter of our survival as a civilized species without which we reduce ourselves to savagery.

Shuster warned about the danger of failing to see value in everyone, every nation regardless of size or consequence. A few years after he returned from Persia, in an article for the *Annals of the American Academy of Political and Social*

Science, Shuster wrote that he "wished to say a few words on the rights of small nations to independence" and then went on to write:

> ...there are a great many nations in this world, contributing to its welfare and civilization in a high degree, and making life both interesting and profitable for all of us, which could never by any reasonable probability become great powers. If these nations are to be wiped out, if they are to become subject peoples, merely because of their indisposition...or their inability... to become great military powers, the world will live in centuries more of strife.[529]

Iran's attempt to gain control of its own national destiny—efforts similar to those made by Shuster—was at the center of a discussion between Dr. Mohammad Javad Zarif, the Iranian Foreign Minister, and members of Code Pink, an organization dedicated to promoting peace and justice throughout the world, who visited Iran in February 2019. According to Jackie Spurlock, a former Peace Corps volunteer in Iran and a member of the delegation, Zarif told the group that "we are all representatives of a common bond among peoples. We are all one. One government getting security by making others insecure can never work." In describing the history of the last fifteen years, he said, "Our nuclear buildup [prior to 2015] was not to get a bomb, not even for nuclear energy. We just wanted to make the political point that you can't tell us what to do. We wanted to maintain our pride and dignity, only that. We do not want to be told 'you can do this or you cannot do that!' Our crime is we want to be independent."[530]

Since 1979, the United States has had very few people

fluent in Persian and with direct experience in Iran itself making policy about Iran. Yet, as the Code Pink delegation discovered, and as so many travelers to Iran are still discovering, there is a deep reservoir of good will between the two countries that can be the basis for enriching both.

Despite our moral cavities—and they are many and they are glaring—America has been more than its history. It has been an ideal. It has stood for something good. Our most powerful weapon is not now, nor has it ever been, our military arsenal nor our technology nor our wealth, but our ideals. Respect for the dignity of the individual regardless of color, creed, sex or background, our integrity, the keeping of a bond once made, the adherence to just laws, the right of folks to master their own affairs have been a beacon of hope to people around the globe. What Shuster and American missionaries before and after him, and Arthur Millspaugh two decades later, and Peace Corps volunteers in the 1960s and early 1970s left behind was a reservoir of good will based largely on those ideals.

Shuster's struggle and the struggle of that second Majles, a struggle like that of Gandhi, Mandela, King and so many other "losers," is a testament to the fact that, in human affairs, it is not, in the long run, who wins the dice throw, not who has the most and biggest guns or the largest economy or the wiliest diplomats, or whether or not a country is safe for investments. Freedom and dignity are neither Western nor Eastern nor do they belong to any particular religious, philosophical or ethnic group. They belong to the entire human family. If we assert that we are going to respect the "independence and integrity" of a person or a nation, it is in our best interest then to do just that…or not make the assertion at all.

As King declared in his *Letter from Birmingham Jail*, "right defeated is stronger than evil triumphant." A West Point cadet puts it slightly differently but with the same general meaning when he prays, "Endow us with a courage that is born of loyalty to all that is noble and worthy" and "make us choose the harder right instead of the easier wrong."

About fifteen years ago, another accountant, Roger Doost, reflecting on the Shuster mission, wrote, "...perhaps the so-called 'real world' should reconcile with the conduct and attitude of Morgan Shuster if the human race is to survive."[531] In other words, moral principle, knowing that we can be trusted to negotiate honestly, openly and fairly—that is the essence of realpolitik.

That is the "something worthwhile" that we can still leave behind.

That is why I have written this book.

Appendix

The text from Articles IV and VI of the will of Shu'a al Sultaneh:

IV. "A cette date, je possède à la Banque d'Escompte une somme de 18,000 Tomans au comptant, en compte courant, et je possède également une somme de près de 20,000 tomans à la Banque Imperiale, qui, à cause d'une certain différence, ne me l'a pas payée et qui retient injustement mon solde créditeur. Mes executeurs testamentaires tacheront évidemment à poursuivre cette affaire et à ne point laisser se perdre le droit de mes héritiers mineurs."

[As of this date, I hold, at the Banque d'Escompte, the sum of 18,000 tomans in the current account and I also hold the sum of about 20,000 tomans at the Imperial Bank which, because of a certain difference, has not been paid to me and unjustly holds my credit balance. The executors of my will obviously will attend to this matter and not allow the rights of my minor heirs to be lost.]

VI. "Mon unique dette, à cette date, consiste en une obligation de 46,000 tumans envers ma mère Nozhat-es-Saltana, sur laquelle obligation j'ai déjà payé 3000 Tumans. Il reste donc un solde de 43,000 tumans dont je suis redevable à ma mère d'après cette même obligation imprimée et rédigée de la main de Montakhab'd Dowla....

Outre cette dette due à ma mère, je ne dois plus rien absolument à personne à quelque titre que ce soit. Et si une obligaton venait à être exhibée par une personne quelconque, *elle doit être reconnue comme fausse et falsifiée.*

Je suis absolument quitte de toutes dettes outré celle relate ci-dessus."

[My only debt at this date consists of an obligation of 46,000 tomans to my mother Nozhat es-Saltana, on which obligation I have already paid 3000 tomans. There remains on this a balance 43,000 tomans for which I am indebted to my mother according to this same obligation, printed and written by the hand of Montakhab'd Dowla....

Aside from this debt due to my mother I owe absolutely nothing to anyone. And if an obligation comes to be shown by any person, *it must be recognized as totally false.*

I am absolutely free of any debts other than that related here.]

From W. Morgan Shuster, *The Strangling of Persia* (New York: Greenwood, 1968), 152.

Glossary

anjeman - society or association

arbab - landlord

bast - sanctuary

bazaar – the market place; the merchant class

chador - full-length covering worn by women largely in cities rather than in tribes. It covers the head and falls to the ankles and is held in front by the hands.

dolat - the government

feda'i - literally, a faithful one. A person who is willing to sacrifice his life for something or someone. This should not be confused with the suicide bombers of the early twenty-first century. A feda'i will sacrifice his own life but not willingly take the lives of innocent civilians.

ghalian - water pipe (hookah)

kadkhoda - village headman

kafir - an infidel; a non-Muslim

ketabche - The little notebook kept by pishkars in which tax notations were kept.

luti - a hired thug, ruffian

maidan - a public square in a Persian city or village. Depending on the size of the city, besides a central maidan, there are often a number of smaller ones as well.

Majles - literally, place of sitting; Parliament

maliat - taxes on land

mellat - the people or nation

mojtahed - senior cleric

mostafi - One of eight senior tax overseers in the central treasury office responsible for revenue collection from two or more province.

pishkar - collector of local taxes

Safavid - dynasty that ruled Persia from 1501-1736

sardar - a senior military official roughly equivalent to a general

Shariah - Islamic law

sholugh - disturbance; noisy gathering

toman - unit of Persian currency

ulema – upper level of the Shi'ite clergy

vaghf - endowment to a religious institution in either money or property to be used for charitable purposes

vatan - homeland

Notes

Chapter I

1.- Abbas Amanat, *Iran: A Modern History* (New Haven: Yale University Press, 2017), 213.

2.- Although Queen Elizabeth had been aware of the Sherley trip and had not disapproved of it, this was not a diplomatic mission.

3.- Another count has 260 sons by only 158 wives. See Michael Axworthy, *History of Iran, Empire of the Mind* (New York: Basic Books, 2008), 178. Either somebody stopped counting or stopped caring. Or both.

Chapter II

4.- Lord George Curzon, *Persia and the Persian Question*, 2 vols. (London: Longmans, 1892), I, 433.

5.- About mid-century, the toman was worth roughly ten English shillings sterling. Lady Mary Leonora Woulfe Sheil, *Glimpses of Life and Manners in Persia* (London: John Murray, 1856), 388.

6.- The Twelvers believe that, following the death of the Eleventh Imam, (the dome of whose shrine in Samarra, Iraq, was blown up by extremists in 2006), his only son and heir was hidden or "occluded" in order to save his life. The heir, the Twelfth or Hidden Imam, will return at the right time, presumably in a time of crisis, to bring about the rule of God on earth.

7.- Curzon, *Persia and the Persian Question*, I, 441.

8.- Sheil, *Glimpses*, 393.

9.- Ibid.

10.- In 1901, a British-born Australian, William d'Arcy, secured oil rights to the entire country except for the five northern provinces for a period of sixty years. In return, the shah would receive 16% of the revenues. Drilling did not actually begin, however, until 1908.

11.- Ibid., 383. Lady Mary apparently missed the similarity between Persian practice and the contemporary custom in Great Britain of purchasing or inheriting military rank.

12.- W. Morgan Shuster, *The Strangling of Persia* (New York: Greenwood, 1968), xxxiii.

13.- The notation system in the ketabches was something called *siyaq*, which literally means 'sequence' or 'flow.' The figures were in an abbreviated Arabic notation derived from the Arabic names for the numerals. See Peter Avery, *Modern Iran* (New York and Washington: Frederick A. Praeger, 1965), 149.

14.- Shuster, *Strangling*, 287. Another view of the mostafis comes from Peter Avery, who finds them "by and large incorruptible" if only from the risk of punishment if the revenues were not returned to the government. According to him, "The failure of revenues to reach the government in amounts proportionate to expenditure requirements was not so much due to malpractices on the mostafis' part as to revision of assessments and the abuses of powerful notables who...generally compounded with the government, often over the mostafis' heads, for a sum in settlement of taxes and much less than what was due...." See Avery, *Modern Iran*, 149.

15.- Edward Stack, *Six Months in Persia*, 2 vols. (New York: G.P. Putnam's Sons, 1882), II, 256, 281.

16.- Arthur Millspaugh, *Americans in Persia* (Washington, D.C: Brookings Institution, 1946), 11.

17.- James Bassett, *Persia. The Land of the Imams* (New York: Scribner's, 1886), chs. 4-7.

18.- For the text and translation into English, see http://movarekhan.com/blog/agha_mohammad_khan_qajar_advice/. There is a sad irony in this advice in that, arguably, one of the most enlightened treatises on government ever written, the *Siyasat-Nameh* (*Book of Government*), came from the pen of a Persian statesman, Nizam-al Mulk, in the eleventh century. As the vizier to the Seljuk sultan, Alp Arslan, he emphasized the need for justice in governing his realm. He recognized the existence of classes and urged the sultan to give each class its rightful due but that included an insistence on protecting the poor.

19.- Avery, *Modern Iran*, 81.

20.- The story of Persia's favorite beverage, tea, almost deserves a chapter of its own. Tea had long been imported into Persia from India. But in 1898, the Persian consul in India, Mohammad Mirza, Kashef al-Saltaneh, knowing that the British authorities would never allow him to learn the secrets of tea production, disguised himself as a French planter in order to work in the tea plantations and factories of northern India. Then, covered by his diplomatic immunity, he smuggled about 3000 saplings out of India and brought them to the province of Gilan, where the climate and quality of the soil resembled that of northeastern India. The result literally revolutionized the agricultural economies of Gilan and the neighboring province of Mazandaran. Despite being a direct descendant of Fath Ali Shah, Kashef al-Saltaneh vigorously supported the Constitutional Revolution. His mausoleum and a tea museum are located in the city of Lahijan, the heart of Gilan's tea production.

21.- Robert McDaniel, *The Shuster Mission and the Persian Constitutional Revolution* (Minneapolis: Bibliotheca Islamica, 1974), 29.

22.- Michael Axworthy, *A History of Iran. Empire of the Mind* (New York: Basic Books, 2008) 194.

23.- McDaniel, *The Shuster Mission*, 33.

24.- Ibid., 18.

25.- Homa Katouzian, *Iran. Politics, History and Literature* (New York: Routledge, 2013), 77.

26.- A superb treatment of Persian nationalism published on the eve of the 1979 Revolution is Richard Cottam's *Nationalism in Iran* (Pittsburgh: University of Pennsylvania Press, 1979).

27.- See A. Maurice Low, *American People. A Study in National Psychology*, 2 vols. (Boston and New York: Houghton Mifflin, 1911).

28.- Katouzian, ibid.

29.- The name derives from Shiat Ali, the Party of Ali.

30.- Stack, *Six Months in Persia*, 291.

Chapter III

31.- Lady Mary Sheil, *Glimpses of Life and Manners in Persia* (London: John Murray, 1856), 141. Sir Justin Sheil served in that post from 1849-1852.

32.- Ibid., 389-90. Lady Mary notes that her figures are derived from "an authentic source, as authentic, at least, as a Persian authority can be considered...."

33.- Ibid., 393.

34.- Initiated in 1839 as a program of reform and modernization, the Tanzimat (1839-1876) had aimed at a number of reforms including the establishment of an academy of sciences and a postal system as well as reforms in the army and in the civil and criminal code.

35.- Abbas Amanat, ed., *Taj al-Saltana, Crowning Anguish, Memoirs of a Persian Princess from the Harem to Modernity. 1884-1914* (Washington, D.C: Mage Publishers, 1993), 124.

36.- The crime of this woman was her argument for equal rights for women.

37.- Peter Avery, *Modern Iran* (New York and Washington: Frederick A. Praeger, 1965), 114.

38.- Arthur Millspaugh, *Americans in Persia* (Washington, D.C:, The Brookings Institute, 1946), 13.

39.- Abbas Amanat, *Pivot of the Universe* (Berkeley, Los Angeles: University of California Press, 1997), 17ff.

40.- Cited in Robert McDaniel, *The Shuster Mission and the Persian Constitutional Revolution* (Minneapolis: Bibliotheca Islamica, 1974), 22n.

41.- Michael Axworthy, *A History of Iran* (New York: Basic Books, 2008), 194.

42.- Amanat, *Crowning Anguish*, 32.

43.- Edward Stack, *Six Months in Persia*, 2 vols. (New York: G.P. Putnam's Sons, 1882), II, 284. The *qanats* are subterranean irrigation canals.

44.- Edward G. Browne, *Year Amongst the Persians*, 3rd ed. (London: Adam and Charles Black, 1950), 99. For a fictionalized account of how ordinary Persians suffered from the concessions, see Rabeah Ghaffari, *To Keep the Sun Alive* (New York: Catapult, 2019), 142-152.

45.- See Rogers Platt Churchill, *The Anglo-Russian Convention of 1907* (Cedar Rapids, IA: The Torch Press, 1939), 215.

46.- Anis ad-Dowla's protest against the Concession had less to do with patriotism, however, than with shaming the Atabak who had accepted it and whom she loathed. See Firuz Kazemzadeh, *Russia and Britain in Persia, 1864-1914* (New Haven and London: Yale University Press, 1968), 112-13, 117. The strong influence of Anis ad-Dowla as well as other members of the harem on the Court is covered by Abbas Amanat in his Introduction to *Crowning Anguish*.

47.- Hamideh Sedghi, *Women and Politics in Iran. Veiling, Unveiling, and Reveiling* (New York: Cambridge University Press, 2007), 41.

48.- Avery, *Modern Iran*, 102.

49. E.G. Browne, *The Persian Revolution of 1905-1909* (Cambridge: University Press, 1910), 57.

50.- Ibid.

51.- Browne, *Year Amongst the Persians*, 99.

52.- Amanat, *Crowning Anguish*, 127.

Chapter IV

53.- Abbas Amanat, ed., *Taj al-Saltana, Crowning Anguish. Memoirs of a Persian Princess from the Harem to Modernity. 1884-1914* (Washington, D.C., Mage Publishers, 1993), 223.

54.- This is the concession that gave the Bakhtiari khans the opportunity to negotiate a separate deal in 1907 with what became the Anglo-Persian Oil Company in which the khans agreed to provide protection in return for 5% of the profits for 75 years. See Chapter 1, n.

55.- Amanat, *Crowning Anguish*, 264.

56.- Co-education had been established in the schools by Christian missionaries.

57.- Hamid Naficy, *A Social History of Iranian Cinema*, 4 vols. (Durham, NC: Duke University Press, 2011), I, 40.

58.- His bill from a Paris hotel for a single day, September 17, 1902, was £240. That did not include other purchases and outside expenses. See Edward G. Browne, *The Persian Revolution of 1905-1909* (Cambridge: At the University Press, 1910), 105.

59.- Nazeer Ahmed, "The Constitutional Revolution in Persia-1906" in *Encyclopedia of Islamic History*, 3.

60.- Browne, *Persian Revolution*, 112.

61.- Amanat, *Crowning Anguish*, 319.

62.- Browne, *Persian Revolution*, 112.

63.- The physical pain of being beaten on the soles of the feet, though excruciating, was less perhaps than the humiliation of not only having one's feet bared in public during the caning but by the inability to cover them in the aftermath.

64.- Browne, ibid., 112.

65.- Cf. Chapter 16.

66.- Mangol Bayat-Philipp, "Women and Revolution in Iran" in *Women in the Muslim World*, Lois Beck and Nikki Keddie, eds. (Cambridge, MA: Harvard University Press, 1978), 298.

67.- W. Morgan Shuster, *Strangling of Persia* (New York: Greenwood, 1968), 194.

68.- Ibid., 191-92.

69.- Thousands of women attempted to join and were prevented from doing so by British authorities. See Mangol Bayat-Philipp, "Women and Revolution," ibid.

70.- Delegates were required to possess property valued at no less than £200 and, interestingly, were required to be able to speak Persian. See the "Electoral Law of September 9, 1906, Article 4" in Browne, *Persian Revolution*, 355-6.

71.- According to Nikki Keddie, as late as the end of the twentieth century, slightly over 50% of the population had Persian as their first language, although, as she points out, Persian has long been the cultural language of the area. See Nikki Keddie, *Qajar Iran and the Rise of Reza Khan, 1796-1925* (Costa Meza, CA: Mazda Publishers, 1999), 5.

72.- It might be worth recalling that when America's own Founding Fathers met in 1786 to draft the Constitution of the United States, they had faced almost none of these barriers. And even at that, freed from any superior outside force unlike that facing Persia, the cohesiveness of the American Republic was not at all a foregone conclusion as the Civil War eighty-seven years later proved.

73.- Fundamental Laws of December 30, 1906, Article 2. Cited in Shuster, *Strangling*, 337.

74.- Supplementary Fundamental Laws of October 7, 1907, Article 30. Ibid., 349.

75.- Article 8. Ibid., 346.

76.- The earlier alliance of women's groups with the ulema suffered a rupture when, under the influence of the clergy, the Constitution denied women either a vote or a place in the government. Despite the often heroic role they played in support of the Revolution, in a listing of eight categories of people excluded from participation in voting or holding office, women were listed first, placing them ahead of murderers and thieves who were listed in the next to last category for exclusion. See Browne, *Persian Revolution*, Article 3, 356. Nonetheless, they continued to support the Revolution. Many sold their jewelry to contribute capital for establishing the first National Bank of Iran. See, e.g., Sima Bahar, "A Historical Background to the Women's Movement in Iran" in *Women of Iran. The Conflict with Fundamentalist Islam*, ed. Farah Azari (London: Ithaca Press, 1983), 171.

77.- Articles 1 and 2, Supplementary Fundamental Laws, Shuster, *Strangling*, 345.

78.- A Jewish representative actually was seated in the Majles but withdrew when he encountered anti-Semitism from other members. The Jews then chose a leading member of the clergy who was one of the leaders of the Constitutionalist movement, Ayatollah Abdullah Behbehani, to represent them. See Michael Axworthy, *A History of Iran* (New York: Basic Books, 2008), 204.

79.- Fundamental Laws, December 30, 1906, Article 23. Cited in Shuster, *Strangling*, 340.

80.- Shuster, *Strangling*, 240-41.

81.- Cited in Browne, *Persian Revolution*, 123.

Chapter V

82.- Edward G. Browne, *The Persian Revolution of 1905-1909* (Cambridge: University Press, 1910), xi.

83.- Charles Chenevix Trench, *The Road to Khartoum. A Life of General Charles Gordon* (New York: Carroll & Graf Publishers, Inc.,1978), 108.

84.- The fight was over control of Manchuria and Korea.

85.- Harold Nicolson, *Portrait of a Diplomatist* (Boston and New York: Houghton, Mifflin Company,1930), xii.

86.- Ibid., 45.

87.- Ibid., 49.

88.- Cited in ibid., 183.

89.- The Convention was an integral part of the Triple Entente that included France along with Russia and Great Britain.

90.- Sir Edward Grey, *Twenty-five Years. 1892-1916* (New York: Frederick A. Stokes Company, 1925), I, 161.

91.- Ibid.

92.- Ibid., 148.

93.- Ibid., 162.

94.- Nicolson, *Portrait*, 184.

95.- George N. Curzon, *Persia and the Persian Question*, 2 vols. (London: Longmans, Green and Co., 1892), II, 593-97.

96.- Cited in Nicolson, *Portrait*, 176.

97.- Curzon, *Persia and the Persian Question*, II, 605-606.

98.- Cited in Browne, *Persian Revolution*, 173.

99.- Sergei I. Witte, *The Memoirs of Count Witte* (New York: H. Fertig, 1967), 433-34.

100.- Browne, *Persian Revolution*, 186-7. The article was part of a four-part series published in the Persian newspaper in Calcutta, the *Hablu'l-Matin*, in September 1907.

101.- Cited in Firuz Kazemzadeh, *Russia and Britain in Persia, 1864-1914* (New Haven and London: Yale University Press, 1968), 350.

102.- Ibid., 494-95.

103.- See the entire communique in Browne, *Persian Revolution*, 190-92.

104.- Michael Axworthy, *A History of Iran. Empire of the Mind* (New York: Basic Books, 2008), 195.

105.- Cited by W. Morgan Shuster, *Diary*, November 16. This was part of a speech Curzon gave at the Inaugural Banquet of the London Persia Society on November 15.

106.- W. Morgan Shuster, *Strangling of Persia* (New York: Greenwood, 1968), xxi.

Chapter VI

107.- Firuz Kazemzadeh, *Russia and Britain in Persia, 1864-1914. A Study in Imperialism* (New Haven and London, 1968), 189, citing V.A. Kosgovskii, *Iz tegeranskogo dnevnika polkovnika* V.A. Kosogovskogo (Moscow, 1960), 133.

108.- Articles 18 and 25, Fundamental Law, December 30, 1906, in Shuster, *Strangling*, 340.

109.- Edward G. Browne, *Persian Revolution of 1905-09* (Cambridge: University Press, 1910), 13.

110.- Shuster, *Strangling*, 22.

111.- Browne, *Persian Revolution*, 139-40.

112.- Shuster, *Strangling*, xxiii.

113.- Browne, *Persian Revolution*, 162.

114.- Ibid., xxxiv.

115.- Ibid., xxxv.

116.- *Manchester Guardian*, Sept.10, 1980, 7e cited in Mansour Bonakdarian, *Britain and the Iranian Constitutional Revolution of 1906-1911* (Syracuse: Syracuse University Press), 123.

117.- Shuster, *Strangling*, xl.

118.- Cf. Chapter 16.

119.- Browne, *Persian Revolution*, 269.

120.- For this particular episode see e.g., Mangol Bayat-Philipp, "Feminism and Nationalist Politics in Iran, 1905-1911" in *Women in the Muslim World*, ed. Lois Beck and Nikki Keddie, (Cambridge, MA: Harvard University Press, 1978) as well as Mansoureh Ettehadieh, "The Origins and Development of the Women's Movement in Iran, 1906-41" in *Women in Iran from 1800 to the Islamic Republic*, ed. Lois Beck and Guity Nashat, (Urbana and Chicago: University of Illinois Press, 2004).

121.- See, e.g.,Michael Zirinsky "American Presbyterian Missionaries at Urmia During the Great War" at:www.iranchamber.com/religions/articles/american-presbyterian-missionaires-zirinsky.pdf, 2, footnote.

122.- Ahmad Mansoori, *American Missionaries in Iran. 1834-1934* (Ph. D. diss., Ball State University, 1985), 55-56.

123.- Abraham Yeselson, *United States-Persian Diplomatic relations, 1883-1921* (New Brunswick, NJ: Rutgers University Press, 1956), 98. In reluctant compliance with the American policy of strict non-intervention, Doty had urged Baskerville to stop training the group and withdraw his support for the Nationalist cause. When Baskerville refused, arguing that he was not taking up arms against any "lawful government" but simply trying to help a distressed people defend themselves against "lawless rapine and murder," Doty threatened to withdraw his passport. Ibid., 99.

124.- Shuster, *Strangling*, xli.

125.- He would not be crowned until July 1914. According to Shuster, the lad was "surrounded wherever he went by a large and expensive coterie of parasitic gentlemen who styled themselves members of His Majesty's court." Ibid., 47.

126.- Kazemzadeh, *Russia and Britain in Persia*, 548.

127.- Shuster, *Strangling*, 231.

128.- Kazemzadeh, *Russia and Britain in Persia*, 549.

129.- Ibid., 555-6.

130.- Ibid.,560, citing telegram Grey to O'Beirne, November 18, 1910.

131.- Ibid., 576.

132.- Edward G. Browne, *Letters from Tabriz. The Russian Suppression of the Iranian Constitutional Movement*, ed. Hasan Javadi (Washington, D.C. Mage Publishers, 2008), 17-18.

133.- Poklewski-Koziell had previously served as a former secretary at the Russian embassy in London.

134.- Kazemzadeh, *Russia and Britain in Persia*, 602, citing a telegram from the Minister of Foreign Affairs to the Minister in Tehran, December 29, 1910/January 11, 1910; S.D.D., 3, 310.

135.- Robert McDaniel, *The Shuster Mission and the Persian Constitutional Revolution* (Minneapolis: Bibliotheca Islamica, 1974), 108.

136.- Browne, *Letters from Tabriz*, 22.

137.- Shuster, *Strangling*, lv.

138.- Browne, *Letters*, 23.

139.- Homa Katouzian, *State and Society in Iran* (London, New York: I.B. Tauris, 2000), 60.

Chapter VII

140.- Arthur Millspaugh, *The American Task in Persia* (London: T. Werner Laurie Ltd., 1925), 12.

141.- Edward Grey, *Twenty-five Years. 1892-1916* (New York: Frederick A. Stokes Company, 1925), I, 163.

142.- Robert McDaniel, *Shuster Mission and the Persian Constitutional Revolution* (Minneapolis: Bibliotheca Islamica, 1974), 113.

143.- For the work of the missionaries, see e.g., Ahmad Mansoori, *American Missionaries in Iran. 1834-1934* (Ph. D. diss., Ball State University, 1985).

144.- Arthur Millspaugh, *Americans in Persia* (Washington, D.C., The Brookings Institution, 1946), 17.

145.- W. Morgan Shuster, *Diary* (Washington, D.C: Library of Congress), entry of May 18, 1911.

146.- Abraham Yeselson, *United States-Persian Diplomatic Relations, 1813-1921* (New Brunswick, NJ: Rutgers University Press, 1956), 39-41.

147.- W. Morgan Shuster, *Strangling of Persia* (New York: Greenwood, 1968), 3.

148.- Yeselson, *United States-Persian Diplomatic Relations*, 111.

149.- Possibly the firm of Carlisle and Johnson where he had worked before going to Cuba.

150.- Ibid., 112.

151.- McDaniel, *Shuster Mission*, 113 and 115, ff.

152.- Shuster, *Strangling*, 4.

153.- Millspaugh, *Americans in Persia*, 18.

154.- Grey, *Twenty-five Years*, 163.

155.- Jennifer Siegal, *Endgame. Britain, Russia and the Final Struggle for Central Asia* (London and New York: I.B. Tauris, 2002), 102.

156.- Renamed George Washington University in 1904.

157.- See *Columbian* 1898 (yearbook) (Washington, D.C.: George Washington University Archives), 69.

158.- Edgar G. Bellairs [Charles Ballentine] *As It Is in the Philippines* (New York: Lewis, Scribner & Co., 1902) 56.

159.- "Honors for Washington Boy" in *Washington Post* (1877-1922), July 26, 1901, 2.

160.- His meticulous attention to detail can be seen, for instance, in W. Morgan Shuster, Third and Fourth Reports of the Collector of Customs for the Philippine Islands. (Manila: Bureau of Public Printing), September 1, 1905.

161.- Bellairs, *As It Is*, Ibid.

162.- Cited in Firuz Kazemzadeh, *Russia and Britain in Persia, 1864-1914* (New Haven and London: Yale University Press, 1968), 584.

163.- Shuster, *Strangling*, 41.

164.- Ibid., 251. Ruritania is the fictional country that provides the setting for three novels by Anthony Hope, the most famous one being *The Prisoner of Zenda*. The fly-fishing allusion was not entirely sarcastic. That really was Grey's favorite pastime and he really had written a treatise on the sport, published in 1899.

165.- Ibid., 32.

166.- Ibid., 4.

167.- Letter to Sir George Barclay in ibid., 374. His knowledge of Persian culture remained limited. For instance, in a footnote, he defines "sayyid" as a "holy man" when, in fact, the term refers to a descendant of the Prophet Mohammad. Ibid., 296.

168.- He was also fluent in Spanish and German. "Honors for Washington Boy", *Washington Post*, (July 26, 1901), 2.

169.- Shuster, *Strangling*, 272.

170.- Edward G. Browne, *The Persian Revolution of 1905-1909* (Cambridge: University Press, 1910), xv. Browne ascribes the more negative characteristics primarily to members of the Persian court.

171.- Ibid., xx.

172.- Ibid., xv.

173.- Edward G. Browne, *A Year Amongst the Persians. Impressions as to the*

Life, Character, & Thought of the People of Persia. 3rd ed. (Cambridge: University Press, 1950), xv.

174.- Shuster's term in *Strangling*, 28.

175.- Browne, *Persian Revolution*, 261.

176.- McDaniel, *Shuster Mission*, 78-9.

177.- Shuster, *Strangling*, 28. The emphasis is Bizot's.

178.- Ibid., 272.

179.- Kazemzadeh, *Russia and Britain*, 576.

180.- Ibid., 574.

181.- Shuster, *Strangling*, 4.

182.- Ibid., 6.

Chapter VIII

183.- Mrs. Shuster would later be described as a "delightful woman from Kentucky – you all – sweet personality." See Turin Boone, *Persian Diary*, unpublished, 2.

184.- W. Morgan Shuster, *Strangling of Persia* (New York: Greenwood Press, 1968), 12.

185.- Shuster, *Diary*, May 15. The leg of the journey by carriage was from the little hamlet of Pir Bazaar (Old Bazaar) to Rasht. It took an hour and a half to go three miles.

186.- Boone, *Persian Diary*, 50.

187.- Shuster, *Strangling*, 10.

188.- He does admit that Persia is an "attractive and comfortable place to live" with an "agreeable climate and clear, dry and bracing weather." Nonetheless, the omissions of his physical surroundings are startling, and repeated in Tehran where he says relatively little of the city's architecture, bazaars, palaces, or gardens except to note that every house has a garden of flowers, fruits, and fountains. (Ibid., lx) On the other hand, the omissions might have been understandable. Fifteen years later, Vita Sackville-West, who, although delighted with Persia in general, found its capital "a squalid city of bad roads, rubbish-heaps, and pariah dogs; a few pretentious buildings, and mean houses on the verge of collapse." See Vita Sackville-West, *Passenger to Tehran* (New York: Moyer Bell, 1990), 77.

189.- Shuster, *Strangling*, 12.

190.- There were twelve gates, three at each of the four corners of the wall that then surrounded the city.

191.- Shuster, *Strangling*, 11.

192.- Ibid., 15. In the long *Diary* entry for May 15, and in the manner of a most meticulous accountant, Shuster lists the staff at Atabak which numbered fourteen as well as the monthly salary of each member. The head cook received the highest at twenty tomans a month and the lowest at four tomans went to two kitchen boys. Two soldiers were also stationed at the gate to the complex.

193.- Shuster, *Strangling*, 12.

194.- Ibid., 16.

195.- Ibid., 269.

196.- Ibid., 37.

197.- Ibid., 37, 54.

198.- Ibid., 37.

199.- Ibid., 27.

200.- Ibid., 30.

201.- Ibid.

202.- Ibid., 33. Barclay would serve as the British minister to Tehran from 1908-1912. Poklewski-Koziell served as Russia's envoy from 1909-1913.

203.- Ibid., 31.

204.- Ibid., 32-3. The French minister was also in the tent "but either missed his cue" to meet Shuster, or, for one reason or another, changed his mind. During his entire stay in Tehran, Shuster never did meet the man.

205.- Ibid., 118.

206.- Ibid., 35.

207.- Ibid., 15.

208.- Ibid., 16. Shuster would change his assessment of Nasr al-Mulk and find him a "most unfortunate choice" for Regent. He was, Shuster later decided, "a profound egoist [who] could look at no question except in its bearing upon him and his dignity." Ibid., 239.

209.- Ibid.,19.

210.- Ibid.

211.- Ibid., 62. A photo of Amir Azam and his personal staff in Shuster's *Strangling of Persia* shows a man of truly abundant girth and a "personal staff" numbering well over fifty.

212.- Ibid., 19.

213.- Ibid., 242.

214.- Ibid., 36.

215.- Ibid., 240-41.

216.- Ibid., 21. In a footnote, Shuster notes that Baha'is were greatly disliked and up to modern times cruelly persecuted but "now tolerated, and include many of the most enlightened and patriotic Persians." He does not say whether any of the Atabak staff actually were Baha'is.

217.- Ibid., 22.

Chapter IX

218.- W. Morgan Shuster, *Strangling of Persia* (New York: Greenwood, 1968), 21. It is unclear whether the emphasis is Shuster's or Lecoffre's.

219.- Ibid., 41.

220.- Ibid., 316-17.

221.- At that time, the toman was worth about 90 cents, American. See ibid., 289ff.

222.- Ibid., 303.

223.- Ibid., 289-90.

224.- Ibid., 38.

225.- Ibid., 308.

226.- Ibid., 20.

227.- Ibid., 303.

228.- Ibid., 49.

229.- "Report of the Parliamentary Finance Regulations Commission" in ibid., 356-58.

230.- Shuster, Diary, June 8, 9, and 15.

231.- Ibid., June 13, Only two or three members opposed the bill.

232.- Peter Avery, *Modern Iran* (New York and Washington, D.C: Frederick A. Praeger, 1965), 154.

233.- Shuster, *Strangling.*, 297.

234.- Ibid., 282.

235.- Ibid., 68.

Chapter X

236.- W. Morgan Shuster, *Strangling of Persia* (New York: Greenwood, 1968), 297.

237.- Ibid., 61.

238.- Shuster, *Diary*, June 3.

239.- Ibid., 295.

240.- Ibid., 296.

241.- Ibid., 20.

242.- Ibid., 55.

243.- Ibid., 304.

244.- Ibid., 42.

245.- E.G. Browne, *The Persian Revolution of 1905-09* (Cambridge: University Press, 1910), 231.

246.- Shuster, *Strangling*, 55.

247.- Ibid.

248.- Ibid., 56.

249.- Ibid., 59-60.

250.- Ibid., 60.

251.- Ibid., 61 and *Diary*, June 16. When Moore asked Shuster what he thought of the Sepahdar's abrupt departure, Shuster replied that he thought it the action of an "erratic man."

252.- Ibid., 66.

253.- Shuster, *Diary*, June 23.

254.- Shuster *Strangling*, 62.

255.- Ibid., 65-66.

256.- Ibid., 298-301.

257.- Shuster, *Diary*, June 24.

258.- Shuster, *Strangling*, 66.

259.- Ibid., 302.

260.- Ibid., 53.

261.- Ibid., 54.

262.- Shuster, *Diary*, August 7.

263.- Shuster, *Strangling*, 53.

264.- Ibid., 67.

265.- Ibid.

266.- Ibid., 79.

267.- Ibid., 67-68.

268.- Ibid., 69.

269.- Ibid., 80.

270.- Shuster, *Diary*, July 17.

271.- Mansour Bonakdarian, *Britain and the Iranian Constitutional Revolution, 1906-1914* (Syracuse: University Press, 2006), 255, citing *Manchester Guardian*, August 1, 1911, 9f and London *Times*, August 1, 1911, 5d.

Chapter XI

272.- W. Morgan Shuster, *Strangling of Persia* (New York: Greenwood, 1968), 74, 69-70.

273.- Robert McDaniel, *The Shuster Mission* (Minneapolis: Bibliotheca Islamica, 1974), 146.

274.- Shuster, Strangling, 70.

275.- Ibid.

276.- Ibid. 74.

277.- Ibid., 373-4.

278.- Ibid.,73.

279.- Shuster, *Diary*, July 28.

280.- Ibid. and the text of Barclay's note to Shuster, 377.

281.- Firuz Kazemzadeh, *Russia and Britain in Russia, 1864-1914* (New Haven and London: Yale University Press, 1968), 586.

282.- Like the idea of a gendarmerie, the idea of a Swedish officer was not new. Throughout the spring of 1911, there had been negotiations with several Swedish army officers to instruct and lead a gendarmerie to be formed under the Ministry of Interior, and on May 18, the Majles having completed the contracts, voted on them. A month later, the Swedish government designated three officers, Captain Hjalmarson, Lieutenant Skjoeldebrand, and Lieutenant Petersen to fill the posts. These three men, none of whom had had any experience in Persia, would not reach Tehran till the middle of August. See McDaniel, *The Shuster Mission*, 146-7.

283.- Kazemzadeh, *Russia and Britain in Persia*, 587.

284.- Ibid., 587-88.

285.- Shuster, *Strangling*, 78.

286.- Ibid., 79.

287.- Ibid., 80.

288.- The term is Shuster's in ibid., 264.

289.- Shuster, *Strangling*, 73.

290.- Ibid., 377-79.

291.- Shuster, *Diary*, August 10.

292.- Kazemzadeh, *Russia and Britain in Persia*, 590.

293.- Cited by Shuster, *Strangling*, 75.

294.- Kazemzadeh, *Russia and Britain in Persia*, 590.

295.- Shuster, *Strangling*, 254.

296.- Jennifer Siegel, *Endgame. Britain, Russia and the Final Struggle for Central Asia* (London and New York: I B. Tauris, 2002),106, citing secret Poklewski-Koziell telegram August 8, 1911.

297.- Kazemzadeh, *Russia and Britain in Persia*, 590-91.

298.- Shuster, *Strangling*, 391.

299.- Kazemzadeh, 591.

300.- Steven Ward, *Immortal. A Military History of Iran and Its Armed Forces* (Washington, D.C: Georgetown University Press, 2009), 102.

301.- Shuster, Strangling, 190.

Chapter XII

302.- W. Morgan Shuster, *Strangling of Persia* (New York: Greenwood, 1968), 83, and "Persians Welcome Ex-Shah," New York Times, July 23, 1911.

303.- Firuz Kazemzadeh, *Russia and Britain in Persia, 1864-1914* (New Haven and London: Yale University Press, 1968), 511, citing Sir George Barclay to Sir E. Grey, No. 18A Confidential, Tehran, February 10, 1910; F.O 371/956.

304.- When Mohammad Ali had been deposed, Hartwig had been removed and transferred to Belgrade where he would remain until 1914.

305.- Kazemzadeh, 603, citing telegram to the Diplomatic Officer assigned to the Viceroy in the Caucasus, No. 877, July 1/14, 1911.

306.- Robert McDaniel, *The Shuster Mission and the Persian Constitutional Revolution* (Minneapolis: Bibliotheca Islamica, 1974), 139-40.

307.- Shuster, *Strangling*, 84.

308.- Ibid., 88 and *Diary*,

309.- Shuster, *Diary*, July 15.

310.- Ibid.,*Strangling*, 90.

311.- Ibid., 93. Shuster agreed with Arbab Kaikhosro that Samsam's plan would amount to infanticide. See Shuster, *Diary*, July 21.

312.- Ibid.

313.- Ibid., 87.

314.- Ibid., 97.

315.- Ibid., 86.

316.- Ibid., 97.

317.- Ibid., 98.

318.- Ibid.

319.- Ibid.

320.- Shuster, *Diary*, June 4.

321.- Shuster., *Strangling*, 103-04.

322.- Shuster, *Diary*, July 22.

323.- Shuster, *Strangling*, 116.

324.- Ibid., 112-15.

325.- Ibid., 115.

326.- Ibid., 121.

327.- Ibid., 116.

328.- Shuster, *Diary*, July 22.

329.- Shuster, *Strangling*, 94.

330.- Ibid., 116.

331.- Shuster, *Diary*, August 2.

332.- Ibid., August 9. Shuster learned of this meeting a few days after it had occurred.

333.- Ibid., July 20.

334.- Shuster, *Strangling*, 108.

335.- McDaniel, *The Shuster Mission*, 146.

336.- Ibid., 110. Again, Shuster's emphasis.

337.- Ibid., 109.

338.- Ibid.

339.- Ibid., 111.

340.- Ibid., n.

341.- Ibid., 100.

342.- Ibid., 103.

343.- Shuster, Diary, August 5.

344.- It might be remembered that the provision of security in that area was not disinterested on the part of the Bakhtiaris. See Chapter 2.

345.- Shuster, Diary, June 9.

346.- Shuster, 123.

Chapter XIII

347.- Robert McDaniel, *The Shuster Mission and the Persian Constitutional Revolution* (Minneapolis: Bibliotheca Islamica, 1974), 158.

348.- See Steven R. Ward, *Immortal. A Military History of Iran and Its Armed Forces* (Washington, D.C., Georgetown University Press, 2009), 103.

349.- W. Morgan Shuster, *Strangling of Persia* (New York: Greenwood, 1968), 115-116.

350.- McDaniel, *Shuster Mission*, 155.

351.- Shuster, *Strangling*, 124.

352.- Ibid., footnote.

353.- McDaniel, *Shuster Mission*, 145 n.

354.- Ibid., 153-4.

355.- Shuster, *Strangling*, 117.

356.- Ibid., 124-128.

357.- Photos of the execution are in Shuster, facing pages 127 and 130. The reason for executing Arshad immediately in the field rather than taking him prisoner was that Ephraim Khan felt that if Arshad had been brought to Tehran alive, some foreign legation would have had a pretext for interceding on his behalf. (*Diary*, September 7.)

358.- Ibid., 130.

359.- Ibid.

360.- Ibid.

361.- Ibid., 134-5.

362.- Ward, *Immortal*, 104.

363.- Shuster, *Strangling*, 135.

364.- Shuster, *Diary*, July 22 and September 13.

365.- Shuster, *Strangling*, 157.

Chapter XIV

366.- Interestingly, in neither this proposal nor in the June 13 Law was there any mention of revenue from *vaghf* holdings. Nor does Shuster even mention them in his *Strangling of Persia*. Whether it was by instinct, observation, or conversations with members of the Majles or possibly from progressive members of the ulema, throughout his entire tenure in Persia, he managed to avoid directly antagonizing that most powerful bloc.

367.- Ibid., 306.

368.- Ibid., 305-307.

369.- Cf. Chapter 12.

370.- Robert McDaniel, *The Shuster Mission and the Persian Constitutional Revolution* (Minneapolis: Bibliotheca Islamica, 171.

371.- Cf. Chapter 11.

372.- Shuster, *Strangling*, 304.

373.- Shuster, *Diary*, September 10.

374.- Shuster, *Strangling*, ibid.

375.- Ibid., 305.

376.- Shuster, *Diary*, September 23.

377.- McDaniel, *The Shuster Mission*, 169.

378.- Ibid., 161,

379.- Cf. Chapter 5.

Chapter XV

380.- W. Morgan Shuster, *Strangling of Persia* (New York: Greenwood, 1968), 140.

381.- Ibid.

382.- Ibid., 141.

383.- Ibid.

384.- Ibid., 142.

385.- Perhaps this was Mirza Ali Asghar since Shuster mentions that he spoke Russian.

386.- Firuz Kazemzadeh, *Russia and Britain in Persia, 1864-1914* (New Haven and London: Yale University Press, 1968), 614.

387.- Shuster, 148. So toxic was the relationship between Pokhitanof and Poklewski-Koziell that neither Pokhitanof nor his family and staff attended the official Christmas Ball at the Russian legation that year. Practically every other member of the European colony did attend.

388.- Ibid., 145.

389.- Ibid., 147.

390.- Kazemzadeh, *Russia and Britain in Persia*, 616.

391.- Shuster, 146. Another property, "Chizeh" near Gulhak, was seized without difficulty.

392.- Shuster obtained this information from a Persian telephone employee who understood Russian and "overheard" the discussion. Ibid., 151.

393.- Shuster, ibid., 197.

394.- Ibid.

395.- Ibid., 152. See Appendix for the full text.

396.- Sometime before the invasion, Shu'a had taken out Turkish citizenship in order to avoid prosecution by Persian authorities.

397.- Kazemzadeh, *Russia and Britain in Persia*, 616.

398.- Ibid.

399.- Ibid., 617.

400.- Ibid.

401.- Shuster, 148.

402.- Sir Edward Grey, *Twenty-Five Years, 1892-1916* (New York: Frederick A. Stokes Company1925), I, 162.

Chapter XVI

403.- Cf: Chapter 11.

404.- Firuz Kazemzadeh, *Russia and Britain in Persia, 1864-1914* (New Haven and London: Yale University Press, 1968), 613.

405.- Barclay to Shuster, October 3, in W. Morgan Shuster, *Strangling of Persia* (New York: Greenwood, 1968), 382.

406.- Shuster to Barclay, October 5, 1911, ibid., 382 and *Diary*, October 3.

407.- Letter to the *Times*, ibid., 371.

408.- Ibid., 333. The mention of Morocco and Tripoli refer to the Agadir crises.

409.- Poklewski-Koziell to Shuster, ibid., 397.

410.- Ibid., 153.

411.- Shuster, *Diary*, October 17.

412.- Ibid., *Diary*, October 19 and *Strangling*, 153.

413.- Shuster, *Strangling*, 371.

414.- The full text of the *Times* letter is reprinted in ibid., 358-371.

415.- Ibid., 161.

416.- Shuster, *Diary*, November 12.

417.- "The Lost Independence of Persia" in *The Nation*, (London: Covent Garden), Vol. X (October 7, 1911, to March 20, 1912), December 2, 1911, 369.

418.- Ibid., 384-85.

419.- *The Nation*, Vol. X, October 21, 1911, 115.

420.- Robert McDaniel, *The Shuster Mission and the Persian Constitutional Revolution* (Minneapolis: Bibliotheca Islamica, 1974), 177.

421.- Ibid., 172, citing the *London Times*, Oct 18, 1911.

422.- Shuster, *Strangling*, 157.

423.- *The Nation*, X, November 4, 1911, 187.

424.- Ibid., 178, citing the paraphrase of a telegram reporting a conversation between Nasr al-Mulk and Louis Mallet. Mallet was the assistant Under-Secretary of State for Near and Middle Eastern Affairs.

Chapter XVII

425.- W. Morgan Shuster, *Strangling of Persia* (New York: Greenwood, 1968), 157-8.

426.- Ibid., 157.

427.- Robert McDaniel, *The Shuster Mission and the Persian Constitutional Revolution* (Minneapolis: Bibliotheca Islamica,1974), 179.

428.- Ibid., 177.

429.- Shuster, *Strangling*,158-59.

430.- Ibid.

431.- McDaniel, *Shuster Mission*, 190 n, citing the German representative.

432.- Shuster, *Strangling*, 158.

433.- Ibid., 159.

434.- Lecoffre did leave for Tabriz on November 10 and Schindler left for Shiraz the next day. Shuster, Diary, November 10.

435.- Shuster, *Strangling*, 160.

436.- Ibid., 161.

437.- Ibid., 400.

438.- Ibid., 161.

439.- McDaniel, *Shuster Mission*, 184.

440.- Ibid., 186.

441.- Shuster, *Strangling*, 162. Here, as McDaniel points out, Shuster was "clearly in the wrong" since the Russians had demanded only that the gendarmes be removed and replaced by Cossacks, and the Cossacks as well as the gendarmes were technically under the authority of the Persian government, so it really was up to the Cabinet to decide which forces would occupy the property. Cf. McDaniel, *Shuster Mission*, 184.

442.- Shuster, *Strangling*, 161.

443.- McDaniel, *Shuster Mission*, 184.

444.- Ibid., 193.

445.- Shuster, *Strangling*, 165.

446.- Ibid., 166-68.

447.- Ibid., 167.

448.- Ibid., 169.

449.- Ibid., 166.

450.- Ibid., 172.

451.- Ibid., 173.

Chapter XVIII

452.- W. Morgan Shuster, *Strangling of Persia* (New York: Greenwood, 1968), 175-77.

453.- Ibid., 181.

454.- Robert McDaniel, *The Shuster Mission* (Minneapolis: Bibliotheca Islamica, 1974), 192. Khiabani was killed in an uprising against the Russians in Tabriz in 1920.

455.- Shuster, *Strangling*, 182.

456.- Ibid., 184.

457.- Ibid., 183.

458.- Ibid., 206, 209.

459.- Ibid., 187-8.

460.- No. 243, 7 December 1911, L/P&S/11/2, India Office Records, cited in Firooz Kashani-Sabet, *Frontier Fictions* (Princeton: University Press, 1999), 141.

461.- Shuster, *Strangling*, 210.

462.- Ibid., 184.

463.- Ibid., 187.

464.- Turin Bradford Boone, *Persian Diary*, unpublished, 1956, 2. Boone and his wife arrived in Tehran on December 15, 1911, that is, about two weeks after the rejection of the Ultimatum. He had been appointed secretary to Cairns who was Director of Taxation and Principal Assistant to Shuster.

465.- Shuster, *Diary*, November 5, viz., the day the order from Grey was delivered to Stokes by Barclay.

466.- Cited from the speech by H.F.B. Lynch, Chair of the Persia Committee given in Shuster's honor January 29, 1912, in Shuster, *Strangling*, 401.

467.- *The Nation*, Vol. X, (October 7, 1911-March 30, 1912) (London: Covent Garden), December 16, 1911, 460.

468.- Shuster, 188.

469.- Ibid.

470.- Abraham Yeselson, *United States-Persian Diplomatic Relations 1883-1921* (New Brunswick, NJ: Rutgers University Press, 1956), 119.

471.- Shuster, *Strangling*, 189.

472.- Ibid., 190.

473.- Ibid., 191.

474.- Ibid., 198.

475.- Mangol Bayat-Philipp, "Women and Revolution in Iran" in *Women in the Muslim World*, ed. Lois Beck and Nikki Keddie (Cambridge, MA: Harvard University Press, 1978), 303.

476.- Mansour Bonakdarian, *Britain and the Iranian Constitutional Revolution of 1906-1911* (Syracuse: University Press, 2006), 287.

477.- Homa Katouzian, *State and Society in Iran, The Eclipse of the Qajars and the Emergence of the Pahlavis* (London and New York: I.B. Tauris, 2000), 67.

478.- Ibid., 68.

479.- Shuster, *Strangling*, 203.

Chapter XIX

480.- W. Morgan Shuster, *Strangling of Persia* (New York: Greenwood, 1968), 199.

481.- Ibid.

482.- Ibid., 204.

483.- Turin Boone, *Persian Diary*, unpublished, 1956, 4.

484.- Shuster, *Strangling*, 209.

485.- Ibid., 213.

486.- Ibid., 213.

487.- Ibid., 214.

488.- Ibid., 215-216.

489.- Boone, *Diary*, 9.

490.- Shuster, *Strangling*, 219.

491.- "Diary of the Week" in *The Nation*, Vol. X, (October 7, 1911-March 30, 1912) (London: Covent Garden), (December 30, 1911), 535.

492.- Shuster, ibid.

493.- Ibid., 223.

494.- Ibid., 316-17, ff.

495.- Harold Nicolson, *Portrait of a Diplomatist* (New York: Houghton Mifflin, 1930), 259.

496.- Boone, *Diary*, 17.

497.- Shuster. 320.

498.- Boone, 42.

499.- Turin Boone, *Persian Diary*, 19.

500.- Ibid., 13.

501.- Boone, 8.

502.- Boone, 12.

503.- So rigid was Russell in blocking the funds to the American departure that Boone referred to him as "demented." Ibid., 20.

504.- Merrill had come in September to take charge of the Treasury Gendarmerie.

505.- Homa Katouzian, *State and Society in Iran* (London, New York: I.B. Tauris, 2000), 65.

Chapter XX

506.- W. Morgan Shuster, *Strangling of Persia* (New York: Greenwood, 1968), 225-226, 229.

507.- Ibid., 225. Shuster didn't expect to ever receive the portrait.

508.- Ibid., 398.

509.- Ibid., 388.

510.- Ibid., 226.

511.- Ibid., 229.

512.- Ibid., 226.

513.- Ibid., 230.

514.- Ibid., 405.

515.- Cited in E.G. Browne, *The Press and Poetry of Modern Persia* (Cambridge: University Press,1914), 252.

516.- *The Nation* (New York: New York Evening Post Company), Vol. 93, 540. Parsifal is the innocent hero of Richard Wagner's 1883 opera by that name.

517.- *The Nation*, Vol. 95 (New York: New York Evening Post Company, 1912), 80.

518.- Ibid.

519.- Shuster, *Strangling*, Dedication and xv.

520.- Ibid., 334.

521.- Mansour Bonakdarian, *Britain and the Iranian Constitutional Revolution of 1906-1911* (Syracuse, NY: University Press, 2006), 324. The other recommendations were preventing the restoration of the shah to the throne and withdrawing Russian troops from Persia.

522.- Shuster, 330n.

523.-Cited in Firoozeh Kashani-Sabet, *Frontier Fictions* (Princeton, NJ: University Press, 1999), 142.

524.- *The Nation* (New York: New York Evening Post Company, v. 93, 619.

525.- Boone, *Diary*, 44.

526.- Ibid., 50.

Chapter XXI

527.- Turin Boone, *Persian Diary*, unpublished, 49.

528.- W. Morgan Shuster, *The Strangling of Persia* (New York: Greenwood, 1968), xiii.

529.- W. Morgan Shuster, "Acquisitive Statesmanship" in *The Annals of the American Academy of Political and Social Science*, Philadelphia, September 1915, 1, 5.

530.- See PCIA Advocacy Bulletin at advocacy@peacecorpsiran.org.

531.- Roger Doost, "The Unsung American (accounting?) Hero: W. Morgan Shuster" in *Managerial Accounting Journal*, Vol. 19, 2 (1 February, 2004), 313.

Index

A

Afghanistan 79, 81
Agadir 177, 178, 229, 318
al-Afghani, Jamal al-Din 104, 126
Alau ad-Dowla 67, 68, 240, 241, 250
Alexander 79, 124, 153, 176, 235
Alexander I, Tsar 79
Algeciras, Conference of 77
Amir Azam 142, 160, 161, 214, 309
Amir-i Mufakhkham 202, 206
Amir Kabir 64, 71, 112, 124, 151
Anglo-Russian Convention 75, 95, 96, 99, 128, 170, 174, 177, 182, 211, 229, 243, 256, 271, 281
anjemans 64, 68, 95, 173
Anzeli 80, 95, 131, 160, 166, 190, 208, 235, 237, 258, 268, 274
Arbab Kaikhosro 135, 188, 314
Arshad, Sardar 201, 202, 203, 204, 205, 206, 316
Astara, massacre at 80, 101, 106, 181, 191, 192, 201, 208
Atabak (also see Amin al-Saltan) 63, 64, 66, 95, 112, 134, 144, 181, 188, 190, 218, 235, 254, 255, 273, 308, 309
Atabak Park 134, 188, 254, 273
Ayin ad-Dowla 68
Aynu ad-Dowla 66, 99
Azerbaijan 63, 101, 103, 107, 114, 183, 197, 238, 239
Azud al-Mulk 102, 103

B

Baghdad 77, 177, 178, 182
Bagh-i Shah 97, 207, 217, 273
Baharistan 96, 97
Bakhtiari, tribesmen, demands for money 101, 186, 190, 191, 197, 201, 202, 203, 204, 206, 207, 211, 214, 240, 241, 245, 246, 249, 254, 258, 264, 265, 286, 299, 315
Baku 131, 183, 208, 235, 238, 274
Bandar Anzeli 80, 208
Banque d'Escompte 149, 165, 167, 211, 222, 277, 292
Baqer Khan 100, 161
Barclay, Sir George 87, 106, 128, 138, 139, 140, 142, 155, 158, 164, 165, 167,

168, 171, 173, 174, 175, 176, 178, 195, 198, 199, 211, 215, 220, 224, 227, 228, 229, 232, 234, 242, 243, 263, 268, 273, 306, 308, 312, 313, 318, 321
Baskerville, Howard 100, 101, 114, 117, 136, 275, 304
Beddoes, Colonel H. R. 135, 139, 215
Behbahani, Abdullah 103, 104
Benckendorff, Alexander von 176, 178
Berlin to Baghdad Railway 77
Bizot, M. 127, 128, 151, 307
Browne, E. G. 84, 124, 125, 126, 127, 128, 129, 134, 143, 144, 170, 285, 299, 300, 301, 302, 303, 304, 306, 307, 310, 324
Bryce, James 112, 121

C

Cairns, F. S. 131, 219, 220, 268, 269, 321
Columbian University, Shuster at iv, 120, 124
Constitutionalists 97, 98, 99, 101, 104, 136, 184, 186, 258, 275
Constitutional Revolution iv, 62, 69, 73, 100, 114, 126, 148, 157, 247, 278, 299, 303, 304, 305, 312, 313, 315, 316, 319, 322, 324
Cossack Brigade 96, 97, 102, 158, 174, 184, 191, 200, 221, 224, 265
Curzon, Lord George 82, 83, 85, 88, 96, 233, 271, 302
Customs 62, 63, 65, 66, 94, 113, 118, 120, 121, 131, 132, 137, 149, 150, 164, 165, 166, 167, 168, 201, 210, 268, 306

D

Dar al-Fanum 114
de Hartwig, N. G. 97, 182
Dickey, Bruce G. 131, 141
dollar diplomacy 117
Doty, William 101, 304

E

Ephraim Khan 106, 186, 187, 188, 192, 193, 201, 203, 204, 205, 207, 217, 246, 249, 254, 265, 316

F

Fath Ali Shah 99
Firuzkuh 201, 202, 203, 207
Fundamental Laws 62, 72, 300, 301

G

325

Germany 77, 79, 107, 174, 177, 178, 229, 283
Gomesh Tapeh 181, 182, 183, 184, 207, 208
Gordon, Charles "Chinese" 75, 301
Grey, Sir Edward 80, 81, 82, 84, 86, 89, 96, 98, 103, 105, 106, 107, 108, 113, 119, 122, 128, 155, 168, 172, 173, 174, 175, 176, 178, 225, 227, 233, 234, 236, 242, 243, 244, 245, 246, 247, 248, 251, 255, 256, 260, 271, 275, 277, 281, 285, 302, 304, 305, 306, 313, 318, 321

H

Haase, Major 192, 193, 201, 204, 207
Hakim al-Mulk 192, 214, 215
Haycock, E. C. 235, 238
Herat 88
Hills, Ralph 131
Hormuz Khan 131, 133, 154
Hussein Quli Khan 107, 117, 186, 187

I

Imperial Bank 65, 104, 150, 152, 158, 165, 166, 171, 201, 206, 233, 278, 292
India 74, 77, 78, 79, 80, 81, 83, 84, 88, 89, 150, 170, 171, 176, 189, 212, 235, 253, 256, 261, 287, 321
Isfahan 80, 88, 95, 99, 101, 107, 125, 133, 169, 186, 190, 196, 197, 212, 228, 235, 238
Izvolsky, Alexander, Russian Minister of Foreign Affairs 79, 86, 172

K

Khiabani, Shiekh Mohammad 252, 321
Knox, Philander, American Secretary of State 117, 118, 257, 270

L

Lecoffre, M., Controlleur 148, 149, 151, 238, 239, 241, 242, 245, 247, 251, 254, 255, 278, 285, 309, 320
Liakhoff 97, 98, 102
London Times 100, 136, 231, 312, 319

M

Majlis 152, 171, 193
maliat 148, 149, 152, 213, 294
Marling, Charles 97
Mashhad 80, 114, 206, 215, 270

McCaskey, Charles 131, 139, 141
Merrill, Colonel, J. N. 179, 219, 220, 270, 323
Millspaugh, Arthur 112, 290, 305
Mirza Ali Asghar 63, 218, 317
missionaries 101, 113, 114, 115, 117, 123, 133, 141, 276, 290, 299, 305
Mohammad Ali Shah 134, 181, 182, 197, 200, 203, 268
Moore, W.A., London *Times* correspondent 100, 136, 139, 231, 260, 311
Mornard, Joseph 94, 95, 150, 164, 165, 166, 167, 168, 169, 174, 195, 268, 269, 277
Morocco 77, 177, 199, 230, 318
mostafis 153, 154, 163
Mozaffar 62, 63, 65, 74, 96, 99
Mu'avin al-Dowla 158, 159
Mutashamu as-Saltaneh 142, 166, 189, 249

N

Nasr al-Din Shah 75, 101, 126
Nasr al-Mulk 96, 103, 142, 155, 161, 188, 236, 258, 264, 270, 271, 309, 319
Nation, The 62, 71, 233, 236, 276, 279, 319, 321, 322, 324
Naus, Joseph 65, 66, 68, 94, 95, 164, 165
Neratov, A. A. 172, 173, 175, 221, 224, 228, 237, 238
New, George 206, 215

Nicolson, Arthur 79, 80, 82
Nicolson, Harold 301, 323
Nuri, Sheik Fazullah 104

O

O'Beirne, Hugh 105, 304

P

Panther gunboat 177
Persia Committee 84, 125, 243, 275, 277, 321
Philippines, Shuster in 118, 121, 122, 123, 125, 129, 131, 132, 170, 286, 306
Pokhitanov, Ivan Fedorocich 99
Poklewski-Koziell, Stanislav 106, 138, 139, 140, 142, 158, 164, 165, 166, 168, 173, 178, 179, 190, 195, 219, 220, 221, 222, 223, 224, 225, 227, 228, 230, 231, 237, 238, 240, 241, 246, 247, 248, 263, 267, 269, 273, 304, 308, 313, 317, 318
Potsdam Agreement 213, 242
Protocol of 1909 102, 107, 108, 183, 194, 196, 217, 232

Q

Qazvin 67, 102, 104, 114, 133, 169, 193, 254, 274, 275

R

Rahim Khan 99, 101, 106, 187
Rasht v, 80, 95, 99, 101, 104, 114, 132, 154, 160, 190, 196, 247, 268, 279, 307
Russell, Charles 113, 118, 133, 141, 142, 267, 270, 323

S

Salaru ad-Dowla 160, 183, 185, 201, 202, 203, 206, 207, 208, 217, 222
Samsam al-Saltaneh 101, 181, 186, 201, 202, 213, 214, 240, 244, 250, 266
Sardar Arshad 201, 202, 203
Sardar-i Muhiy, Walking Arsenal 191, 206
Sattar Khan 100, 161
Sazanov, Sergei Dimitrovich 119, 172, 173, 177
Schindler, Alexander 235, 320
Seligman Brothers 105, 135, 211, 216
Sepahdar-i Azam, Mohammad Vali Khan x, 101, 139, 142, 157
Sharia 70, 71, 104, 294
Sheil, Justin 157
Sheil, Lady Mary 157
Shi'ite, Shia 64, 294
Shiraz 81, 125, 169, 198, 228, 235, 320
Shu'a al-Saltaneh 67, 181, 185, 201, 217, 218, 219, 222, 223, 227, 230, 237, 242, 246, 248
Spring-Rice, Cecil 85, 86, 106, 128
Stokes, Major, Claude Bayfield 169, 170, 171, 172, 173, 174, 175, 176, 177, 178, 179, 189, 195, 197, 198, 212, 227, 228, 229, 230, 232, 235, 239, 251, 255, 278, 285, 302, 305, 318, 321

T

Tabriz iv, 80, 95, 99, 100, 101, 103, 104, 106, 114, 125, 136, 160, 161, 169, 197, 220, 238, 239, 242, 245, 252, 254, 258, 262, 264, 267, 268, 277, 285, 304, 320, 321
Taft, President William 116, 118, 121, 122
Taj al-Saltana 62, 63, 299
Taqizadeh, Sayyid Hassan 104, 143, 261, 262
Tbilisi 267
Thucydides 284
Tobacco Concession 87, 98, 126

Turkomanchai, Treaty of 78, 81

U

ulema 64, 67, 68, 70, 71, 103, 104, 286, 294, 300, 316
Ultimatum 237, 247, 248, 249, 250, 251, 253, 254, 255, 257, 261, 262, 263, 266, 267, 268, 284, 286, 321

V

Vadbolski, Prince 184, 224, 265
Vosuq ad-Dowla 215, 237, 239, 244, 246, 254, 257, 263, 266, 285

W

Wood, A. O. 100, 152, 158

SELECT BIBLIOGRAPHY

Ahmed, Nazeer. "The Constitutional Revolution in Persia in 1906" in *Encyclopedia of Islamic History*. https://historyofislam.com/contents/resistance-and-reform/the-constitutional-revolution-in-persia.

Amanat, Abbas. *Iran: A Modern History*. New Haven and London: Yale University Press, 2017.

_____. *Pivot of the Universe: Nasir al-Din Shah Qajar and the Iranian Monarchy, 1831-1896*. Berkeley and Los Angeles: University of California Press, 1997.

_____, ed. *Taj al Saltana. Crowning Anguish. Memoirs of a Persian Princess from the Harem to Modernity. 1884-1914*. Washington, D.C. Mage Publishers, 1993.

The American Monthly Review of Reviews "Record of Current Events," (September 1911), 161-164.

Avery, Peter. *Modern Iran*. New York, Washington: Frederick A. Praeger, 1965.

Axworthy, Michael. *A History of Iran. Empire of the Mind*. New York: Basic Books, 2008.

Bahar, Sima. "A Historical Background to the Women's Movement in Iran" in *Women of Iran. The Conflict with Fundamentalist Islam*. Edited by Farah Azari. London: Ithaca Press, 1983.

Bassett, James. *Persia, The Land of the Imams*. New York: Scribners, 1886.

Bayat-Philipp, Mangol. "Women and Revolution in Iran" in *Women in the Muslim World*, edited by Lois Beck and Nikki Keddie. Cambridge, MA: Harvard University Press, 1978.

Beck, Lois and Nashat, Guity, eds. *Women in Iran from 1800 to the Islamic Republic*. Urbana and Chicago: University of Illinois Press, 2004.

Bellairs, Edgar G. [Charles Ballentine] *As It Is in the Philippines*. New York: Lewis, Scribner & Co., 1902.

Bonarkdarian, Mansour. *Britain and the Iranian Constitutional Revolution of 1906-1911*. Syracuse, NY: Syracuse University Press, 2006.

Boone, Turin Bradford. *Persian Diary, 1911-1912*. Assembled and copyrighted by Isabella Boone, 1956.

Browne, E.G. *Letters from Tabriz. The Russian Suppression of the Iranian Constitutional Movement*. Edited by Hasan Javadi. Washington, D.C. Mage Publishers, 2008.

Browne, E.G. *The Persian Crisis of 1911. How It Arose and Whither It Will Lead Us*. Cambridge: Priv. Print. At the University Press, 1912.

_____. *The Persian Revolution of 1905-1909*. Cambridge: At the University Press, 1910.

_____. Year Amongst the Persians. Impressions as to the Life, Character, & Thought of the People of Persia. 3rd ed. Cambridge: University Press, 1950.

_____. *The Press and Poetry of Modern Persia*. Cambridge: University Press, 1914.

Catalogue of the Law School of The Columbian University for the Academic Year 1897-98. Washington, D.C: Hartman & Cadick, Printers, 1898.

Churchill, Rogers Platt. *The Anglo-Russian Convention of 1907*. Cedar Rapids, IA: The Torch Press, 1939.

Columbian (yearbook) 1898. Washington, D.C., 1898.

"Honors for Washington Boy" in *Washington Post* (1877-1922), July 26,1901, 2.

Cottam, Richard. *Nationalism in Iran*. Pittsburgh, PA: University of Pennsylvania Press, 1964, 1969.

Curzon, George. *Persia and the Persian Question*. 2 vols. New York: Barnes and Noble, 1892.

Doost, Roger. "The Unsung American (Accounting?) Hero: W. Morgan Shuster" in *Managerial Accounting Journal*, 1 February, 2004, Abstract.

Ettehadieh, Mansoureh. "The Origins and Development of the Women's Movement in Iran, 1906-41" in *Women in Iran from 1800 to the Islamic Republic*. Edited by Lois Beck and Guity Nashat. Urbana and Chicago: University of Chicago Press, 2004.

Ghaffari, Rabeah. *To Keep the Sun Alive*. New York: Catapult, 2019.

Greaves, Rose. *Persia and the Defence of India, 1884-1892*. London: The Atholone Press, University of London, 1959.

Grey, Sir Edward. *Twenty-five Years, 1892-1916*. 2 vols. New York: Frederick A. Stokes Company, 1925.

Hjelmgard, Kim. *USA Today*, November 5, 2018.

"Honors for Washington Boy" in *Washington Post* (1877-1922), July 26,1901.

http://movarekhan.com/blog/agha_mohammad_khan_qajar_advice/.

Kaine, Senator Tim. "A New Truman Doctrine. Grand Strategy in a Hyperconnected World." *Foreign Affairs*, 96, no. 4 (July/August 2017), 36-53.

Katouzian, Homa. *Iran. Politics, History and Literature.* (New York: Routledge, 2013.

_____. *State and Society in Iran. The Eclipse of the Qajars and the Emergence of the Pahlavis.* London and New York: I.B. Tauris, 2000.

Kazemzadeh, Firuz. *Russia and Britain in Persia, 1864-1914. A Study in Imperialism.* New Haven and London: Yale University Press, 1968.

Keddie, Nikki. ""Iran under the Later Qajars, 1848-1922" in *Cambridge History of Iran*, Peter Avery, Gavin Hambly, and Charles Melville, eds. Vol. 7. Cambridge: University Press, 1991.

_____. *Modern Iran. Roots and Results of Revolution.* New Haven and London: Yale University Press, 2006.

_____. *Qajar Iran and the Rise of Reza Khan, 1796-1925.* Cosa Meza, CA: Mazda Publishers, 1999.

Kinzer, Stephen, *Reset: Iran, Turkey, and America's Future* (Macmillan, 2010), p. 22.

Limbert, John. *Negotiating with Iran.* Washington, D.C. United States Institute of Peace Press, 2009.

Low, A. Maurice. *The American People. A Study in National Psychology.* 2 vols. Boston and New York: Houghton Mifflin, 1909-11.

Mansoori, Ahmad. *American Missionaries in Iran. 1834-1934.* Ph.D. diss. Ball State University, 1985.

McDaniel, Robert A. *The Shuster Mission and the Persian Constitutional Revolution*. Minneapolis: Bibliotheca Islamica, 1974.

Millspaugh, Arthur. *The American Task in Persia*. London: T. Werner Laurie, Ltd., [c.1925].

_____. *Americans in Persia*. Washington, D.C. The Brookings Institution, 1946.

Mirfendereski, Guive. *A Diplomatic History of the Caspian Sea: Treaties, Diaries, and other Stories*. Palgrave Macmillan, 2001.

Naficy, Hamid. *The Artisanal Era, 1897-1941*, Vol. 1 of *A Social History of Iranian Cinema*, 4 vols. Durham, NC and London: Duke University Press, 2011.

Nafisi, Azar. *Things I've Been Silent About*. New York: Random House, 2008.

Nation, The. Vols. IX (April 1, 1911-September 30, 1911) and X (October 7, 1911-March 30, 1912), London: Covent Garden.

Nation, The. Vols. 93 & 95. New York: New York Evening Post Company.

New York Times. "Persians Welcome Ex-Shah," July 23, 1911.

Nicolson, Harold. *Diplomacy*. New York: Harcourt, Brace and Company, 1939.

_____. *Portrait of a Diplomatist. Being the Life of Sir Arthur Nicolson, First Lord Carnock, and a Study of the Origins of the Great War*. Boston and New York: Houghton, Mifflin Company, 1930.

Nizam al-Mulk (Abu Ali Hasan ibn Ali Tusi). *Siyaset Nameh (The Book of Government)*. Translated from the Persian by Hubert Drake. New Haven: Yale University Press, 1960.

Sackville-West, Vita. *Passenger to Tehran*. New York: Moyer Bell, 1990.

Saint-Marie, Joseph J. and Naghshpour, Shahdad. *Revolutionary Iran and the United States: Low Intensity Conflict in the Persian Gulf*. Farnham, Surrey: Ashgate Publishing, Ltd, 2011.

Sedghi, Hamideh. *Women and Politics in Iran. Veiling, Unveiling, and Reveiling*. New York: Cambridge University Press, 2007.

Sheil, Lady Mary Leonora Woulfe. *Glimpses of Life and Manners in Persia*. London: John Murray, 1856.

Shuster, W. Morgan. "Acquisitive Statesmanship" in *The Annals of the American Academy of Political and Social Science*, Philadelphia, September 1915.

_____. *Diary*. MMC3238 Shuster MSS. Washington, D.C: Library of Congress, 1911.

_____.*Fourth Special Report, Covering the Period from July 1, 1904, to September 1, 1905*. Manila: Bureau of Public Printing, 1904 and 1905.

_____. *Third Special Report Covering the Period from September 1, 1903, to September 1, 1904*. Manila: Bureau of Public Printing, 1904.

_____. *The Strangling of Persia. Story of the European Diplomacy and Oriental Intrigue that Resulted in the Denationalization of Twelve Million Mohammedans*.

A Personal Narrative. New York: Greenwood Press, 1968.

Sicker, Martin. *The Bear and the Lion. Soviet Imperialism and Iran.* New York: Praeger, 1988.

Siegel, Jennifer. *Endgame.* London, New York: I. B. Tauris Publishers, 2002.

Stack, Edward. *Six Months in Persia*, 2 vols. New York: G.P. Putnam's Sons, 1882.ed.

Trench, Charles Chenevix. *The Road to Khartoum. A Life of General Charles Gordon.* New York: Carroll & Graf Publishers, Inc., 1978.

United States. Congress. House of Representatives. Committee on Insular Affairs. *Statements of Hon. Wm. H. Taft, Secretary of War, Mr. Wm. Morgan Sister, Philippine Commission*, Wednesday, April 15, 1908. Washington, D.C. Government Printing Office, 1908.

Ward, Stephen. *Immortal. A Military History of Iran and Its Armed Forces.* Washington, D.C: Georgetown University Press, 2009.

Witte, Sergei. *The Memoirs of Count Witte.* Translated from the Original Russian Manuscript and edited by Abraham Yarmolinsky. New York: Howard Fertig, 1967.

Wright, Denis. *The English Amongst the Persians During the Qajar Period. 1787-1921.* London: Heinemann, 1977.

Yeselson, Abraham. *United States-Persian Diplomatic Relations. 1883-1921.* New Brunswick, NJ: Rutgers University Press, 1956.

Zirinsky, Michael. "American Presbyterian Missionaries at Urmia During the Great War" at: www.iranchamber.com/religions/articles/american_presbyterian_missionaries_zirinsky.pdf

"Finding in Morgan Shuster a spirit resembling that of the Peace Corps volunteers who served in Iran from 1962 to 1976, I knew the writing of this book was almost unavoidable," says Joan Gaughan. Her own Peace Corps experience in Iran and her knowledge of the country and its language make her uniquely qualified to evaluate Morgan Shuster's efforts in 1911 to put that country's chaotic finances on a sound footing at a time when Iran was divided between the British and Russian spheres of interest.

Gaughan holds a Ph.D. in history from the University of Michigan and has taught history and humanities in college for thirty years. Her publications include the three-volume *Milestones in Western Civilization*, seven articles in the *Victorian Encyclopedia*, and *The 'Encumbrances': British Women in India, 1615-1858*. She makes frequent presentations at conferences on British colonial history and other topics.

Currently, Gaughan is editor of the Peace Corps Iran Association's newsletter, *Khabar Nameh*, and is co-founder and manager of McKenzie Sporthorses. She lives in Manchester, Michigan.

www.ingramcontent.com/pod-product-compliance
Lightning Source LLC
Chambersburg PA
CBHW021052080526
44587CB00010B/229